TEA, COMICS AND GENDER

or

Yet Another Fucking Trans Memoir

Ellen Mellor

Samarcand Books

Copyright © 2022 Ellen Mellor

Samarcand Books

All rights reserved. ISBN

Paperback: 978-1-8384266-6-8

E-Book: 978-1-8384266-7-5

Also by Ellen Mellor

(Novels)

The Long Sleep

Down Among the Yla

Ghostkin

(Short Story Collections)

Stories From The Corner of the Room

All The Books of Earth

(For children)

The Princess and The Elephant (illustrated by Piper Strange)

Dedicated to

My Family

Without whom I wouldn't be where

or who I am now.

With thanks to my Postkin and

Paper Ghostkin level Patreon patrons:

Dylan Falconer

Karen Nayler

TC O'Neil

Mike Wilkinson

"If there's anything more important than my ego around, I want it caught and shot now."

Douglas Adams

The Hitch-Hikers' Guide to the Galaxy

Foreword

This book wasn't meant to exist.

I was in the middle of working on pieces for my next short story collection *All The Books of Earth* and I had decided that as well as my fiction I wanted to include the various bits of non-fiction I had written as well. This included a collection of quotes and reminiscences about the positive aspects of being trans that I wrote during the week after my bottom surgery called 'Positive Trans-itions' and 'The TERF Form Letter and You' which talked about the similarities between JK Rowling's essay explaining why she was 'gender critical' (aka transphobic) and the 'open letter' written to me by someone who I had considered a friend. I was also going to include an essay I wrote near the start of my transition. A friend told me that she had to write a 'potted history' of her life for the doctor at the Gender Identity Clinic to prove that she was really trans (this, being both ableist as well as gatekeepery as fuck is even more reason that it shouldn't happen). She went to a different GIC from the one I eventually went to but I thought that I knew that I was going to have to prove my transness when I finally got an appointment and, even if it wasn't needed, it would be useful to help get my thoughts in order. Reading over it for inclusion in the collection, I decided to rework it a bit and bring it up to date as it ended pretty much just as things were getting interesting. Aware of how pretentious and wanky it was to write any kind of memoir and also that memoirs by trans people seemed to be quite a popular genre at the moment, I called it 'Yet Another Fucking Trans Memoir'. I had decided that extending it to eight or nine thousand words, effectively doubling the word count of the original, would make it a nice piece to end on. (The 'Tea, Comics and Gender' came quite a bit later, suggested by my lovely friend Dylan.) When I got to 20,000 words and still hadn't reached the point of actually coming out as trans I realised that this thing may have grown bigger than I had initially intended. This is what comes of not actually planning what one is going to write.

However, I persevered and discovered that I was writing almost every day and that the more I wrote the more I was able to write. Despite - or perhaps, because of - the apocalypse, I wrote more in 2020 than I have ever done before - easily topping 90,000 words. *Ghostkin*, by contrast, is somewhere in the region of 95,000 words and took me about five years to write. Those 90,000 words weren't just on this book though. As I was writing this I was also trying to keep up with a regular flow of short stories because I didn't want to fall behind on *All The Books of Earth*. I also decided to start writing a roleplaying game based on *Ghostkin*. Writing all three together didn't quite work out as I realised that I both wanted and needed to finish this first. The stories and the game are still there though, waiting for me to download them from my brain onto the computer. It's just that, as a collection, *All The Books of Earth is* going to be about eight or nine thousand words shorter than I intended because this won't be in there.

So, here we are. A book that was meant to be an essay until it ended up being about twelve times longer than planned but written in about nine months. I'm very proud of it while at the same time terrified that it is the wankiest thing anyone has ever written. Although, considering the competition I'd have to work pretty hard to manage that.

Tea, Comics and Gender

There are a few things about some of the wording I've chosen. When talking about the name my parents gave me when I was born, I use the term 'deadname'. I don't actually say what that name is because it's not one that I associate with myself anymore and, when people do refer to me as such, I find it very upsetting. I understand that most of the time it's just a slip of the tongue and not said to deliberately hurt me but it does still hurt when it happens. I also recognise that the term is quite emotive and can be read to mean that, in my opinion, the person I once was is dead and I want nothing more to do with him. But that's absolutely not true. 'Deadname' is the generally accepted term in the trans community for the name you had before you transitioned and using a different term just muddies the waters. The person I was and the person I am are the same person. It's just that I know who I am now and have stopped conforming to what society says a person assigned male at birth should do and be. My deadname is the most obvious example of that. While I don't miss the time I spent thinking I was male, there are many, many experiences that I had in that time that I absolutely wouldn't wish to lose but I prefer to think of having experienced them as Ellen working under a facade rather than as a man or a boy.

While writing the first draft of the book, I talked about 'my depression' and 'my dysphoria', making them a part of who I was.

When I was editing it, I decided to change to talking about 'the depression' and 'the dysphoria'. Those things are neither mine nor are they any part of me. They are things that I experienced due to various pressures, both internal and external and to accept them as being a piece of me, like my finger or my (gorgeous) breasts, feels wrong. They were obstacles preventing me from being me and needing to be excised. There are points where I quote myself from things I wrote at the time when I do talk about 'my' dysphoria or depression and I chose to leave them as they are.

One final thing before the real book actually starts. Obviously, this is my story and as such my experiences, thoughts and feelings are unique to me and do not relate to anyone else's experiences, thoughts and feelings about being trans or a comic book geek or a tea-drinker. There is a very strong narrative drive that has been created by cis people to describe trans experiences that barely touches on reality and when we don't conform to it we are often seen as being inauthentic. My life really doesn't conform to it. I am a relatively late transitioning transgender, femme lesbian who blocked out and denied any thoughts that she was a woman for most of her life. It took me a long time to get here but now that I am, I'm planning on sticking around and enjoying myself for a long time to come. I mean, I have loads more books to write, not to mention the number of books and comics there are for me to read. I often say that I am planning on living forever because, some day, as heat death of the universe finally approaches, there will be no more books being published. At that point, with no further interruptions from 'people', I'll finally be able to catch up with my To Be Read pile.

Tea, Comics and Gender

A note on content and trigger warnings Because this book deals with my transition in a lot of detail, there are going to be elements of it that may well cause some problems for you as a reader, especially if you suffer from gender dysphoria yourself.

There is a lot of discussion about both gender dysphoria and transphobia. I also talk about sex and sexuality. While I do not go into the details of genital reassignment surgery, I do discuss my experiences leading up to it and afterwards. There is also a picture of my vulva in the first few days post surgery.

Finally, I also talk about the periods of mental illness from which I suffered including suicidal ideation, thoughts of self-harm and general depression.

If you find these things triggering and upsetting and you need to talk to someone about it, I would recommend the following:

MIND Infoline (information and signposting for mental health) - 0300 1233393 (MIND also have a 'Get Help Now' button on their website which gives simple practical advice and information - https://www.mind.org.uk/)

Samaritans - 116 123

MindLine Trans+ (mental health support helpline for trans people) - 0300 3305468

Be Trans Support (North East England based trans peer support) - https://be-north.org.uk/contact-us

Part 1

'Him'

Tea, Comics and Gender

1
Meet the Family

I have never really explained why I called myself Ellen, always saying that I couldn't remember why I had chosen that name.

Well, that's not entirely true. After settling on the name, I decided to keep the reason behind it secret, mainly because I didn't think that it was anyone else's business.

However, I made a pact with myself that if I ever wrote a memoir, I'd reveal the truth.

So here it is:

When I was growing up, one of my favourite songs was Eleanor Rigby by The Beatles. Except when I first heard the song, I misheard the lyrics and thought they were singing about Ellen or Rigsby. I was very confused about what the lead character of Rising Damp had to do with the rest of the song but went along with it for a long time.

I have been female all my life. It just took me until I was in my mid-forties to realise it.

I was born in 1971 in Barrow-In-Furness in Cumbria, renowned as being the place where the United Kingdom's Trident missile- carrying nuclear submarine fleet was built and also for having the highest infection rates in the country during the initial wave of the Covid-19 pandemic in 2020.

My parents, Shaun and Carol, were both from the North East of England but other than that there was nothing that would obviously connect them. My dad's family were very definitely working class stock, my mum very much middle class. Bill, my paternal grandfather, was a Sergeant Major in the army who was deployed to India during World War II. He took his wife, Muriel, and she would often talk of how she was treated like royalty while she was over there, not the least of which was being waited on hand and foot by a loyal coterie of servants. Returning, without her husband who had remained behind but with two daughters in tow and a third child on the way, to a cold flat in Bishop Auckland without even have an indoor toilet was something of a comedown.

My maternal grandmother, Margaret, married a man named John Smith. My uncles, George and Wilf, are non-identical twins born on the first of January 1943. My mother was born in November 1944 although John never saw her as he abandoned the family when Margaret was pregnant. In England in the 1940s when one is as conscious of one's appearance as my grandmother this should have been utterly devastating. And yet both Muriel and Margaret proved how incredibly strong they were, picking themselves up and moving forwards.

Muriel worked hard and made sure that life for her children was as good as it could be. When Bill came home they moved to a house in Heaton and had a second son, Nigel. Margaret started up in business for herself as a ladies hairdresser and made her way on her own until she met Jack Gosney. He didn't see her three young children as a problem and they married soon after. Their relationship was a happy and loving one right up until Jack's death. I know that my mother adored him and although he may not have been her biological father he was definitely her dad and she was his beloved daughter.

Mum and Dad met on a trip to Ford Castle in Northumberland when their respective Methodist Youth Clubs organised a joint excursion. Margaret was appalled. He was an electrician who worked down the mines, hadn't passed his Eleven Plus exam and was definitely not the calibre of man that she was expecting her daughter to marry. Even worse he rode a motorcycle, wore denim jeans ('his work-clothes!') and looked very much like Che Guevara. But her mother's disapproval did not stop her - Mum had obviously inherited a large chunk of her mother's determined streak - and they married. In 1967, shortly after their marriage, they emigrated to South Africa. As you do. I had for years thought they flew out on the day of the 1966 World Cup Final and only recently discovered my mistake. They were actually driving to Scotland for a holiday that day which, as they were just going up to visit her brother George my mum admits that they could have waited a day to go. But, on the other hand, if my dad had been that desperate to watch it he could have insisted on waiting.

Although they weren't sure if they were going to emigrate permanently they certainly made a go of it. Dad had several jobs before finally ending up as an electrician at the West Driefontein Gold Mine while Mum worked in an office in Johannesburg. It was a fairly idyllic life for them but their caring, principled sensibilities - handed down to them by their parents - were appalled and disgusted by the apartheid regime and they quickly realised that there was no way they could stay there. They had gone out to South Africa, innocent and unknowing, convinced that this was a golden opportunity and they would be living in paradise. And, if they could have remained blind to the racism and iniquity in the country that is exactly what it would have been for them. Instead, it opened their eyes and turned them into powerful, committed Socialists who worked for the betterment of everyone, traits I like to think that they passed down to both their children.

Mum was pregnant with my brother when they returned to the UK and Sean was born in Newcastle in 1969. Apparently inter- continental travel while heavily pregnant is a family tradition. Dad had found a job as an electrician in the Vickers shipyard in Barrow in Furness working on warships and nuclear submarines and was already living in Barrow when his son came along. One of the ships he worked on was the HMS Sheffield, famed as the only British ship to be sunk during the Falklands Conflict. On the night of Sean's birth, Dad made it from Barrow to Newcastle in about an hour and a half. Mum and her new-born baby moved to Barrow a fortnight after his birth.

When I was born, I came as something of a surprise to my parents. I was planned (as far as I know) but the truth is that they were expecting a baby girl. When the doctor presented them with what he said was a boy they were more than a little surprised and it took a little bit of time for them to get used to the idea. They had been so convinced of the gender of their new baby that they had only chosen a girls' name and hadn't thought of one for a boy. It was however, a name that had an obvious masculine version. So, on July 29th 1971 I came into the world, a surprising second son with a name that was really only a boys' name by default. Life would have been so much easier if they hadn't listened to the doctor and stuck to their original plan...

I don't have many memories from Barrow, mostly just

flashes and hazy images that may or may not be real: Seeing a charity parachute drop. Going to the nearby park and seeing the ducks in the pond. Being in nursery school and getting told off because while I was making a splatter painting by flicking paint at a piece of paper I was also creating a second work of art on the wall behind me because the energy I was exerting in splashing the paint onto the paper was only matched by the energy at the other end of the arc. I definitely remember getting a little Paddington Bear plaster-of-Paris 'Plastercasters' statue for my birthday one year. It had been made for me by the son of my parents' closest friends, but when I unwrapped it I said something awfully crass and ungrateful about hoping to get a 'proper present' next year. It still makes me cringe. However, more than forty years later, I still have him and he's one of my most treasured possessions, along with the extremely well-loved teddy bear that belonged to my mother when she was a little girl which she bequeathed to me when I was born.

    Life in Barrow was pretty idyllic - I was well-loved by my parent's and have no memories of being treated in any way badly. When I was no more than one year old we got a pet. A beautiful black kitten that we named Smokey. I absolutely adored her and she pretty quickly became 'my cat' or rather I became 'her human' and we were pretty inseparable. She lived a long life, finally dying in her sleep the day before my eighteenth birthday which was sad but at the same time, I recognised that she had been pretty happy and healthy right up until her death. We also had a dog at one point although only for a month or so before having to send it back to the shelter. It was a rescue dog and had obviously been mistreated by its previous owners. While most of the time it was sweet and gentle it could also turn vicious without warning. My parents just couldn't take the chance that it might turn on their young children.

There are a couple of bad memories that I have from my time in Barrow although I am a secondary character in both. The first isn't so much a memory however as it is a reconstruction from hearing the story from my parents. The house on Cheltenham Street in which we lived had a sliding glass door between the front room and the back with a step between them. My brother and I were pretty typical siblings in that we squabbled a lot and fought - sometimes playfully, sometimes less so. During one such fight, I rolled across Sean's arm from the back room, down the step and into the front. It wasn't until several hours later when Sean discovered that he was unable to pick up his cutlery at dinner time that my parent's realised that I had actually managed to break his arm and rush him to hospital. Fortunately, it was only a green-stick fracture and healed quickly and easily.

Another time, Sean and I were playing at the front of the house, swinging on the gate - something we had been told not to do on many occasions - when he slipped. The latch sliced into his leg, opening a long, deep gash in his thigh. Before the blood started to gush out, I remember seeing the muscle of his leg and I'm still convinced that I actually saw a glimpse of bone. That injury needed quite a long period of recuperation although the only sign that remains now is the scar that went from being a vicious, raised welt that took up quite a lot of space on his thigh to a pale, barely noticeable line, hidden by one of his many tattoos.

All through my childhood one of my regular pastimes, along with playing with Playmobil and Star Wars figures, was playing dress up in my mother's clothes. It was completely innocent at that age and she was fine with it most of the time. At one point - although I'm not certain if it happened in Barrow or later when I lived in Newcastle - I remember my mum telling me off for opening up (and of course putting a run in) a brand new packet of tights rather than going for an older pair. I guess that even back then I had standards!

In 1975 we moved back across the Pennines from Barrow to Killingworth, a small town just outside Newcastle. Killingworth's only claim to fame is as the place where George Stephenson first worked on his steam engine design while he was an engineer in the local mine. (Not coincidentally it was also the setting for the *Doctor Who* story "The Mark of the Rani". Yes,. I'm a Whovian geek as well as a comic book geek. Also, yes, it's far too late to return this to the shop and get Janet Mock's autobiography.)

Both sets of grandparents lived in Newcastle so I got to see them regularly. My paternal grandparents lived in a house in Palmersville, quite close to us and we would often visit. My Granda Bill had an allotment and I would sometimes go and help him there. The big draw, however, were the cakes that Granny Mellor made. She was always baking (and did so right up until her death) and had very high standards. If ever a cake was even slightly 'sad' in the middle, she was just as likely to throw it away than she was to serve it, despite our constant assertions that it still tasted amazing and the sadness didn't matter at all to us.

We also saw my maternal grandparents who lived a little further away in Kenton, often going for Sunday tea. Whenever I was allowed, I would go and open up their glass-fronted bookcase in the front room. While a lot of it was taken up with ornaments (including a beautiful metal horse statuette which now has pride of place on my desk) the bottom shelves held some beautiful old books. Amongst them were books of poetry by Keats, Longfellow and Wordsworth and a beautiful old bible that belonged to my great-grandfather. He had been a Methodist lay preacher and his Bible contained cuttings that he had found interesting along with notes in the margins illustrating his thoughts and ideas for sermons. It wasn't so much the content rather than their existence that fascinated me. These things were probably the oldest things I'd seen outside of a museum and I was allowed to look at them. The fact that they were books was a definite bonus.

Books had been part of my life from birth. My house had several shelves of them and my parents always read to me, at least until I learnt to read myself which happened very early - certainly before I started school. I would always have at least one book on the go and often two or three. Back then, one of my favourite authors was Enid Blyton - specifically The Famous Five and the 'Adventure' series. This latter series was very much a carbon copy of The Famous Five in that it was a tale about a group of horrendously upper-middle class children who were desperately English and desperately snobbish. The major difference between the children in this series and Julian, Dick, Anne and George (not to forget Timmy the Dog) was that their pet was a parrot called Kiki. All of the books had titles that were *The Something (Island/Valley/Mountain etc.) of Adventure.* I owned a collection of beautiful first editions of this series that had originally belonged to my father when he was young and I read and re-read them over and over again. Unfortunately, I have no idea what happened to them and I haven't seen them in years.

My favourite was *The Circus of Adventure*. In it an annoyingly foreign young boy, who doesn't understand what it means to be English, has girlishly long hair and keeps bursting into tears, comes to stay with the family one summer. It turns out that he is the Crown Prince of a vaguely Eastern European country, his long hair is one of the country's traditions and he's not allowed to cut it until he becomes king. He gets kidnapped by the evil Count (because of course there's an evil Count) and the kids go to his country to rescue him. While trying to get out of the country and back to good old Blighty they are taken in by a travelling circus. In order to hide the young prince he is disguised as a girl. Of course, they are successful and get back home for tea and cake and lashings of ginger beer and the young Prince vows to cut his hair so nobody can mistake him for a girl ever again! For some reason, that I didn't understand at the time, the young Prince being disguised as a girl absolutely fascinated me and I kept reading and re-reading the book specifically for that section. Here is a brief excerpt of the Prince (Gussy) being made over into a girl:

> *Gussy was not asleep, however. He lay in the small bunk, listening to Ma's deep breathing and sudden snorts. He was very angry and very humiliated. Ma had seen to him properly! She had tried his hair this way and that, and had finally decided that he looked more like a girl with a small bow at each side rather than with one big one on top. She had also looked out some clothes – a longish skirt, rather large, very highly coloured, and decidedly ragged – and a small red blouse with a green scarf tied skittishly round the waist.*

Ellen Mellor

Gussy could have cried with shame.

Blyton, Enid. The Circus of Adventure (The Adventure Series) . Hachette Children's Group.

I desperately wanted something like to happen to me especially as (after some initial piss-taking) the others become friendlier and closer to him as a girl than they had ever done when he had been a boy.

(Writing this section made me check out how much a copy of the first edition would cost me. Discovering it was only ten pounds I decided that I would honour the unaware young girl I was back then by buying it. So, once again, Ms Blyton has a place on my bookshelves.)

I never spoke about these desires because growing up in the 1970s meant that there were no role models for a young trans girl who didn't realise she could actually be a girl. The closest you got to it was Dick Emery in a dress proclaiming 'Ooh, you are awful!' or Les Dawson as Ada. Occasionally, Danny La Rue might turn up. But none of these were what you could call positive examples of someone assigned male at birth but really being female. I certainly don't remember being exposed to anything like Caroline Cossey's outing by the (absolutely unmissed) News of the World in 1976.

It must have been around the time of Caroline's outing that I first became aware of really wanting to be a girl. From the age of five or six I would go to bed most nights desperately wishing that I was a girl, imagining that I would wake up the following morning to discover that I had somehow been transformed into a girl and that everyone would be so happy for me.

Tea, Comics and Gender

As well as Enid Blyton's oeuvre, I had also discovered fantasy and science fiction - although the event that would set my feet firmly upon that path was still to occur. I read books by Nicholas Fisk (*Trillions* and *Grinny*) and John Christopher (The *Tripods* trilogy), reading *Watership Down* several times and loving *A Wizard of Earthsea* and *The Hobbit* but also starting out on Ray Bradbury, Isaac Asimov and Arthur C. Clarke. My dad had Book Club copies of Asimov's *The Bicentennial Man and Other Stories* and *The Foundation Trilogy*, that I read regularly from quite a young age. It was also around this time that I started writing stories, although I very rarely finished anything. The longest piece I completed when I was in First School was a two part *Star Trek/Doctor Who* crossover with which my teacher was very pleased. I remember getting the first part back marked as 10/10 and the comment that he was looking forward to the next instalment.

This was also a bit of a golden age for British televisual science fiction. Little of it actually stands the test of time now but there were shows like *The Tomorrow People*, *Blake's Seven*, *Space 1999*, and *Sapphire and Steel* that are still remembered fondly. That last one scared the crap out of me. One of the stories involved the true meaning of nursery rhymes. The evil entities in the story were depicted as moving lights on the ground. For years afterwards, I insisted on having the landing light on outside my bedroom because of it.

As I may have subtly mentioned, the biggest show on television was, at least for me, *Doctor Who*. I first started watching in 1976, with the story "The Deadly Assassin". I have vivid memories of The Master's rotting visage from that story, of the multiple faces of the Doctor saying 'Who am I?' in "The Face of Death" and Leela discovering that her eyes have changed from brown to blue (or possibly vice versa) in The Terror of Fang Rock". I didn't think I especially missed it when it went off air (although I was sorely disappointed by the huge mis-step that was the mid-90s TV Movie) and it wasn't until its return in 2005 that I realised how much of an influence it had had on my life and what a massive Whovian I actually was. Recently, I realised that although I may have not seen the stories since they were first broadcast, I have not missed a single episode since The Doctor's return to Gallifrey to thwart his arch-enemy once again.

None of those shows nor anything else I had watched (*Star Trek, Sinbad and the Eye of the Tiger, Silent Running*) prepared me for the event to which I alluded earlier. Sitting in the Odeon cinema in Central Newcastle having just been told that was I was about to see happened *A Long Time Ago, in a Galaxy Far, Far Away* when a huge, triangular space ship flew over my head with a gut-shaking rumble. I was entranced. *Star Wars* cemented science fiction into the very core of my being. It turned me into the geek that I am today.

It's pretty inevitable then that fantasy and science fiction would make their way into my internal life. At around the same as I was wishing that I could wake up as a girl, I also started to imagine an entirely new life for myself. I wasn't this ordinary boy in an ordinary house with an ordinary life. I was a princess and, because of some unexplained threat (probably an evil count), I had been magically transformed and placed for my own protection into this situation. Part of the magic was, of course, my inability to remember the truth. At some point soon, everything would be safe again and the wizard who had transformed me would come and remove this awful enchantment and I would go back to being my true self.

The first time I wore makeup occurred when I was about nine or ten. *Kings of the Wild Frontier* by Adam and the Ants had been released in 1980 and my brother and I both really liked it. Adam Ant (and the rest of his band, whose names I can remember due to them being named in *Ant Rap*: "Marco, Merrick, Terry Lee/ Gary Tibbs and yours truly") followed in the footsteps of older artists such as David Bowie by playing with his appearance in a way that differed wildly from most of the other bands of the era being an interesting mix of pirate and Native American but with more and glossier make up. One weekend, my brother and I persuaded our mother to paint our faces to mimic the appearance of Adam Ant. I'm absolutely certain that I enjoyed the experience more than Sean did.

We moved from Killingworth to Heaton when I was about 12, living about two streets away from where my dad grew up. Sean and I both still went to school in Killingworth but slowly started to make friends in Heaton as well. Most notably, a group of boys (and the - very occasional - girl) who were part of a local role-playing group that we both went to. We had discovered role-playing when I had been given a copy of *Basic Dungeons & Dragons* a year or so earlier. This totally hit my geek soul and it quickly grew into an obsession. Over the years, I bought more and more games, certainly more than I could ever reasonably play. Some of my favourite games included *Middle Earth Role Playing*, *Marvel Super Heroes* and *Call of Cthulhu*. While I loved playing every Sunday, I got sort of side- tracked into being the games master for the younger players (mostly because none of the older, more experienced players were prepared to do so) which was not a role with which I was entirely comfortable or happy. I always felt - and still feel - that I am at best a mediocre GM and my strengths definitely lie with being a player character. When I did get to play in a game, I would inevitably choose to play a female character. Looking back I can see that much of the scene in which I found myself at the time was quite toxic. While there were a couple of women who played, the vast majority of players were a very specific type of male. Intelligent but socially awkward, straight single men (there was perhaps one married couple who came along but I don't remember any others and there was certainly nobody who was openly gay). Coupled with this was a deep streak of misogyny that ran through many of the older players and which could be seen manifesting in some of the younger ones who were somewhat starstruck by being around these people with the money to do what they wanted and few, if any, real, 'grown up' responsibilities. The entire set up was a massive boys club with sexist, homophobic jokes constantly being cracked. People noticed that I almost always played a female character and some members of the group remarked loudly upon this face, wondering what it meant, but, when I played a male character that was also noticed and I would be questioned about why I was doing that so, really, I was in a no-win situation.

As I hit puberty, my desire to be feminine went to the next level but also changed its focus. While I had played dress up in my mother's clothes when I was younger, this had stopped as I grew older and my dreams of being a girl had faded. I was still fascinated with girls and 'girlishness' but I had consciously stopped wanting it for myself and had all but forgotten the dreams I had had when I was younger.

But as the testosterone started to flow, my desire for femininity crashed back into my life. I once again started to wear my mother's clothes although far more secretively than I had used to not only because, while it was okay for a child of five or six to play dress up, it was far less so for a teenager to do so but also because it was no longer innocent 'dress up fun'. Wearing those clothes came with an intense rush of sexual pleasure that I neither could nor wanted to deny. But, alongside that joy came a powerful feeling of guilt. I knew that getting excited by wearing girls' clothes was 'wrong' and I really shouldn't have been sneaking them out of my mother's drawers but at the same time I couldn't stop myself. Not only did the feel of soft satin, lace and nylon feel good and sexy, it also felt right. It felt like these were the clothes I should have been wearing.

I didn't know the word for what I was nor that it was something that other people did until my parents rented a video one evening. Sitting watching *The Rocky Horror Picture Show* with them was one of the most exquisitely uncomfortable and embarrassing things I have ever done. I sometimes wonder if they brought it home because they had suspicions about me although, on the whole, I doubt it. Instead it just looked like a fun, science-fiction film. If they had known about the sexual imagery in which the film was drenched I suspect they probably wouldn't have done so. Or at least waited until Sean and I were in bed before watching it.

This was not the only time they managed to unwittingly expose me to sex. The best present of Christmas 1985 (certainly the only one I can still remember) were copies of the two-volume fantasy saga *The War of Powers*. In itself it was just another second rate, sub-Tolkien knock-off. The thing that meant that I read and re-read it over and over again was the hardcore sex which came along (literally and metaphorically) every twenty pages or so - the non- human beings in the book were lizard men whose defining feature was that the males had two penises. There were several occasions when the book described exactly what they did when coupling with a human woman. Those books made the rounds of my school's Sixth Form on several occasions until it was possible to hold them loosely in one hand and they would just naturally fall open to one pornographic description or another. Unsurprisingly, I never let my parents read them and they had no idea until I told them several years later.

So, while watching *Rocky Horror*, I discovered the terms 'transvestite' and 'transsexual' and became aware of what I was. Unfortunately, as Frank's extremely omnivorous omni-sexuality was one of the few overt images I had ever seen of transvestism, it really confused me. As I had done before with comic books and role- playing games, I became more than a little addicted to the film, buying multiple copies of the soundtrack and listening to them over and over again and attending screenings as often as possible which were the most fun thing because of the audience participation that went along with them. Although Frank is definitely the strongest, certainly the most enjoyable, character in the film, I was never able to connect with him. His lifestyle was 'too extreme' for me, his sexuality too powerful. But he did have an effect on me. Despite seducing Janet, Frank was certainly far more interested in the male of the species, he was after all building himself a man and not a woman. There was no real sign anywhere that a man who wore lingerie would or could ever be properly attracted to women. Every time a transvestite turned up on the television, he was associated with being gay (and usually a serial killer but that's a separate thing all together). The only time I can remember it not being the case was in the awful *Two Ronnies* series 'The Worm That Turned' about a literal 'feminazi' dictatorship in which all the men are forced to dress in skirts and dresses, while the women all wore trousers, although the Secret Police all wore skin tight vinyl hot pants because, sexism.

This equating of crossdressing with homosexuality really screwed me up for quite a while, to the extent that one day I came out to my parents although even as I was telling them that I thought I might have been gay, I never hinted at the possibility that I enjoyed lingerie, skirts and make up. This was in the 1980s during the run up to Section 28 being enacted (the Tory legislation that outlawed the 'promotion of homosexuality' by local authorities) when AIDS was starting to run rampant and homophobia was growing equally as much, egged on by the usual media outlets. Despite that, it was still easier for me to come out as a gay boy than it was to tell my parents that I was a transvestite. However, after a while I came to realise that there was a fundamental problem with my burgeoning homosexuality in that I just didn't fancy boys. I was definitely about the girls and indeed finally at the age of sixteen persuaded one - a girl a couple of years younger than I was - called Adele to go out with me. Having a girlfriend was so much fun and kissing her was great (but that's all it was. She was only fourteen at the time) but I was still very interested in her clothes. I never wore anything of hers but I would have given anything to try on her school uniform. My relationship with Adele lasted for six months and then she

Ellen Mellor

dumped me. My reaction to this was to wear girls' clothes more often which became a lot easier to do as I'd finally started to buy my own. Although the fact that this all happened in the mid-80s, I had no idea what I was doing and I had to deal with the embarrassment of buying things meaning that I tried to get in and out of the shop as quickly as I could meant that I made some terrible fashion choices. I remember, in particular, a pale lilac Lycra mini skirt that I thought was really sexy, especially when combined with lace-topped stockings that peaked out from under the hem. This was nothing compared to some of the underwear I bought though. The only silver lining was that this was in a time before digital photography had been invented (or if it had been, it was not available to the likes of me) and the word 'selfie' had not yet been coined. There was no way I was going to take a photo of myself using a film camera and then send it off to be processed.

With the exception of Adam and the Ants which was, to be honest, more my brother's thing than mine, I hadn't really taken much notice of music in the early part of my life. Punk, New Wave, the New Romantics and all of those genres pretty much completely passed me by. The one record that I listened to on a regular basis was a *Goon Show* record which had 'Tales of Old Dartmoor' on one side and 'Dishonoured' on the other. To fit the episodes onto the record, the musical interludes by Max Geldray and Ray Ellington that punctuated the full-length episodes had been edited out. It was not until many years later that I discovered that listening to the Goons and killing myself laughing at Moriarty discovering the English Channel cunningly hidden away in the basement of Dartmoor Prison was my first encounter with a trans woman. The musical director for the Goons was a pre-transition Angela Morley who later worked (uncredited) with John Williams on the soundtrack for *Star Wars*. Music did start to seep its way into my life though. The first ever album that I personally owned was a tape of Queen's 1978 release, *Jazz*. I was given it one Christmas along with my very own Sony Walkman. All unknowing, I put the tape into the player, turned the volume up to maximum and pressed play. The first track of the

album is 'Mustapha' which starts with Freddie imitating a muezzin calling the faithful to prayer with a cry of 'Ibrahim! Ibrahim! Allah, Allah, Allah will pray for you..." Back then. that first cry of 'Ibrahim' was perhaps the loudest thing I had ever heard. Ripping the headphones off, I sat stunned by the sound I had just heard. It didn't take long for me to recover though and I soon tried again, this time with the sound turned down to a more sensible level. After that, I was pretty much hooked and started to listen to more although Queen was (and is) my first and greatest musical love. In July 1986, a few days shy of a year since they had captivated the world at *Live Aid* my mum took me to see them play at St. James Park in Newcastle with support from Status Quo. Inxs has been third on the bill that day but they had had transport issues coming from the previous venue and so were unable to make it. As a result, Quo did an extra forty minutes or so to make up for it. They were loads of fun but Queen was the reason I was there and they did not disappoint. Freddie had the whole crowd in the palm of his hand and played us as expertly as Brian May played his guitar. It was a mind-blowing experience. One of the most joyous moments of the gig for me was singing 'Tie Your Mother Down' to my mother while Freddie sang it to the rest of the audience. It made me laugh then and still makes me smile now.

Puberty is obviously a time of discovery when you work out who you are. And so it was that it was around this time that I discovered another part of myself. One that would come to define me at least as much as my gender. One of the friends I made at the role playing group was a boy a couple of weeks younger than me called Toby.

Not only was he an avid role player but he was also a comic book collector. I borrowed a great many of them from him before I started to collect them myself. When I did start I quickly became a regular visitor to Newcastle's only comic book shop, a tiny little pre-fab shack in the centre of town called Timeslip. Once again, it became something of an obsession, beginning with the *X-Men* which meant trying to collect every single X-related comic there was - and there were a lot (and that was even before I started to think about buying copies of the issues that were published before I started collecting). I'm not going to say that the whole 'misunderstood and hated because of who you are' was a fundamental part of why they chimed so strongly with me but, looking back, there has to be part of that in the mix there. At the same time, I was a teenager and all teenagers feel that they are misunderstood and hated so I can't claim that I was special in anyway with this identification. However, one thing that may have marked me out as being 'not like other boys' was that I identified wholly and entirely with the character of Kitty Pryde/Shadowcat. She was the youngest X-Man and I absolutely adored her. She is still my favourite comic book character. In a lot of ways, my obsession with the X-Men was more about her than it was about anyone else. There are two images of her in particular that really resonate with me. Even now, if I close my eyes, I can see them both. The first is a picture of her drawn by the amazing artist Alan Davis. It's just a picture of her in her Shadowcat costume fixing a computer, assisted by her pet dragon Lockheed and I just love it. It perfectly captures, for me, the strength and beauty of the character. The other is the cover of *Kitty Pryde and Wolverine* issue 1 by Al Milgrom. It's Kitty in a very cute skater outfit with the background separated between her home in upstate New York in the middle of winter and a very generic Japanese city. It wasn't a great story (and as a follow-up to the outstanding Claremont/Miller *Wolverine* series it really gets shown up) but I read it and re-read it because the focus was very much on Kitty and her becoming a bad-ass ninja.

My initial obsession with Kitty happened right in the middle of the vogue for aerobics. My mother had a dark blue leotard and light blue tights outfit that could - if one squinted really hard in a dark room - have been taken for Kitty's Shadowcat costume and I would

regularly 'borrow' these. I guess you could say I was cosplaying but really it was more about imagining myself as being as pretty and bad-ass as she was.

One last thing about Kitty and then I promise I'll shut up about her. Probably. In the movies, she was played by a pre-transition Elliott Page when the world thought that he was a lesbian women. That was, as far as I was concerned, perfect casting. I had always imagined Kitty as being a lesbian and this just confirmed everything for me. My head canon portrays the whole love affair between her and Colossus as a lavender marriage. If ever there was a character who was as gay as a gay thing it's Piotr Nikoleivitch.

It wasn't all fun and games and sexy times. Despite my

best attempts, my parents and my brother both caught me dressed on several occasions. While Sean didn't really care and was good enough not to threaten me with blackmail, my parents were unsurprisingly somewhat shocked. It wasn't necessarily that they were opposed to me wearing girls' clothes, it was just that this was a time when it wasn't understood and was often portrayed as a mental health problem in a way that it mostly isn't any more. While there are still people who try to put forward the 'trans people are mentally ill' trope, most people seem to see it as just a thing that happens and realise that the trope is intensely problematic anyway. If trans people are mentally ill then they need help and treatment rather than opprobrium and hatred. Research has shown that the best form of treatment has proven to be allowing them and helping them to be the person they need to be rather than trying to 'cure' them and turn them back into 'real' men or women. So, my parents weren't angry with me - apart from having invaded my mother's privacy by going into her wardrobe and drawers and taking her clothes - rather they were concerned. There was one occasion I can remember when they sat me down and asked if I thought I needed to speak to anyone. I said that I didn't think I did and promised that I wouldn't do it again. As you can tell, that was a promise that I kept faithfully and I am now a happy and successful straight cis man...

Coming out to people happened relatively early. Again, this is another example of how I differed from your 'average, every day' crossdresser, many - if not most - of whom stay very firmly in the closet. By the age of seventeen a lot of the eroticism that I had associated with crossdressing had already worn off which is why I felt comfortable telling someone. Obviously, there were still times it felt sexy but it was more along the lines of 'putting on sexy clothes make me feel sexy' in much the same way that cis women can feel sexy by wearing nice things. I just had a more obvious reaction to feeling that way. There were however just as many occasions, if not more, when I would put on a dress because it felt comfortable and right for me to be dressed that way.

Angela was one of my closest friends at the time. We met at high school and really got on well. There was no chance of us ever having a relationship that was more than just being friends, although I did ask her out at one point. I think it's probably a good thing that she said no. She quickly became one of my closest friends and the one person to whom I knew that I could tell absolutely anything. We later lost touch for about twenty five years due to one thing and another but as part of my transition, I decided to try to get in touch with several people from my youth and Angela was right at the top of my list. When we met up again it was almost as if the intervening years hadn't happened and we seemed to fall straight back into our friendship.

She was the first person I ever came out to, when I was around about seventeen years old. I was sitting in my parents' bedroom, talking to her on the telephone that was in there when I told her that I liked to dress in women's clothes, then described my outfit, which is a lot less sordid than it sounds as it was just a plain but pretty dress, bra, panties and stockings. Initially she didn't believe me and thought I was joking and it took until I had a chance to dress while I was with her for her to completely accept that I was telling the truth. From that moment on, she was completely supportive. She gave me clothes, taught me about wearing makeup and escorted me for my first outing as a girl into the real world.

The two of us, along with Suzanne, one of our mutual friends from school, went to a quiet little pub called The Northumberland Arms, situated beneath the Eldon Square shopping centre in the middle of Newcastle. It was very much an 'old man' pub in the middle of the week when we went. At the weekend, I believe it had a tendency to get busier and rowdier with football fans congregating there and getting loudly pissed, but that night there can't have been more than five other patrons. So, three young women going in there should probably have drawn more attention than it did. I was very thankful at the time that we were ignored by everyone. I was far too terrified to go to the bar to get the drinks but other than I found myself being quite comfortable and enjoying both being out in public and being 'one of the girls'. Along with that night being my first ever time out in public as a girl there were a few other 'firsts' that evening. It was the first time I ever went to a women's toilet; It was the first time I ever took public transport while in a skirt; and it was the first time I ever ran in high heels - to make sure that we didn't miss the bus. The whole evening went entirely without incident. Almost.

That first time that I went to the loo, Suzanne called out to me. I don't remember what she was saying, probably something about remembering to redo my lipstick while I was in there. However, when she called out to me, she forgot to call me by the name I had chosen (this was before I had settled on Ellen and was using the feminine form of my male name which was the name my parents would have given me had I been assigned female at birth) but instead called out my male name which of course absolutely terrified me. By accidentally outing me like that I was being opened up to ridicule and perhaps more. That it didn't seem to cause even a flicker of interest from the other punters shows how well Angela had chosen our destination. Susanne was incredibly apologetic, but it still took quite a while for my heart to slow down and my desire to leave to subside. The only form of public crossdressing in which I had ever indulged before I started to come out was for a sponsored Comic Relief Fancy Dress Day when I was in Sixth Form. I dressed as a stereotypically 'sexy schoolgirl' - short skirt, fish net stockings and suspender belt. I borrowed the skirt and a pair of French Knickers from one of the girls in my Computer Science class but bought myself the stockings and suspender belt. Amazingly enough, I still own those stockings although that is more because I never wear them and haven't thrown them out due to a misplaced sense of nostalgia rather than due to any supernatural strength that can be ascribed to them. It was fun but as it was seen as 'a laugh', along with all the other boys in drag, it also felt wrong. I didn't want to be laughed at for dressing as a girl. At the time I didn't think that I wanted to be a girl, but I wanted to be able to look like one. Of course, if anyone had suggested that I was doing it for any other reason than because it was funny, I would have been mortified and would have denied it strenuously. Probably to the extent that someone could have legitimately exclaimed 'methinks the lady doth protest too much!'

That was the only time I actually dragged up for a fancy dress party in the days before I started to come out as a crossdresser. I was worried that people would become suspicious of where I had

sourced the clothes and how I was so good at the

makeup. There was in fact one party later on, when C and I had started to live together and were renting a flat in Cullercoats, where I dressed as the Joker in a purple velvet jacket and black silk shirt, my face painted white, hair dyed green and bright red lipstick, a look that was more Cesar Romero than Heath Ledger. One of the guests, a colleague from work, came dressed as a sexy nurse with immaculate makeup and in beautiful high heels that he managed to wear for the entire night without once complaining. A feat that I am still unable to pull off. I wondered then and still wonder now if he had any hidden urges in which he was indulging that evening - which is exactly the reason why I hadn't done the same thing that night.

When I first started dressing, it took quite a while before I worked up the courage to actually go and buy things from high street shops.

The World Wide Web had not yet been invented so I was very restricted in what I could get. I was desperately embarrassed whenever I went into a shop being absolutely certain that everyone was staring at me, and knew I was looking at the pretty underwear specifically so I could wear it. At the time, there was a chain of shops called Transformations which catered to transvestites - offering clothing, makeup, makeovers and the like. The Newcastle branch was down a back alley which just made the whole thing feel even more sordid and it looked and felt exactly like a sex shop. I have been into sex shop a few times, from the really run down horrendous places with hard-core porn playing on screens that make you feel like you're in danger of catching an STD just by going in, to the Anne Summers style shops which are trying to make it a high street thing that is perfectly fine and nothing to be ashamed of.

Tea, Comics and Gender

Although I have bought myself a few things from Anne Summers over the years, I don't think I ever got anything in the vile shops, I went in them more out of curiosity than anything else and, once inside, was overcome with embarrassment. Coming out of them was even worse. Going in, you could wait until the coast was clear before making your move. When leaving you just had to go through the door and hope there was nobody there.

I did go into Transformations occasionally. It was somewhere I could be myself and admit that I enjoyed wearing feminine clothing although I never actually bought any clothes or make up or anything like that from there. The shop aimed itself squarely at the 'slutty tranny' end of the market (don't get me wrong, there's nothing wrong with a bit of sluttiness. It's quite fun.) which wouldn't have been so bad if it all hadn't been so relentlessly down market, sordid and poor quality. The clothes were all obviously really cheaply made from polyester and cheap vinyl. The wigs were very low quality, and the makeup was garish and poor. On top of all that it was also very, very expensive. From what I remember, the most basic set of panties was around about £20 (in the late 1980s - the equivalent of about £60 in 2021) and rapidly increased from there. Even the cost of the most basic outfit could run into hundreds of pounds. On top of the obvious price-gouging for those who were too shy to purchase clothes elsewhere, there was the sheer awfulness of the stuff they sold to help 'feminise' you. The one thing I remember was the breast enhancing cream which was claimed to increase the size of your breasts. This item was apparently the cause of several prosecutions by Trading Standards. I once read something that said that you would have gained more breast enhancement by rubbing standard body lotion into your chest. What I did buy were the cheaply made (but still expensive) erotic novellas that they sold. Little more than photocopied booklets, the stories ranged from forced feminisation to 'having to wear girls' clothes and then discovering that it made your life so much better' to 'everyone thought I was a boy, but something happened that allowed me to discover my true self and everyone loved me' type of stories. I far preferred the latter two scenarios over the former and would while away evenings hidden in my bedroom reading them over and over again. I eventually got rid of them but until then, they gave me a lot of comfort knowing there were other people out there who had the same as me. And they were often erotic as hell which was, of course, something that I really liked.

For me, buying clothes wasn't sordid and secret. I knew what I liked and the best place to get them was in an ordinary clothes shop. I didn't then - nor do I now - have any especially interesting or outré clothing tastes. I am really quite desperately vanilla with no fetishes, so my favourite shops were desperately pedestrian. Almost everything I bought came from either Marks & Spencer or Dorothy Perkins. As I said earlier on, when I first started buying clothes, I was desperately embarrassed to be in the women's clothing sections. Being in the underwear section was even worse. I knew that everyone was staring at me and knew that I was buying that cute skirt or that pair of panties for myself and they were judging me for it. At any moment, someone was going to point at me, laugh and call me a pervert. It took a very long time to realise that nobody cared, least of all the shop assistants. Most people had better things to do than police other people's purchases and my money was just as good as anyone else's. Slowly, I got used to wandering around the shops, looking at all the pretty clothes - most of which would never fit me, and I couldn't have afforded them even if they did. I started to make 'jokes' to the cashier, asking if she (I would only ever say this to a woman, never a man) thought it would suit me. Sometimes, they said that they thought it would, while at others just laughed. Either way was a win and helped me to become more and more comfortable about being in those shops. Finally, I reached the point where I grew brave enough to actually ask to try them on. In places like Marks and Spencer that wasn't a problem as I just went into the men's dressing rooms with my choices. In Dorothy Perkins and the other women's clothes shops it was a little harder. Some places said that they didn't feel like they could accommodate me because it could make their other customers uncomfortable, which I understood and accepted, but even then, they were perfectly polite and pleasant about it, telling me that instead they would be happy to exchange or refund them if they didn't fit. Which usually meant that I would buy the clothes, go to M&S and use their dressing rooms before taking them back if they weren't right. Many though, were absolutely fine with me trying things. They would often check the dressing rooms and ask me to wait until they were clear or at the very least that there weren't any women on view in a state of undress, but they would then allow me in. It was the same when I got brave enough to ask for advice from someone at a makeup counter. Approaching the Clinique counter in Boots was just as nerve-wracking as anything else to do with me indulging my feminine desires in public but my anxiety was quickly calmed when the ladies behind the counter proved how welcoming and willing to help they were, often giving me little lessons and mini-makeovers. Having them take it off once they had done my face so perfectly was always a wrench, but it was always my choice. They did take the sting out of it by giving my samples on a fairly regular basis though. I got to know some of the women behind the counters reasonably well and would often say hello to them when I passed, and they were always pleased to see me. They knew that if they got a crossdresser as a customer, they had someone who would be loyal because he was so happy to have found someone who is accepting of his femininity. Ironically, when I started to wear makeup regularly, I stopped using Clinique makeup and switched to No.7 because there was no way I could afford to pay the prices for Clinique's products.

2 Coming Out (V1.0)

I have never really explained why I called myself Ellen, always saying that I couldn't remember why I had chosen that name.

Well, that's not entirely true. After settling on the name, I decided to keep the reason behind it secret, mainly because I didn't think that it was anyone else's business.

However, I made a pact with myself that if I ever wrote a memoir, I'd reveal the truth.

So here it is:

Growing up, one of my favourite books was 'Call of the Wild' by Jack London. He lived in a town in California called Glen Ellen. I was rereading Call of the Wild when I was deciding on a name and remembered the name of the town. I wanted to have a little personal tribute to one of my favourite writers.

My A-Level results were pretty terrible to be honest. Looking back, I realise that I had chosen entirely the wrong subjects and was heading down the wrong path. I got a B at AS Level Maths because I hadn't been good enough to do the full A-Level which had been decided the previous year when I had failed both the exam in Lower Sixth and the subsequent resit at the beginning of Upper Sixth.

When I was sitting in the classroom just about to start my resit, one of my maths teachers came into the room and told us all that we had to remember that if we failed this we wouldn't be allowed to continue on to do the A-Level. I think that I just gave up then at least partly as a 'fuck you' to that teacher. I got a C in Computer Science - we were a class of three, me and two cis girls, one of whom I was desperately attracted to but with whom I had absolutely no chance. She was beautiful, tall, slender and always immaculately made up. I was actually really jealous of both her abilities and the fact that she could wear the girls' uniform every day. She was the school's best dancer and I had vague daydreams about choreographing a dance piece for her. The closest I ever got to that was getting her to be one of the backing singers (along with Angela) when I and two of my friends did a Blues Brothers skit for a school show - it was originally going to be just two of us - Steffen as Jake and me as Elwood but the third friend insisted on being a part of it and so we created a third brother, long before *Blues Brothers 2000*.

My final A-level was Physics for which I received a grade of 'N'. This was actually something of a surprise to me because I was expecting to fail entirely, so to get a result of 'nearly passed' was far better than I was anticipating. I was really fairly rubbish at Physics. I could never remember equations (which, to be honest was because I was too lazy to actually put in the time needed to learn them which was itself a symptom of having chosen the wrong subjects) and I had the amazing ability of always - always - being able to choose the wrong option when two were presented to me. This unique ability was made even worse because my friend (who had been the third Blues Brother) who sat beside me and got an A would often whisper the answer to me and I would ignore him because I didn't really trust him. It later turned out that I was right not to do so on so many levels.

Even despite my bad results I accrued enough UCAS points to get me onto the Computer Science degree course at Newcastle Polytechnic which I started in September 1989. I hated the course. I hated everything about it. The worst part of it was the maths class. I had to make it to A-Level standard by the end of the first year but just stopped going after three or four lectures. In our first class, the lecturer handed out the entire year's notes on badly Banda machine-copied sheets and then proceeded to read them out to us, even going so far as to copy the examples from the sheet onto the board without any extra explanation. After about six weeks I had a revelation: I didn't mind using a computer as a tool, but I had absolutely no desire to use one as a means to an end. Considering that I had spent the last several years aiming directly at this as a career path, this was pretty devastating. And then I compounded my mistake by not officially dropping out of the course. Instead, I just stopped going to lectures and, because nobody ever chased, I spent the entire year collecting my grant and hanging out with my friends. For some reason though, I did attend the exams at the end of the year. Unsurprisingly, I failed every single one of them, leaving the maths exam after about twenty minutes, although I have to admit to being quite proud of this achievement. Shockingly, I wasn't invited back for year two. I may have been able to start again but I chose not to engage with the process at all failing to attend a meeting with the course leader to which I had been invited, which I rather regret now because doing that was just rude.

The following year was spent working nearly full time in a pub while I tried to work what to do next. The Tap and Spile on Shields Road in Byker was not your standard Shields Road pub in that there was almost never any violence and it sold decent beer. It was one of a chain of real ale pubs and over time I became head bar person. Despite being a total non-drinker, I never tapped a bad barrel and became really quite adept at running the place when the landlord wasn't around. One of my favourite things to do was to reply to the question "What do you recommend" by saying "Well, the lemonade is really good". The landlord himself was a complete git and was quite abusive to his wife. She was a real sweetie and one of the people that I actually told about my crossdressing. She's also the only non-girlfriend I have ever 'got off' with. The only nightclub I ever went to of my own accord was 'Walkers'. Wednesday night was Indie Night and it played all of my favourite music. And some of my least favourite. For some reason, the DJ would always play at least two mixes of Move Any Mountain by The Shamen. I don't like The Shamen generally, but I really fucking detest that track. It got so that I could (and still can) recognise it by the end of first bar of music and immediately get off the dance floor, loudly berating the DJ for playing it a-fucking-gain. One Wednesday, a bunch of us went along and she came with us. Somehow, I'm not sure how but I suspect it had a lot to do with the amount of alcohol she had imbibed and my inherent teenage horniness, I ended up lying on top of her under a table, my tongue in her mouth and hand up her skirt. It's not exactly my finest moment.

Soon after that, I met my third girlfriend. She was a very pretty barmaid at the Dog and Parrot, a pub I often frequented in Newcastle usually before heading off to Walkers. I had been talking to her for a few weeks and finally worked up the courage to ask her out and she agreed. Although it was a very short relationship, no more than a couple of months, we did end up in bed together. It was my first-time having sex and I don't really remember much about it other that it being an incredibly unsatisfying episode for all concerned.

Tea, Comics and Gender

Casting around for something to do and a direction to take, I spent a year at Gateshead College studying a Higher Education Foundation Certificate in Media and Communication Studies. It wasn't an especially arduous course but was fun and something in which I was actually interested. The highlight was making a music video for the song Stand by REM. I believe I may still have a copy of it on a VHS video tape somewhere, but I have no idea where. What I found interesting was that, when I made my version, I hadn't seen the actual video, the similarities between my version and the official video were quite striking. Although mine had fewer topless women dancing around.

After that, in autumn 1990, I went to back to university to study for a degree in Humanities at Teesside Polytechnic. Going to university in Middlesbrough meant that I actually moved out of my home. Not very far, admittedly as Middlesbrough is only about thirty miles down the coast but it was a start. I didn't actually make a decision about what I wanted to do until a few weeks after the course had begun and so I started having to catch up. Starting late also made finding somewhere to live quite difficult and it took a few days of searching before I finally found a room in a house that had three lads in it. While I loved the course, I very quickly ended up really disliking my house mates. They were loud, laddish and generally quite unpleasant. During the week, I tended to live in my room with the door locked wearing lingerie. At the weekends, I went home.

My girlfriend had gone to art college in London that September and saying goodbye was pretty much the last time I heard from her. We may have spoken on the phone a couple of times but even that quickly stopped. Then a couple of months later, on November 11th, I received a letter from her ending our relationship. I'd pretty much worked out that we weren't together anymore by this point, so wasn't upset. I know the exact date I got the letter because it was the day before I went to a Wedding Present gig at Sunderland Polytechnic. I was going with Angela who had moved out of her home at that point and was staying in my parents' spare room. Somehow, she had managed to get a ticket and I hadn't and for some reason (which I suspect was connected with her having a ticket), she was actually meeting up with some of her other friends and then meeting me at the gig. We had agreed that if I couldn't get in, I would lend her some money to get both of us some merchandise. There were about three people in the queue in front of me when they announced that they had sold out. Greatly annoyed, I waited at the barrier in order to hand some money over to Angela who had already gone in. Just as she was coming over, I was told that actually they hadn't sold out and there was a ticket available for me.

The one drawback to the gig being in Sunderland was that I had to miss the end of the gig in order to catch the last Metro home. Once again, Angela stayed behind with her other friends who were going to give her a lift. Living in Heaton - actually in the house that I would later use as Rachel's home when I wrote *Ghostkin* - meant changing trains at Monument station in the centre of Newcastle. The platform for the Metro to Chillingham Road was empty apart from one pretty young woman. Buzzing the intercom, I asked if I had missed the last train and was told that I had, meaning that the only choice I had, as I couldn't afford a taxi, was to walk home. It was annoying but as I'd done it many times before after a night at Walkers, I wasn't complaining too much

Tea, Comics and Gender

Walking up the steps out of the station, I saw the young woman who had been on the platform and overheard my conversation with the intercom person. Smiling at her, I asked where she lived. She replied that she lived in Heaton, so I offered to walk her home. Bearing in mind that I had long dark hair and was dressed all in black with a long, black trench coat, it was reasonably surprising that she said yes.

As we walked back, she told me her name, that she was a first- year student at Newcastle Polytechnic studying French, Russian and Politics and had just been to a Freshers Russian evening at the Cooperage, a pub that had been in the same building on the Quayside since the fifteenth century. She had had quite a lot of vodka to drink and was really rather drunk. We talked and laughed together the whole way back to her place. Looking back, it felt like I had known her for my whole life rather than for half an hour.

When we got to her door, I asked if she would like to go out on a date with me sometime. To my total amazement - and I think somewhat to hers - she once again said yes. The following evening, when I went to work in the pub, I asked if I could have the following night off as it was a Wednesday night and I wanted to take her to Walkers. Getting the go ahead, I rang her and once again she surprised both of us by saying yes.

In the beginning our relationship was one that only happened at the weekends as I met her during the first few months of my own degree at Teesside. But, even so, it quickly went from strength to strength - I remember traipsing through heavy snow that winter to hand deliver love letters to her.

Ellen Mellor

Middlesbrough in the early 1990s was not a very nice place, surrounded by chemical factories with air that was not exactly the freshest thing ever. There is a story I heard once that the director Ridley Scott, who was born and raised in Cleveland, based the opening of *Blade Runner* with its flaming chimneys and dark towers on his childhood memories of seeing the chemical factories burning off excess gases. It had improved since then and has (as far as I understand it) continued to improve but in the early nineties it was still pretty grotty. To the extent that it smelled in summer. I have very mild asthma but living in Middlesbrough caused it to become a lot worse. On top of that, I woke up one morning to discover my eyes were stuck together with gunk, something that really freaked me out. Discovering that I had quite severe conjunctivitis (which I blame on Middlesbrough's polluted atmosphere), combined with the fact that I really disliked my house mates and really liked C and wanted to be closer to her more often, convinced me that it was time to give up on Middlesbrough and move home. I spent the next two and half a years commuting to poly, first on the bus and then, when I learnt to drive, by car. Travelling back and forth like this was only really possible because it wasn't exactly an intensive degree course. In my final semester I had four hours of timetabled lectures and all the parts of the degree I had chosen - which had by this time allowed me to specialise, turning from a Humanities into an English degree - were either coursework only or seen exams. Which, to be honest, rather annoyed C. Her degree was practically full time and she had weeks of exams at the end of the whole thing. The hardest thing I had to do was write my final year 'dissertation' a ten-thousand-word essay on post-modern comic books. I also got to write an essay in one of my seen paper exams about why

Watchmen should be included on the syllabus. It has been said on several occasions that I don't actually have an English degree but a comic books degree. And I really can't find it in myself to disagree. Although I also wrote an essay about the Talking Heads concert movie *Stop Making Sense* as a post-modern deconstruction of a rock concert so, it wasn't entirely about the Postmodernist aspects of Superman wearing his trunks outside his tights and the gendered implications of cape-wearing.

Very early on, I knew that C was the one. This was the woman with whom I really wanted to spend my whole life. And if that was the case, then I knew that I had to be honest with her. Telling her about my desire to dress in women's clothing, despite being sure that she would be okay with it, was perhaps the hardest thing I had ever done in life. Nothing else - not my A-levels, not dropping out of university, not telling my parents that I thought I might be gay, not telling Angela about dressing, not even going to the pub in a skirt - was as difficult as telling C that I liked to wear lingerie, dresses and make up.

We had been together about six months and things were going really well, to the extent that I was regularly spending the night, sharing her single bed. I had been trying to work up the courage to tell her for several weeks. Finally, of course, when I managed to do so I did it in one of the worst ways I possibly could have chosen.

It was half past one in the morning, and we were finally settling down for sleep. In fact, I think she may have already actually been mostly asleep. I managed to blurt out the words "I have something to tell you."

Which woke her up. Unfortunately, I then clammed up

and couldn't say anything else. For the next ten minutes, I struggled, while she tried to stay awake. Then, just as she was succumbing to sleep again, I managed to get out the words to tell her that I was a transvestite. That I enjoyed wearing women's clothing. Her reply was "Oh. Okay. Can I go back to sleep now." It obviously didn't matter to her at all. I was still me and she still loved me. She was just very tired and needed sleep. I, however, was absolutely thrilled and so I asked her to marry me. Now THAT woke her up. It wasn't a serious proposal, rather it was a reaction to her not kicking me out bed. Up until this point I'd been fairly certain that she was special, but this absolutely confirmed it.

A few weeks passed before she saw me in a skirt and, as I had hoped, it didn't faze her at all. It neither turned her on nor off. She just didn't care - as far as she was concerned, what I wore didn't change who I was. It was just something I enjoyed that gave me comfort and so was fine by her. Over the years, she bought me lots of lovely, girly presents - clothes, jewellery and the like - and every time she proved to me how much she cared for me, loved me and supported me. I know that without her, I would never have had the courage or the strength to become who I am now.

C's third year at university was a gap year in which she spent six months in Moscow (experiencing winter there which entailed partially frozen, cheap Russian champagne 'slushies' in Red Square on New Year's Eve and being told off by babushkas for not wearing a hat) and six months in Bordeaux (spending the spring and early summer there). While I wasn't able to go to Russia, I did spend a few weeks in Bordeaux with her, sharing her tiny single bed and driving around the country with the others of her group.

Tea, Comics and Gender

During the time she was away, I wrote to her every day. To make things more interesting, I would find different things on which to write - clear plastic, tin foil and the like as well as interesting bits of paper which I bundled up and sent weekly.

When she returned, C found it very difficult to get back into the swing of things with life back in Blighty. While she was able to manage at uni, she found that her year away had given her a taste for being by herself. One evening when I was around at her place, she told me that she wasn't sure if she wanted to continue our relationship. While I had been stuck at home attending my second year in Middlesbrough, I had been pining for her and desperately missing her. We had always had what seemed sometimes to be an almost psychic level of understanding of one another so to discover that her feelings had changed like this was devastating. I don't know if she took pity on me for breaking down in tears or if she just wasn't sure enough of her feelings to want to go through with splitting up but, after a shaky couple of months, we did seem to get back onto an even keel.

After university - in which C got a 2:2 in French and Politics and I gained a 2:1 in English - neither one of us managed to find immediate entrance into the world of high salaries and exciting jobs that having successfully completed a degree in the Humanities should have entailed. (Quick joke: Why doesn't an English student look out of the window in the morning? It gives them nothing to do in the afternoon...) Instead, we ended up working pretty dead-end jobs but at least we were together. Initially we rented a Tyneside Flat (a specific design of flat that is prevalent throughout much of Newcastle and Gateshead) in Heaton before then moving to a gorgeous, but bizarre flat in Cullercoats which we managed to get because one of the people who lived there before us had been a long-time friend of C's. So, when she and her partner moved out, we moved in. It was the top floor of a converted house with almost every room on a different level from the others. The front room looked East directly out of over Cullercoats Bay and there were several occasions when C, getting up at the crack of dawn for a shift in a nursing home, would come and wake me to show me a particularly gorgeous sunrise. I was not necessarily very impressed by this.

As well as living together we also worked together for a time. C got a job in a company which tracked advertising for other companies. She was brought on in order to bolster the Foreign Publications department which meant that she got to read things like *Le Monde* and French *Vogue*. Shortly after she started more vacancies came up and the staff were asked if they knew anyone who would be interested. I applied for a position in a project looking at computer magazines and one of C's friends from university, Kathryn, went for one in the same department as C. (Kathryn had nick-named her 'Scary C' while they were in Bordeaux because she was very good at organising things and refused to take any shit. For example, she once told off a lecturer when he grew exasperated at a room full of girls and one gay guy for not knowing that the initials 'OM' stood for Olympic Marseilles which is, or was or will be or something, apparently one of the best football clubs in France.)

We both got the jobs although, oddly, we knew we had them before we even went for our interviews because we had been told to come along dressed in work clothes as we would be starting immediately afterwards. It wasn't a great

Tea, Comics and Gender

job. The managers of the company were pretty terrible and would have had difficulty organising the proverbial piss-up in a brewery. I know for a fact that it's much better now because, although C and I both left after about eighteen months there, Kathryn stayed on and moved up the ranks. The one positive thing that I took from that place was my friendship with Jean.

Jean was another member of the Foreign Languages department and we hit it off almost immediately. She is a ferociously intelligent, wonderful older woman. She and her partner Roger are Dylan-loving folkies as well as being extremely knowledgeable wine connoisseurs and I adore them both. Jean is also a massive geek. The first time we met, she was wearing a John Totleben illustrated *Swamp Thing* t-shirt. Her comic book collection is a thing of beauty, and she has many, many comics which I thoroughly covet and a great many more 'real' books than I do. Once we discovered each other we were nearly inseparable and would spend all our breaks and lunch times talking about this stuff. We would boast that we could clear a room by having incredibly in-depth discussions about comic book minutiae, including such wonderful topics as our favourite letterer (which for me is and always will be Todd Klein although Tom Orzechowski and John Workman also hold a special place in my heart).

I finally, officially, came out to my parents in my early twenties. I went to see my mother one day while my father was at work. I love my father but the thought of telling them both together was just too scary. When I finally said the words, she was absolutely fine but asked the two questions that always seem to be asked in these circumstances: Was I gay and did I want a sex change? I replied no to both of them. At the time, I didn't think I was lying I was just so deep in the closet - to myself as well as to anyone else - that my best friend was a faun called Mr Tumnus. Rather than having the courage to tell my father myself, I asked if she would tell him. The next day, he rang me at work to tell me he loved me no matter what. After that, I started to come out to more and more people - including my brother. Not a single person walked away from our friendship. Many of them said that it made sense, that it illuminated a lot of things I had said and done over the years. Having friends who were so supportive meant that I felt able to start dressing more and more often

Difficult though it is to admit, things were not as perfect as they might have seemed. I was with a woman that I adored and who loved and supported me. I had friends around whom I could wear a skirt pretty much whenever I wanted. I had a family that supported me and loved me. And yet, I had still had issues. Issues that I didn't, couldn't, allow myself to see. After university, I still had no idea what I wanted to do with my life and drifted from job to job, never looking to improve my prospects and complaining about how much I hated my job. It felt like I was being forced down a career path of being an office administrator; something for which I had no interest or enthusiasm. I did try new things but not even they didn't lead to anything positive. I spent a couple of years working in Waterstone's bookshop running the science fiction section. In theory that should have been the perfect career but after a few months the bloom faded from the rose. As the managerial position became more about central purchasing and dictating the stock that the shops would hold it became less and less a place where those who worked there felt like they had any autonomy and were able give their sections a certain amount of personality. Instead, it became more about stocking the books that would earn them the most profit. Ultimately, I would have been got just as much job satisfaction from stacking tins of beans as I did from making stacks of the latest blockbuster or ghost-written memoir by a soap star or footballer.

Over the years, every single job I did had one thing in common. They were starter level, few if any offered the prospect of moving upwards and paid terribly. Meanwhile, I saw those around me moving onward and upwards, getting better jobs and more money. It's only now, looking back that I realise that I wasn't able to do that because I didn't particularly like myself and didn't feel like I deserved better. If I had challenged myself to improve, it might have started to uncover other things. Things that I was not ready to face and wouldn't be for many years to come.

Every so often I tried to find other transvestites who could understand why I did what I did without me having to explain myself. I went to a few support groups but always found them deeply depressing. I had absolutely nothing in common with most of the other people. The groups often seemed to consist of a bunch of blokes wearing dresses standing around talking about cars and football. I couldn't relate to them. I know that cars and football are not solely male things, indeed I know many men - both cis and trans - who have no interest in either one of these things and several women who do, but it was just the most obvious example of why these places were really not for me. I would, more often than not, ultimately find myself talking to the trans women who were there which still didn't make me realise the truth. Nor did my occasional ruminations to myself that if ever C and I were to split up I would probably start to live full time as a woman - with the proviso that we were never going to split up, so it absolutely wasn't a problem. The only person I have actually kept in touch with from those groups is a crossdresser called Janet who is lovely, sweet and insists on buying me nice packets of tea whenever we meet up.

Living close to my parents, they would often come around for a cup of tea. One afternoon my mum came over with some important news. She and my dad were separating. While I'm sure that there were signs, I had no idea and this totally took my breath away. I collapsed in tears, which was far from an ideal response. Neither one had done anything wrong, rather they had just grown apart and they weren't happy together anymore. I think it's ultimately been for the best, but it was a rough period for all of us.

Through this period of the mid to late nineties both C and I attempted to enter the world of education from the other direction. C successfully passed her Post Graduate Certificate of Education and started teaching Modern Languages in a school in West Denton, a very deprived area in the west end of Newcastle with pupils whose parents and grandparents had been unemployed and had every expectation of ending up the same way. Some of these children had never even made the journey from the area in which they lived into the centre of town. It was very much a trial by fire for her and one that she passed with flying colours, getting used to facing down kids who towered over her when they decided they'd had enough and wanted to leave the classroom.

Tea, Comics and Gender

I was somewhat less successful when I chose to try and teach English. The only thing I really learnt doing the course was that there was absolutely no way in hell I should ever teach. I could just about manage the bottom sets and I was okay with the top sets but had endless trouble with the middle sets. The ones who had the pupils that were bright enough to learn but couldn't be bothered and were more interested in causing trouble. I had no idea how to engage with them and they knew it meaning that when I went into a school and actually tried to teach, I quickly lost control and never succeeded in gaining it back. I joke now about how one of my issues was that I had no come back for the constant complaint that they just didn't like to read because it is not a phrase that I can understand in any way but it's true. I had no idea how to communicate with these children whose interests and ideas were almost entirely alien from my own. It was not a failing on their part, it was how they had been brought up. Part of my job was trying to instil in them a love of books and literature and I failed utterly. I am still convinced that the only reason I passed the course was to ensure that the university kept its pass rate up and because they knew that I would never actually use my qualification. Really, the only positive thing to come out of it was that I used part of my student loan to buy myself a pair of medical grade prosthetic breasts. And, considering that I have never yet earned enough money to even considering starting to repay it (and as long as I continue that streak until I'm fifty when the loans get written off), they were essentially free.

C taught at West Denton for a few years, I worked at Waterstone's, and we were happy together. We had bought our first flat together, a one-bedroom place in a lovely 1920s converted town house overlooking Heaton Park and we were in a state of unwed bliss. And then C came home from work one day and said to me "Do you fancy going and living in France?"

I thought about it for all of a second and a half before replying "Yes."

3
Up and coming in Paris and London

I have never really explained why I called myself Ellen, always saying that I couldn't remember why I had chosen that name.

Well, that's not entirely true. After settling on the name, I decided to keep the reason behind it secret, mainly because I didn't think that it was anyone else's business.

However, I made a pact with myself that if I ever wrote a memoir, I'd reveal the truth.

So here it is:

To put it simply, my favourite character in The Waltons was Grandma Walton, played by Ellen Corby. She was smart, funny, caring and wise - basically all the things I wanted to be. By taking her name, I hoped for some 'sympathetic magic' to work itself and make me like her. I shall leave it to those who know me to decide whether or not it worked.

C had realised that her ability to speak French had deteriorated while she had been working in West Denton. The majority of her job was about discipline and crowd control and very little of it was about actually teaching French. After all, some of the children she was teaching were essentially functionally illiterate in English and so trying to teach them French was never going to work. We were still young and free and so it seemed like an ideal time to go and do something else. C spent about six months looking at various places - at one point it seemed like there was a change that we might end up in Mauritius - but eventually she landed a job as a secretary in a pharmaceutical firm based in La Défense, the business district on the outskirts of Paris. She went over to start work and look for somewhere to live. I joined her a month or so later.

The sweetest thing that happened at Waterstone's occurred when I left there. My going away present was a really rather beautiful lacy bra and pantie set. It made me feel so very accepted and loved by the people with whom I had worked. One of them, Kristine, is still someone I consider to be one of my very closest friends.

Finding a place to live in Paris was actually really, really difficult. The renting situation is very different from here in England - rather than making an appointment to go and see a place and then being able to look around by yourself before making an offer, French (or at least Parisian) renting is done almost the entirely opposite way. An open house is advertised, everyone goes along, hands over their paperwork and then waits for a decision about who gets the place. It took us weeks to find somewhere to live. C had been living in a hostel near the Gare de Lyon and I joined her there when I went across. Those first few weeks were not easy. C had to go to work which meant that sometimes I had to go and look at the properties by myself. My French was only slightly better than non-existent, having given it up in order to study German at O-Level instead. I could, just about make myself understood and in turn could just about understand what I was being told but it was far from ideal and undoubtedly added to the difficulties we had in persuading the owner to rent to us. There were a couple of times where it looked like we were going to have to give up and come home - a prospect which was difficult at best because we had rented out our flat. However, eventually we were successful and found a tiny little flat in an extremely Parisian little apartment block in the eighteenth arrondissement, on the northern side of the Butte Montmartre upon which stands the Sacre-Coeur. It was tiny and it was very, very basic but it was our home in Paris and it was wonderful.

I spent the first few months just finding my feet and learning the language, finally being able to follow conversations but only if I concentrated. If I got distracted or let my mind drift for a few moments I would be utterly bewildered by how the discussion had moved on. One of the highlights of that time was taking the RER out to La Défense and meeting C for lunch. The place she worked had the most amazing canteen. It was incredibly cheap; the selection was amazing and everything was cooked completely fresh. You would stand and watch the chefs cook your fish or your steak or your pizza or whatever it was you had decided to have for lunch that day, it would be the best thing I had eaten that week and cost no more than twenty or thirty francs - this was about a year or eighteen months before the EU would formally adopt the Euro. As we got to the end of our stay, we saw more and more things being priced in both Francs and Euros in anticipation of the change.

One of the real perks of C's job, other than the food, was the extremely cheap annual pass she was able to get for the Louvre. We could jump all the queues and just pop in for an hour or so to look at one particular room or have a little wander. My favourite part was the Grecian statue exhibit. They were just so beautiful. Of course, we saw the Mona Lisa and, to be honest, I came away from it being less than impressed. I don't know if it was because I didn't think much of the picture itself or because it was encased in a thick glass box, surrounded by tourists taking flash photos of it and ignoring all the other amazing works of art that were being damaged by their thoughtlessness. But whatever the reason, I just didn't really get the excitement.

I did continue dressing 'en femme' (when in France and all that...) while living in Paris but had to curtail it a little as I just didn't have the space for my day-to-day wear never mind feminine attire. I did manage a couple of nights out though, once with a Parisian crossdresser support group to a small restaurant and once for dinner at the flat of an English crossdresser who living in Paris.

Eventually I felt confident enough to start actually looking for a job and found employment in a small comic book shop on the Rive Gauche. There was an area leading up from the river along Rue Dante to the Boulevard Saint-Germain which held several English language comic shops. I did discover another one later in another part of the city but the majority of them were all clustered here.

Checking on Google Street View I see that the shop in which I worked is no longer there. This doesn't surprise me as the owner was not exactly a smart businessman. He was very probably an alcoholic, or at least came into the shop drunk on a semi-regular basis. The assistant manager was a lovely guy and knew exactly what he was doing but it was difficult for him to do his job when the owner would come into the shop, open the till, take out some money and go over to the Tabac (bar) across the street. I was employed essentially to deal with the British supplier, although I also served customers. One of the hardest parts of my job was trying to understand the title of the comic that a customer was asking for - especially when they were on the phone. During one particular conversation the customer asked if the latest issue of 'Pri-shaare' was available. I have not done justice to the amount of mangling that he did to the title. It was truly unintelligible and took about five minutes to work out that he was actually asking about 'Preacher'. 'Spawn' and 'The Simpsons' were also titles where the accent vexed me somewhat. On the whole, I enjoyed the job. It wasn't too stressful and gave me plenty of time to sit around and read comics. I also, occasionally, got to take the piss out of Americans who, when they came into the shop and asked if I spoke English occasionally (depending on how arsey I was feeling at the time) got the reply 'better than you'.

After about six months or so, working in the comic shop started to pall a bit. It was mainly due to the very low salary (which was made even lower by the ease with which I could buy comics. Comics with staff discount can still make a sizeable hole in your bank balance when you buy a lot of them) but also because of the owner's attitude. Over the months I worked there, he got worse and started to get more drunk more often which made me feel uncomfortable when he was around. He was never threatening to me, but he was a very loud, quite aggressive drunk and would go off on rants about his ex-wife. I started to look for a new job, surprising myself by finding one quite quickly working at UNESCO as an audio typist. It wasn't exactly the best job in the world, but it paid significantly more than the comic shop did, especially as working in UNESCO meant that I didn't pay taxes. Again, it wasn't exactly a hard job, but it gave me a lot of typing practice which has served me very well ever since.

Living in Paris was one of the best experiences I have

ever had. It was absolutely magical and there are memories I have that will stay with me forever. Eventually, it became pretty much like living in any other city but, every so often, I'd be walking along a street, and I'd catch sight of the Eiffel Tower or Notre Dame or something like that and it would hit me all over again: 'Fucking hell. I'm living in Paris!' But eventually, it was time to return to Blighty. Living abroad was never intended to be a permanent thing and both C and I agreed that it was time to head home. Or at least, sort of home. Back to the land of warm beer and hot tea anyway.

Rather than coming back to Newcastle, we decided to give London a shot. C is actually a Londoner, being brought up in Westminster, literally one street away from the Abbey Road Recording Studios. I have crossed that famous crossing on many occasions, often rolling my eyes at the tourists stopping all the traffic to take photos of one another standing bare foot in the middle of the road. (I have taken a photo of someone doing this, when Katrina came to London for a few days but being a hypocrite in no way undermines my original point.)

Finding a place to live was significantly easier in London and we got a rather nice little place in Highbury, about ten minutes' walk away from the old Arsenal football ground. C started teaching in Hackney and I got a job in a bookshop in Islington. It was a brand- new shop in which I worked from before it opened for business, stacking the shelves and the getting the place ready for opening. Management weren't the nicest people, not only because they didn't give me the science fiction section (they gave it to a guy who, quite frankly, didn't have the depth of knowledge that I do) but also because, when I went for a position in the store as an Events Coordinator, I didn't get it because, when talking about my time in Waterstone's, I referred to 'we' instead of 'they' which the people interviewing me chose to interpret as meaning that I still felt that I owed loyalty to Waterstone's. I didn't last very long there and subsequently managed to get a job working in City & Guilds coordinating and editing exams in such exciting and diverse subjects as plumbing and flour milling. At least it paid reasonably well.

One of the reasons we went to London was because C's father, Guy, was ill. He was getting on in years and it was all finally catching up to him. He had had an amazing life though. He was an army Captain during World War II and saw the Allied bombing of Caen from a hill overlooking the town. He celebrated at the time but subsequently saw it for the war crime it was, causing him to become a Communist upon his demobbing. After the war, he became a film editor. His most prestigious job was working with Orson Welles on the film Mister Arkadin (which was subsequently cut to shreds by the studio and released as Confidential Report). Once while in Paris, Orson asked Guy if he would take Orson's ex-wife out to dinner basically because he was too nervous to do so. Guy agreed, which is how he came to have dinner with Rita Hayworth. Guy also spoke about drinking with Erroll Flynn and David Niven and about doing Foley work on the 1952 version of Ivanhoe - in fact, C can't watch the battle scenes without imagining her father bashing pots and pans in time to the clashing of fake swords against fake armour. He and a few friends also set up a small film company. It didn't survive very long but, while it was a going concern it made a small piece of movie history. His film company was responsible for the famous advert for 'Strand Cigarettes'. It is a beautiful piece of work, atmospheric and noirish depicting a lone man lighting up with a beautiful jazzy soundtrack before a very posh man intones that 'you are never alone with a Strand'. It's readily available on YouTube and, if you haven't seen it, I'd really recommend watching it. Movie lore claims that this advert was responsible for destroying the company because it associated the cigarette with being alone, but Guy was firmly of the opinion that it was just a bloody awful cigarette.

Guy had always been a huge Francophile and almost all of the family holidays were to France. It was fitting that his birthday was on the 14th of July.

While living in London, I didn't do much in the way of crossdressing other than in the comfort and privacy of my own home. It is, however, the time from when the first pictures of me in dressed in a skirt come. They are really very chaste images of me in a skirt and top (at the time, I also had a cheap wig along with my expensive falsies), although there were one or two of me lifting my skirt to show off the top of one of my fishnet stockings. It was also around this time that I started to wear exclusively female underwear. While it may not have been as accommodating to the genitals that I had at the time (fortunately, I was not exactly well-endowed and so didn't really have many issues with things falling out), wearing it felt much more comfortable. Looking back, this was almost certainly another unrealised manifestation of my gender dysphoria. I did keep a few pairs of male underwear for occasions when it was necessary for me to take my trousers off in front of someone else.

Apart from hating London - I found it too big, too expensive, too dirty and too full of really quite unpleasant people - C and I had quite a good time while we were there. I made some good friends, although I am sad to say that I didn't really manage to keep in touch with them once we left, something which is entirely on me because I am terrible at communication. The one friend with who I have managed to just about keep in contact is Simon. We met when I started working at City & Guilds and pretty much immediately hit it off, not least through a shared love of Doctor Who. Simon was, and is, a very out and proud gay man and I actually told him about my crossdressing very soon after we met.

The biggest and most exciting event which occurred while we lived in London was also one of the three biggest and most exciting events of my life - I'll talk about two and three presently. In December 2002, C told to me that she was pregnant. We had been sort of trying for a baby for a few months - to the extent that we weren't using any protection but didn't really have a timetable or a desired outcome - and so for it to happen so quickly was quite a shock although a really good one. C had just started working as a supply teacher at a Catholic school in Hackney so, as an unmarried atheist she was understandably a little worried about how the news of her pregnancy would be received by the Headteacher. His response was to come out from behind his desk, give her an enormous hug and tell her that he would help in any way that he could.

Living where we were, C's maternity unit was at the Whittington Hospital. We did discuss whether or not this meant that our child would end up being a Cockney but could never really decide. Quite early on, at her second or third ultrasound scan we heard the foetus's heartbeat, fast and strong and regular. In theory, it should have been one of the most exciting sounds we had ever heard. In practice, I managed to burst the bubble somewhat by remarking that it sounded like a helicopter, although, indulging in my enjoyment of wordplay, I referred to it as a 'heckylopter'. From that moment on, the foetus was named 'Hecky'.

Hecky wasn't the best-behaved foetus in the world, giving C morning sickness every single day. Fortunately, it was relatively mild - she would throw up first thing in the morning and afterwards was pretty much good to go for the rest of the day, but it lasted literally for the entirety of the pregnancy. The last time she vomited was the morning before she gave birth.

We did do our best for our child though while it gestated inside C. And, in order to save the mum-to-be from any discomfort, I refrained from insisting that we watch *Alien*. We actually started ensuring that Hecky would have a reasonable taste in music by going to an R.E.M. gig in June a month before the due date. It was the first and, so far, the last time, our child would dance in public. I had been used to seeing and feeling movement around her stomach, but this was really something else. Although she wrapped her belly in order to muffle the sounds, there were occasions when C had to actually leave the auditorium in order to allow Hecky to settle down.

Hecky was due to be born in mid-July, which potentially could have intersected with either Guy's birthday on the 14th or mine on the 29th. Sadly, Guy didn't live to see the birth of his second grandchild (the first being C's niece who had been born a few years earlier), dying a few days shy of his birthday.

As the due date came and went, I joked about how the

baby had better not come on the 29th because there was no way I was going to share my birthday with anyone else - especially someone who would inevitably steal my thunder. In the end though, that day came and went without incident, although by this point it was getting worrying and C was on the verge of being taken into hospital to be induced. Coming home from work on the 31st of July I was presented with C sitting on a cushion on the floor moaning in pain every so often as she felt another contraction. It finally happened. C was in labour. The birth was not what you could describe as smooth sailing. The baby's head had not engaged and was not progressing down the birth canal nor had C's water broken. There followed an extremely difficult 36 hours as things grew more and more tense. I took C into the hospital first thing the following morning and they started to monitor her, giving her gas and air to help with the pain of the contractions, although that made C throw up even more so was quickly discarded. Her first midwife was awful with a really terrible bedside manner, looking at readings from the various instruments and machines that C had attached to her and then making a face or saying something negative without actually explaining the problem. At one point, she even tried to take C's blood pressure while she was in the middle of a contraction. C, not one to suffer fools gladly at the best of times, swore at her and told her to back off. We quickly decided that we couldn't deal with her and told the ward sister that we needed someone else. That second midwife was a student, although she had worked as a registered nurse for many years and was just in the middle of retraining. She was lovely - kind, considerate, understanding and took the time to actually explain what was going on. We really liked her, and she made C so much calmer and more relaxed.

Ellen Mellor

But, no matter how calm C was, the birth was just not progressing. After a day and a half (our lovely midwife went off shift, stating confidently that she wouldn't be seeing us again and wishing us well), basically nothing had happened. C's cervix stayed firmly undilated and her waters intact. And it just went on and on and on. Lovely midwife came back on shift the following morning and was shocked to see us. I don't know if she said something but reasonably soon afterwards, they decided that drastic action was needed. The baby was starting to get into some distress and needed to come out now. Within twenty minutes, C was wheeled into an operating theatre, and I was gowned and masked, sitting at her side, holding her hand while a surgeon on the other side of a green barrier performed an emergency c-section. Within about fifteen minutes it was all over. M was born at around 8.30 on the morning of the second of August 2003.

I went across to where the nurse was cleaning and weighing our new-born baby. Seeing M just lying there and knowing that I had had a part in the creation of this tiny life and that I was suddenly responsible for someone other than myself was overwhelming. And terrifying.

C and M stayed in hospital for about a week. And it was one of the hottest weeks of the year. Once again, there was a mixture of helpfulness and otherwise. C almost got into despair with breast feeding because she was so unsure about how to do it and it felt like nobody was going to help her, acting like she should just know it because she was a mother. It wasn't until she went to a mother and baby group several weeks later and one of the organisers took M's head and basically shoved it onto her boob that she worked out what she needed to do.

Tea, Comics and Gender

When they were discharged, I picked them up and drove them home. Driving down Holloway Road with the most important cargo I had ever carried was one of the scariest things I have ever done. I don't think I'm an especially terrible driver, but I was more careful than I had ever been before. I was desperately conscious of the tiny precious package that was in the arms of the somewhat larger and older but still precious package sitting next to me.

One evening in late September 2003, I received a phone call from a woman with an accent that marked her out as being from one of the Southern states of the USA. She told me that she was ringing from Athens, Georgia and because I was a member of their fan club was offering me the opportunity to go and see R.E.M. in a free, secret concert in Shepherd's Bush a few weeks later. The initial disbelief quickly gave way to excitement, and I of course accepted. Arranging for C's mother to look after M, this would be the first time we went anywhere without bringing our child with us. While it may have been okay(ish) for us to take a foetus to a gig, taking a very new baby was not going to happen. Which is a shame because it was a great gig. R.E.M. were always much more suited to the small, intimate gig rather than huge stadium gigs. (The first time I saw them was at Milton Keynes Bowl on my birthday in 1995. It was quite disappointing and lacking in atmosphere.) This though was the perfect venue for them. Comparing this gig to the Queen concert in 1985 is impossible as they are so different that they are barely the same thing. Freddie was captivating there, and Michael was captivating here but in an entirely different way. The former made you want to worship him and engendered an almost cult-like feeling while the latter made you feel like he was singing directly to you, that you were an individual.

C took six months maternity leave and then went back to work, although she wouldn't be there for very long as we had decided that it was it time to return to Newcastle. We didn't renew the contract on our flat in Highbury, instead moving into C's mum's flat in Westminster. It's a lovely place: A garden flat opening out into an enormous private garden for the people who live in the square around it (very like the one at the end of the film Notting Hill). It's a very affluent neighbourhood (although it wasn't when Guy and Phillida first moved into the flat in the sixties) and there were often famous people in and around the area - when C was young, Boy George used to live in a flat on the other side of the garden and would loudly play his own music. Chrissie Hynde (of The Pretenders) lived over the road with Jim Kerr (of Simple Minds) at one point as did one or other of the Gallagher brothers (of Oasis). Clive Swift (Keeping Up Appearances) lived next door to them for a long time. We once took M to the local playground and saw Paul Weller (of The Jam) there with his children (I was very good. I didn't go over and say hello to him or anything. He was having family time and deserved not to be disturbed). Once, when C was younger and worked in a local Jewish market, Herbert Lom (Inspector Dreyfuss from *The Pink Panther* movies) asked her where the mushy peas were (which disappointed her terribly as mushy peas are terrible things). I once walked right past Paul McCartney (of... yeah, I'm not going to go there) as I was going to the Tube station.

The flat is, however, really rather small with only two bedrooms, one of which is little more than a box room. I always found it astounding that C, her brother and her sister all grew up there, sleeping in that room and all managing to end up (relatively) sane and still talking to each other. I don't think I could have done it with my brother. There were occasions when a three bedroomed house wasn't big enough to hold us both. The three of us stayed there for a few months and I don't think we made it too awful for her mum but eventually we were able to move back to Newcastle.

One other thing of note happened before we moved back though. C and I had often kind of desultorily discussed getting married and had decided that it would happen, at least partly because now that we had M there needed to be some kind of backup in case there was ever any reason for a hospital visit and I was the only adult available. Technically, with us being unmarried, medical staff would not be allowed to carry out any procedures on my child based only on my say-so. I'm still not certain that getting married actually solved the problem as M came along before the marriage certificate but fortunately, we never had to test it. There have been hospital visits - especially early on when M suffered from quite serious croup - but either C was always there, or I was never challenged. However, we had discussed it and had at least in theory agreed that it was going to happen at some point.

Walking around Camden Market one afternoon, we came across a jewellery seller. Finding a ring that we both liked, I looked at C and said to her 'shall we get two and say that they are engagement rings?' She agreed, so when we went back to her mum's flat, we were able to show off our matching rings (for which we paid the outrageous sum of £10 each, plus an extra fiver to get mine resized) and announce that we were engaged.

4
My First Transition

I have never really explained why I called myself Ellen, always saying that I couldn't remember why I had chosen that name.

Well, that's not entirely true. After settling on the name, I decided to keep the reason behind it secret, mainly because I didn't think that it was anyone else's business.

However, I made a pact with myself that if I ever wrote a memoir, I'd reveal the truth.

So here it is:

When I was a teenager, I was absolutely fascinated by Ellen Terry. I thought she had the most romantic life and was one of the most beautiful women I had ever seen. I was pretty much obsessed with 'Choosing', a portrait of her painted by her first husband. In my mind, she was the 'perfect woman' - beautiful, talented and very much in charge of her own life. Taking her name was very much a constant reminder to myself to be the best I could be - whatever my gender.

Moving back to Newcastle was really quite lovely. We had sold our flat earlier on as we had realised how much hassle it is to rent out places and we probably didn't have the best temperaments for being landlords. Initially, we rented a flat in High Heaton for a year or so and then, when the landlord turfed us out to install his son, a second one a street away for another six months.

In the year during which we were in the first flat, C and I got married. Incidentally, this is my second major life changing experience. It was a wonderful day. C looked beautiful in a burgundy top and skirt which came from a little boutique at the top of our street in Paris. We got married in North Shields registry office, walking together to the front of the room to You're My Best Friend by Queen. During the ceremony, M decided that there was a definite problem with other people being the centre of attention and ended up sitting on C's lap.

Our wedding party was in the Cluny pub. Although we followed tradition by having a first dance, we chose the decidedly untraditional "Too Much Too Young" by The Specials for it. We thought it was particularly appropriate. My mother baked our wedding cake for us - a huge chocolate cake that was actually four ordinary cakes put together and covered in chocolate icing and Smarties. It wasn't until sometime later that we found about the mishap that had occurred earlier that day earlier that day. The cake had been left in the dining room until they were ready to go, and everything was fine until my mother discovered that the door had been left open and their beautiful but really rather stupid golden retriever, Sam, had gone in and proceeded to chow down on the cake. Fortunately, he had (a) only taken bites from two of the four cakes, the other two were still intact and untouched and (b) not poisoned himself with all that chocolate. So, rather than a calm and relaxed morning she, her husband, C's sister and her partner who were staying there ended up fleeing around in a mad panic, baking, icing and decorating replacements. We look back on it now and laugh but at the time my mother was more than a little frazzled by the whole thing. She managed to keep it well hidden although she may have had one or two more gins that evening than she would have otherwise.

As we approached the end of the contract in the second flat, we started looking around for somewhere else to live. This time, though, we were intending to buy. Looking around, we found a place that seemed to be just about exactly what we were looking for in Forest Hall, no more than fifteen minutes' walk from where I had grown up. It had gardens front and back, was the right price and we could move in reasonably quickly. It wasn't perfect - the front room had laminate flooring that I hated from the moment we moved in - cold underfoot and ugly. Unfortunately, it took a long time before we were able to replace it, at least partly because we were terrified of the state of the wooden flooring beneath. We also quickly discovered that the previous owners had been enthusiastic DIY-ers. Enthusiastic but rubbish, leaving huge, roughly patched holes in the wall. In one case the hole had been filling it with scrunched up newspaper and then papering over the top. In another place we discovered a lump of wood that had something like eighteen nails hammered into it to

keep it in place. While these issues would have stumped me, C was unphased. Not un-annoyed but able to fix them. She has always been the practical one. We had a running joke that, pre-transition, the gender roles in our relationship were perfectly normal, just a little mixed up.

On our return to Newcastle, I got a job at Newcastle College working in the Sixth Form office. Although I mostly liked the people I worked with, I quickly grew to hate the actual job. There was basically nothing for me to actually do - a theme that would continue for the next several positions. It took me a while to be open about my crossdressing - not that I ever came to work in a skirt. Although I took a couple of people into my confidence earlier on, it wasn't until a Christmas night out when I chose to wear nail varnish that I told the rest of my colleagues and that was, on the whole, only because one of them objected to me wearing the varnish. She wasn't exactly overjoyed with the revelation that painting my nails was not the only 'feminine' pastime in which I indulged.

Working there was a nightmare. I would spend hours just desperately trying to make it look like I was doing something. It was one of those situations where people would joke that they wished that they had a job which would allow them to do nothing without realising how difficult it is. In its own way, not having enough to do is as stressful as having too much and as time went on, it really started to take a toll on my mental health. I didn't realise it to begin with, but this was my first descent into depression. And then, one day, I found myself sitting in tears in my car in the car park before work, seriously wondering if the world would be a better place if I wasn't in it. Fortunately, rather than following this thought further down the path, it shocked me enough to make me to go my doctor and seek treatment.

At the same time, I was starting, for the first time, to seriously question my gender. Talking to C about how I felt, she said that she would stand by me and support me in whatever path I chose but didn't know if she would be able to stay with me if I transitioned. It was difficult to hear her say that but at the same time, I understood and accepted it. Ultimately, I decided that I needed to move forwards and explore where this led, so I went to see my doctor and asked for a referral to the Gender Identity Clinic.

Tea, Comics and Gender

It is actually a relatively good thing to be trans, seeking aid in your transition and living in Newcastle. The Northern Region Gender Identity Service (NRGDS) was at that time based in Sunderland with a clinic in the Royal Victoria Infirmary in Newcastle. I mean, it's still terrible but we don't have it as bad as people in other parts of the country who have to travel many miles to one of the seven Gender Clinics in the country. (Two more 'experimental' clinics have opened with one more promised but they are, as far as I am aware, extremely limited.) For example, until recently Welsh trans people had to travel to London for their appointments. So having one in the centre of town was something of a boon. At that time, the waiting list was also relatively short and so I found myself, no more than six months later, in a bathroom in the RVI putting the finishing touches to my makeup and slipping on a skirt in order to go and speak to a doctor. In the intervening months I had had the crisis which had sparked the realisation that I was depressed and started on a course of anti-depressants and also come to the conclusion that I wasn't actually looking to transition but that it had been all wrapped up in the depression. That it wasn't necessarily about me wanting to be a 'different sex', I just didn't want to be who I was. I still wonder what would have happened if I hadn't had the possibility of transition to act as a pressure release. It's not something upon which I enjoy dwelling as I think I know the answer and it's not one that I want to explore.

Questions have to be asked though: If I wasn't trans and looking to transition why, when I met with the doctor, was I taking so much care with how I looked, making sure that I had as feminine an appearance as possible? If I was just a crossdresser, then why did I feel the need to go along at all?

I said at the time, it was just a safety net and a chance to talk to someone, but I think that even then I subconsciously knew the truth. I wonder if, even as I sat there explaining that I had changed my mind and that I didn't want to transition, if the doctor was thinking 'okay, we'll see you in a few years'?

Although I was feeling better and mentally more stable, I was still looking for a new job, eventually finding one in a local council as an admin assistant and support officer for a team of people, none of whom actually really needed any support. Once again, I found myself reduced to scrabbling around trying to find work to do. It didn't help much that shortly after I got the job my line manager went off on maternity leave to be replaced by the one person in the team with whom I really didn't get on. She was a very prim and proper fundamentalist Christian, and I am a loud-mouthed atheist with very little respect for authority or propriety. The two of us should never have been in the same room as one another, never mind in the same team, never mind allowing one to have authority over the other. Shockingly, our relationship fell apart. We tried to remain professional but damn it was hard. Neither of us could resist saying what we thought and although we never actually had an out and out argument it was very much a cold war of politeness and distance. This made it even harder for me to do a job which barely existed in the first place.

This was also the first time I attempted to get into organised union work. I was and am a firm believer in the power of the unions and know that if workers come together, we can increase our strength and have our demands and needs met properly rather than having to work at the whims of management and of the government. Of course, in a time when a Socialist leader of the Labour Party can be attacked and brought low by the efforts of the media, the Tories and certain elements within the Party itself, I am aware just how naive that sounds. Nevertheless, I still stand by these beliefs. Looking at what I could do to try and make things better for myself in terms of the amount of work I had to do, I decided to put myself forwards as a shop steward for Unison going through the training and proudly proclaiming my new position. And then I went to my first union meeting as a steward.

One of my work colleagues had asked that I say something about what he felt was a lack of communication from those higher up

in the union hierarchy. I duly mentioned this and was then harangued for the next ten minutes by the chair of the meeting about how the members were basically lazy bastards who refused to get off their arses and then had the temerity to complain that they weren't being told anything. To say that I was shocked and surprised by this attack would be something of an understatement. I came out of that meeting feeling like I had just been through a major disciplinary meeting and that I had only just escaped with my job. If this was how a new and inexperienced member of the team was going to be treated for asking a simple question, then this was not something of which I wanted to be a part. While remaining a member of the union, I immediately resigned from my post and never interacted with any of the members of the 'Inner Circle' again.

As time went on, I found myself getting depressed again with insomnia returning to haunt me. I don't usually have trouble getting to sleep but when I'm feeling crap I tend to wake up very early. No matter what time I go to bed I don't sleep past three or four o'clock. While working for the Council I had around about six months of waking up at that time. Needless to say, I was a mess. I re-started the anti-depressants - the realisation that I should never have stopped them was a rough one - and was actively looking for other work, although rarely got interviews and didn't get the job if I did.

In 2008 the global financial crisis occurred. Working in the public sector during this time meant that I was at the front line of government austerity measures, and I quickly became one of the 'victims' of the cuts made to Local Authority funding. The night after I was told I was being made redundant was one of the best night's sleep I had had in months. The knowledge that I would soon be out of there made me so happy. Obviously, I had worries about money but that was very much secondary (at least partly because I knew that C had enough money to keep us going for a while) to being able to look after my deteriorating mental health.

I spent the next few years bopping back and forth around temp jobs - including a stint working at the school I used to go to and to where M would go the following year. I kept saying that I wanted to be paid for my writing but never really doing anything about it. I was writing but it was incredibly intermittent and even when I did finish something I rarely actually tried to do anything with it. I had sent off a few stories to magazines when I was younger but never managed to get anything accepted. The one time I did succeed, the magazine went bust before it could be printed. I had written stories when I was young but had stopped for several years only occasionally being inspired to put pen to paper. Few of them stand out. The one exception is a story called *The Gamma-Six Affair*. It isn't going to be collected or re-printed because, objectively, it's not really very good and has a lot of issues with it - not least of which is that the one major character who dies in it is the trans woman who was basically fridged in order to motivate the protagonist. However, it's memorable for a couple of reasons. Firstly, there is the place and time in which I wrote it. I don't remember exactly which year it was, but it was in the mid-nineties. C, my brother Sean, his then-girlfriend and I went on holiday together to Northern France. One day, we went to the beach at Arromanche on the Normandy coast. While the other three were having fun in the sea, I was sitting on the sand with a notepad writing.

(A small digression - we stopped in at C's parents on the way back home and C was raving about Arromanche and how amazing it was that she was able to walk out so far with the water only reaching her calves. Her father replied that he remembered. He was there in 1945 and walked in the other direction.)

The story itself was reasonably long but upon re-reading it I realised and was also told by almost everyone else who read it that there was so much more that could be said. From these small roots were to eventually come the oak tree that was The Long Sleep. It took a very long time to write. There were times I would stop writing for months on end followed by periods of writing on a semi-regular basis. But I kept working and eventually, it was at a place where I could look at it and feel that it was actually finished. I spent a few years trying to find an agent and/or a publisher but to no avail.

Rather than admit defeat and accept the fact that it wasn't worth publishing, I decided to self-publish, choosing the name 'Samarcand Books' for my publishing concern - a title that came from a combination of the initials of my name (as it was then) and the first few letters of 'C's name.

The Long Sleep was first published in 2012 to almost no acclaim whatsoever. It got a few good reviews (all of which are still on Amazon, so if you are desperate to know my Deadname go and look there as it is mentioned several times in those early reviews) but not a great many sales. This has been the case for all of my books so far but it's not really about the reviews or the sales. They're nice and I would request that you go and write one for this and any other books of mine that you have read as it does drive sales but at the same time, they aren't really why I write (when I do). To be honest, writing is relaxing and pleasurable. It is purely a means in and of itself. Even if no-one else were to ever read a single word I had written again, I don't think it would stop me from writing. It may not necessarily encourage me to speed up, but it wouldn't slow me down.

My second novel, *Down Among the Yla*, only took me about five years to write and publish. It was a story that came from a single image in my head of a woman lying in mud and using it to create a golem, The golem imagery was something I had played with before when writing a piece of Marvel Comics fanfic - "Body & Soul" which is included in *Stories From The Corner Of The Room* with all the identifying marks filed off. I had done quite a lot of research into golem at the time and knew that there was still more I could do with them. From that initial image and my unused research came a book that was entirely different to my previous one. Where *The Long Sleep* was a science fiction detective novel with some decidedly 'adult' elements (I'm still proud of the sex-dream I wrote in it) to it, *Down Among The Yla* was a much more YA friendly fantasy novel.

Ghostkin came next, although I actually published *Stories From The Corner of The Room* while working on that. *Stories* was a collection of... well... stories... from the previous decade or so. It didn't include any of my really early stuff, at least partly because I didn't have copies of them. I knew that I had printouts of a couple of stories that I had written in the early nineties but only unearthed them recently.

Ghostkin was written faster than *Down Among The Yla*. Each book has been both longer and written faster than the previous one.

The Long Sleep took around about ten years to write and is just under 76,000 words long. *Down Among the Yla* took about five years and is 83,000 words. *Ghostkin* is 97,000 words and took around about two years. This book took nine months and is over 110,000 words in length. Still not quite at the speed of Terry Pratchett, but getting there...

At roughly the same time as finishing the first draft of *Ghostkin*, I realised that I wasn't actually a crossdresser at all. I was instead a transgender woman.

I don't actually have any idea what it was that pushed me over the edge this time. I wasn't especially depressed or unhappy. My life was reasonably good. I didn't particularly hate my job (I was working in a university print shop and while it was another admin job it wasn't actually too bad) and I was writing. In theory, I should have been great. But I wasn't. I now realise that my gender dysphoria was rapidly increasing without me realising or understanding what was happening. I was feeling less and less able to be intimate with C. When I tried it just felt more and more wrong and became increasingly difficult to be able to 'perform'.

Then, in about September of 2014, it finally hit me like the proverbial ton of bricks. I finally worked out what the problem was and why I was feeling so at odds with my body. It was because this shouldn't be my body. The hair on my chest, the stubble on my chin, the genitals between my legs. All of these were not things a woman should have. And that was who I was. I was not him. I was her.

The realisation was debilitating. It physically hurt me. This was on a different level to how it felt when I had first thought that I needed to transition. This was so much worse.

Facebook was a place which I had always hated. I'd been on there for a few years but very rarely posted anything. In January 2015, I created a second account, this time as Ellen. I was open about it being a second account but not why I had created it. The old one under my Deadname still remained but this new one would become my main connection to the site. Weirdly, I started to post far more often with this new account than I ever did with the old one. In late January, I wrote that I thought I'd posted more in the couple of weeks I had been using the new account than I had ever done on the old one.

Being able to be Ellen on Facebook was a form of escape for me - a place where I could just be myself without having to refer to 'him'. But I still needed to do something about the real world. The first step was to tell C. Over and over again I would screw up the courage, feeling my stomach roil and my throat go dry as I would prepare myself to once again tell the woman I loved that I was not the person she thought I was, but this time with far more conviction. And every time, I would fail, pulling back from speaking and hating myself a little bit more for my cowardice. Over the next few months, I became more and more angry and withdrawn. I stopped seeing friends and pretty much stopped talking because there was this thing that I needed to say before I could say anything else, and it just wouldn't come out. It can't have been nice for C and M having to live with me during that time and I am truly sorry that I put them through it. Eventually, though, I got there and told C the truth. Of course, it being me, I handled it really pretty badly.

Ellen Mellor

Dad and Sean

Mum in South Africa

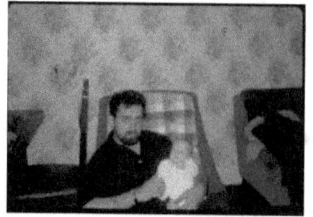

My mum's parents: Jack and Margaret Gosney

My dad's parents: Bill and Muriel Mellor

Sean and Me – 1978

Bathing M at his grandmother's place in London

Part 2

Her

"If I'm going to have a past, I prefer it to be multiple choice."

— Alan Moore, The Killing Joke

1
Coming Out (V2.0)

I have never really explained why I called myself Ellen, always saying that I couldn't remember why I had chosen that name.

Well, that's not entirely true. After settling on the name, I decided to keep the reason behind it secret, mainly because I didn't think that it was anyone else's business.

However, I made a pact with myself that if I ever wrote a memoir, I'd reveal the truth.

So here it is:

There was a character who appeared in Minnie the Minx in The Dandy for about three issues in the late 70s. She was a punk (or at least as close to punk as DC Thomson comics could go, which wasn't very...) and was originally intended to be spun off into her own strip. Unfortunately, her appearance coincided with the furore around Action (the British precursor to 2000AD rather than Superman's home) and it was decided that portraying a punk character was a bad idea, so she was dropped and never seen again. Her appearances stood out for me as far more memorable than other Minnie stories and I always wondered what happened to her. The character's name was Ellen Erth.

Telling C was in many ways a replay of telling her I was a crossdresser. It happened at about 3.15 on the morning of February 23rd, 2015. I had been tossing and turning for at least an hour - again - all while desperately trying not to wake C up and wrestling with the knowledge that I was lying to her by not telling her the truth but also not able to make myself do it. C is usually a pretty sound sleeper, but I still managed to wake her. She held me and asked the question that I had never before answered truthfully. Was I okay?

Finally, shakily, I answered her. Although not directly, I didn't say "I'm a woman" or "I'm transgender" or "I need to transition" or anything like that. Instead, I told her that I thought that I needed to go back to the Gender Identity Clinic.

I write all this so accurately because I wrote it all down the next day. As bad as I am at writing prose, I am infinitely worse at keeping a diary. I have tried over and over again throughout my life,

managing to keep it going for a week or two before letting it lapse. This time though, I thought that keeping a journal would be a useful method of recording what was happening and a way of getting my thoughts out of my head. This time I actually managed it (off and on) for nearly two whole months before stopping.

The following pages are (some of) those journal pages. There is a certain amount of editing. It was all written in a stream of consciousness style so it may not always make sense and may contradict itself at certain points.

23rd February 2015

I'm sitting here in the front room, reading The Ultimates, listening to Kevin doing electrical stuff in the kitchen and my head [is] feeling fuzzy and totally unfocused. I found myself thinking that it could be useful and helpful to start recording my thoughts. This could be the start of a journey.

Tea, Comics and Gender

I was awake at 3.15 this morning, trying not to toss and turn but I must have done something because at 4.00 C asked me if I was okay and what the problem was. This was really the opening I needed. I'd been trying to get her to ask me something like that for weeks, so I could avoid just having to come out with it cold. I might have just kept putting it off and putting it off and continued feeling bad about myself and having a churning stomach when I thought about it and hating myself a little more for being such a coward. Which sounds stupidly melodramatic.

I still didn't come out with the words "I (think) I need to transition". Instead, I told her that I needed to go back to the Gender Identity Clinic. I still hated saying it though. It's really the last thing C needs to hear at the moment. I mean, there is no good time to hear that your husband feels like he needs to be a woman - or whatever the fuck this is - but 4am in the morning, when you have just come back from dealing with your mother who has just come out of hospital and you have to go to work where you are bullied and overworked and stressed has to count of some of the shittiest timing there ever could be. I didn't want to tell her but after last time when I kept my thoughts and feelings hidden and ended up suicidal (nearly suicidal - the desire to transition then was more to do with a pressure release than anything else), I promised her and myself that I wouldn't hide anything like this from her again. The fact that it took six months to tell her is bad enough but lying and telling her it was nothing would have been infinitely worse.

I say it's been six months, but that is just a guess really. It certainly hasn't been much less, but it may have building subliminally before then. But I think that it was last September/October time that the thought that maybe my gender was becoming a problem manifested itself consciously. It's also the first time I had a problem sexually. It's not because I'm no longer attracted to C., I still love her deeply and find her very sexy but I just didn't seem to be getting the pleasure from it that I always did. As I said to C, it feels like there is some kind of disconnect between my penis and me. In some ways, it doesn't feel like it is part of me?

I am still worried that there are other reasons for feeling like this, that it is, once again, a release that would go elsewhere if I didn't have the 'go to' of transitioning. I mean, I've been unemployed for nine months and had no permanent employment since being made redundant from the council. I believe that a large part of the reason I haven't had any interviews is because I am male (although of course, this week I have two interviews and that hasn't relieved things at all). C's work and everything there has led to us becoming a bit more than distant than we've been in a long time (i.e. Very little intimacy apart from back tickles, talking mostly about her job and what's going on there, her working all the hours, thinking about it when she isn't and feeling fairly permanently tired) - none of which I begrudge her and I understand and want to help and do whatever I can but I can't help but admit that has added to my stress (Can I sue her school for emotional distress?)

Has the fact that I am taking the opportunity unemployment has presented to dress more often meant that I want more? Has it become so mundane that it doesn't satisfy anymore? It doesn't feel like that. Wearing a skirt and make-up etc., being hairless just feels right to me and not doing that - especially if it's for an extended period of time - makes me unhappy. It's always been like this, but the length of the extended periods is shortening.

I talked to C last month about the possibility of spending a time as Ellen and even then, saying it would be for a few days or a week, I knew that I wasn't being honest. That if I started, I wouldn't want to stop. I joked about getting bored of it after a few days, but I am pretty certain that's all it was. I may be wrong - I might be wrong about all of this - but I think that getting up in the morning, putting makeup on, a skirt and heels or whatever would be something I could do every single day for the rest of my life without it getting old.

Of course, if I were to transition to whatever extent that happens then it wouldn't be necessary to go to the extent that I do now to present feminine. If I had electrolysis, I could get rid of my facial hair, I wouldn't have to plaster my face with foundation; If I had breasts I wouldn't have to wear false ones. I could wear more [unreadable] clothes and still appear feminine. Appear female.

Even now, when I've had a shower, I'm clean-shaven and my hair is brushed, I see someone feminine looking at me from the mirror. When I'm brushing my teeth in my nightie, I see a woman. When I can't see Ellen, when I can only see {Deadname}, that's when it feels wrong. I don't want to see that anymore.

But on top of all of this, in a lot of ways more importantly than anything else, whatever else happens, I need to make sure that C and M are happy. The thought of not being with her anymore makes me want to cry again. When I cried this morning, part of it was a cathartic reaction to finally having told her, but another big part of it was the fear that I was going to lose her. I know that she will always be there to support me and will love me but being apart from her would be hell. But if I stayed male to be with her - would that be any better? If what I am feeling is true, I would continue being unhappy and self-hating and I'm scared that I could start to blame C for it. And then I could really lose her and have lost out on the chance of being happy with myself.

I really feel - although again I have to face up to the possibility that I could be deluding myself again - but I do really feel that C could adapt and learn to accept me as a woman while still remaining my wife. Our sexual relationship has never been a major component of our lives, it has been far more about a deep, loving companionship.

We have both mostly enjoyed the sex when it happened, but I think there are different things we could do that would satisfy that side of things. It is obviously something I have thought about and we would have to discuss it, but I feel we could work out.

I also don't think my personality would change that much. Being able to be Ellen so much, to be so accepted, has meant that the more feminine aspects of my psyche have become fairly well integrated. I could be wrong - I have no real idea what hormones might do to me psychologically, but I think that the support I've had over the years will mean that I'm pretty well sorted out (although, having said that, if I was 'sorted out' would I want to transition?}

On the whole, I think that the major differences in our relationship will be how I look - breasts and hips. I have no huge desire to get rid of my penis - at least at the moment - although I know that it may well get smaller and mean that I can't get hard but, as I said, there are alternatives.

M is another worry. I think and hope he would be okay with it, but I am also very aware that it might very well make him a target. I hope it won't, or if it is that it gets stamped on very hard (if it doesn't then I'll stamp hard on the school), but I know he's going to find it quite confusing. He handles my dressing amazingly well and I hope he copes as well with this, but I am going to have to make sure that there is some sort of support in place for him. I do worry how having a crossdresser for a father, never-mind a TS, has or will affect him. If it will make it harder for him to form relationships or anything like that. But, on the whole, I think (hope) that he's resilient enough and accepting enough (god knows, he's demonstrated that on loads of occasions) to be able to get through this - whatever else happens, I am determined to be there for him. I am and always will be his dad.

I don't think there is a lot else I can say at the moment. There are things I need to do:

1. Get myself re-referred to the Gender Identity Clinic - I have a doctor's appointment tomorrow morning so hopefully that will be sorted then or at least the wheels will be in motion on that.

2. Get fit and lose weight - I imagine that hormones must be a fairly traumatic thing to do to your body, especially as you are getting older as I am. So being fitter and healthier has to be a good thing, not counting the other reasons (high cholesterol) for doing it. I still think that doing the Great North Ride this year is a good thing but now it will be a waypoint rather than an aim. Additionally, it might make it easier for C being with a fit and healthy person of whatever gender

rather than the overweight, out-of-condition [I crossed out the word 'man' here but didn't replace it with anything] I am now. Next week, when we get M's bike back from my dad's I'll bring mine back as well. And I'll get out on it. If I get one of these jobs, I'll cycle there. And I am going to eat less crap. Cut out going to Greggs. Eat less chocolate. Smaller portions. Maybe this will be the thing to finally get me out of my apathy and make me get fit.

There is a lot to unpack in this initial splurge of thoughts and feelings. Firstly, there was me blaming my gender for not getting interviews. I don't really remember what I meant by this, and it sounds appalling out of context. I think it was all part of my frustration and hatred with being seen as and having to present as male when it was more and more obvious to me that it wasn't who I am. I was looking for an excuse other than the fact that I am rubbish at interviews in order to justify not getting these jobs for which I felt I was perfectly qualified. Although, possibly, the arrogance of going in there feeling like I was perfectly qualified to get the job may have been one of the reasons I didn't get it.

Then there is the contradiction there around my feelings about my penis. (God, just writing that makes me shudder.) First, I say that I feel disconnected from it and then I say that have I no 'huge desire' to get rid of it. The latter bit sounds like a lie to me and I'm just trying to convince myself for some reason. Maybe to make it easier for

myself to do this thing that I was obviously going to be doing whatever happened. If I didn't want surgery, then the whole thing would have been so much simpler.

Lastly, there is the use of the term 'TS' - short for

'transsexual'. This was purely a sign of my lack of knowledge around 'trans stuff'. I discovered pretty quickly that that term was outdated and thought of in many circles as pretty derogatory focusing, as it does, on the sex part and not the gender part thus medicalising us even more. If our 'sex' needs changing, then we absolutely must need all the hormones and surgery and everything. The fact that I did need them is neither here nor there. I quickly stopped using that term and feel absolutely no connection with it now. There are some people who do use that term to describe themselves and, if they do, then all power to them, but it's not me.

Of course, while all this was happening, real life was also happening. We were in the midst of a long and protracted kitchen refurbishment which was so much hassle - Homebase who were supplying the kitchen were just terrible, delivering everything in dribs and drabs, not communicating with us and lying to us when they did. Looking at my Facebook post for that day, gives an entirely different look at my priorities. I was a bloody good actress even then...

23 February 2015

We've had the first problem with the kitchen - which, considering how long this has been going on is quite an achievement (ten years? Twenty?). The vinyl flooring which we hoped would be delivered and fitted tomorrow isn't coming until Friday (which is in large part our fault, because we didn't order it until last week and the guy said that this was a strong possibility). We still need to start building stuff when the kitchen arrives on Wednesday, because the plumber has to come on Friday to connect the gas hob and the sink and he's working over the weekend and on holiday next week. So. Hopefully the fitters will arrive reasonably early on Friday (we were second on the list when we booked, so we should be okay) and, as soon as they have gone, we need to get in there and put the three units which need to be in for the hob and sink to be sited, hopefully before Nev the plumber arrives. God, it's just non-stop excitement here, isn't it?

Not a single mention of any issues with my gender identity or anything other than issues with purely physical matters. Ironically, of

course, my comment that "it's just non-stop excitement here" was in its own way completely true.

Also - quick spoiler alert so you don't hold your breath waiting for it - I didn't do the Great North Ride and still haven't (yet).

24th February 2015

I had my doctor's appointment this morning when I asked Dr. McBride to refer me to the GIC. It was still hard to say. I stumbled through a very truncated version of my 'story'. She was good, listening and asking some questions - mostly about how depressed I felt and whether or not that needed looking at. I don't think it does.

It turns out that they don't have a computerised version of the letter from the last time I went to the GIC which has prompted me to find my copy. It's useful to look back and it's quite interesting to see what has changed and what hasn't - mostly it's about how often I dress. It seems like the time I spend as Ellen has increased dramatically - is this because I wear women's clothes as part of my daily routine (the only male thing I am wearing at the moment is a shirt covering the feminine t-shirt I have on) or because 'she' has been coming to the fore more strongly? I suspect it's both, although which one influences the other, I have no idea.

As I was coming back, dad rang, asking where I was, as he was coming over for a cup of tea. Without thinking, I said I was at the doctors. Which means, when he comes over, he is going to ask why and I'm going to tell him the truth. It's certainly something I was planning on telling him, but he is going to know sooner or later. I am certain he'll be okay with it - but that doesn't stop the nerves with it. At least he can't stop long to interrogate me, as I need to think about getting ready for my interview this afternoon.

9pm

It's been a tiring day, physically and emotionally. I've been feeling quite weepy for quite a lot of it. It started with talking to the doctor. Then there was the worry of telling dad which didn't happen in the end because he didn't come around in the end and then must have forgotten when I saw him later in the afternoon. Then there was a call from Homebase saying that part of the kitchen wasn't coming tomorrow. And then getting to the interview to discover that it is tomorrow. So, on the whole, a pretty fucking awful day.

I have briefly spoken to C and told her that there are things we need to talk about, although with everything that's going on it may not be until after the kitchen is in. We need to work out when I'm going to start living as Ellen; when we are going to tell M and the rest of the family; how we are going to tell them; what C feels is going to be as much as she can take. I actually have very little for which to criticise my GP in regard to my transition (or anything else to be honest). They - and especially Dr Blomfield - have been very supportive and have been cheerfully allowed me to guide them in respect of the things I needed. They didn't even charge me when I needed a letter from them in order to change the details on my passport and driving licence - partly because I already had a form letter ready for them to just sign but they could still have charged if they had been of a mind to do so. The only place they really let me down was when I asked for a 'bridging prescription' - a low dose of hormones in order to help with the dysphoria while I waited for the GIC to get its arse in gear. I didn't really expect them to do so but I was really quite annoyed when the doctor (not Dr. Blomfield) said that they felt that they didn't have the experience necessary to do it safely. My immediate thought was 'so look for guidance?' It's not exactly an unheard-of request so it's likely that there is some guidance out there - indeed I took some papers with me that I had found which actually gave some guidance. If they say this to every trans person who comes along asking for help, then they're never going to get the experience. They have to start somewhere... I understand that it can be scary to do something that they have never done before but it's not as if they will have never prescribed HRT to a cis woman and this is broadly the same - it's even the same stuff. There isn't (yet) a 'Just For Trans' HRT patch 'with added glitter'...

February 25th 2015

This is rapidly getting harder than I anticipated. I knew it wouldn't

be easy, but I guess it's like child birth - you never know how it's going to feel until it actually happens. And, in a way, to really push the metaphor, there is an element of birthing a new person - it's just that she isn't a baby, she is me.

C and I had a discussion last night and we both ended up in tears. She is really scared and confused and having trouble with the whole thing. Which is totally understandable. She had only had two days to come to terms with the idea that I need to transition whereas I have, in a way, been preparing for it for a long time, even before I started to understand that it was where I was heading.

She found it hard to articulate what the problems would be, just that she didn't know if she could handle it. One of the things she said was about society would react. I said that society was changing and growing better all the time which is true. Thinking about it afterwards, though, I think that we can pretty much ignore most of society. Society voted the Tories in and a dog to win Britain's Got Talent. Society is showing support for UKIP. Society buys The Sun because of Page 3 and makes Eastenders and X-Factor the most successful shows on television. I think the only society we should worry about is that which affects us directly - our family and friends. There may be problems with idiots, but they would have caused problems whatever happened, even if I remained as I am now. And considering how many problems I have had up to now, I can't see it increasing significantly when I do transition.

This morning, C went out to work forgetting to say goodbye to me as she went out of the door as she usually does and I over-reacted. I texted her saying she hadn't said goodbye. I feel stupid now thinking about it; bad that I will have made her feel bad for no reason (and I am certain it was just that she was thinking of something else, as she said - and I wish I hadn't done it. But I'm wishing quite a lot of things were different this week. So, one more doesn't make that much difference.)

C said last night that she does need to speak to someone about this, to get some outside support. I hope she does it quite quickly so she can [gain] another perspective on the matter and hopefully work things out.

Although at the moment, things are looking pretty bleak, I still believe that, with time, C will come to terms with it, and we can find some way of staying together - even if it is just as companions and close friends. After all, as I said last night, she won't be living with a woman, she will be living with me. We just need to find a way for us to both be comfortable with where I end up.

This entry illustrates very clearly how incredibly naive I was about transition and also about how 'society' can be ignored. I appeared to forget that while I may want to ignore society, it very definitely will not want to ignore me. It did really seem like society was getting better all the time back then, that things were improving and that we would soon live in a country in which trans people would have the same rights as everyone else. Fast forward five years to mid-July 2020 and things have in fact managed to get so much worse. Not a week goes by - sometimes not a day - without some media outlet publishing a transphobic lie. Within the next few days there is the possibility that the Tory government (that the ignorable society kept voting for) could repeal some or all of my rights and try to force me to use male public toilets - ignoring their own consultation on reform to the Gender Recognition Act because the 70% of those who were in favour of reform were 'influenced by trans activists'. The most successful author in the world has just revealed to the world the depths of her transphobia.

Essentially, in the last five years, acceptance and support for trans people has taken a huge step backwards. If I had known then where this was all going would I have changed my tack? To be honest, I doubt it. I may even have gone at it harder and with more ferocity. I have never been one to back away and there's no way I'm going to do so now. I do know that the vast majority of society - whoever they may have voted for in Britain's Got Talent - support trans people.

Ipsos Mori published the results of a poll last week which said that most people are comfortable with transgender people to a greater or lesser extent (https://www.ipsos.com/ipsos-mori/en-uk/majority-britons-say- transgender-people-face-discrimination-britain). But there is an increasingly loud minority of people, supported by most of the major British media organisations (the BBC, the Guardian, The Times, The Daily Mail, The Sun have all, in the last few weeks, published anti- trans rhetoric or reported on issues to do with transgender people without actually talking to trans people about it), that are pushing to have all of our rights stripped from us.

C did actually go and look for some support and discovered that none of the support organisations for people who are having difficulties with their marriage have any clue when it comes to someone's partner coming out as trans. She had a couple of counselling sessions, but they couldn't give her any useful advice at all. She was very much on her own in this.

26th February 2015

Today hasn't been a day when I have particularly been able to focus on gender issues. Instead, it's been all about the kitchen - starting with spending two hours this morning painting it and then discovering that something else wasn't delivered yesterday - necessitating a half hour phone call to Homebase. At least that is being delivered on Monday. However, another thing (wine racks) is out of stock until 27th March.

On the whole, getting this stuff sorted has really made everything else that bit more stressful.

I haven't entirely avoided thinking about gender though. What I have been doing is worrying about C, hoping that she is going to be able to find a way to live with it. I had a pleasant little daydream of us re-marrying with me in a pretty wedding dress. But it didn't last long. At the moment, I know I can't think about that. At the moment, the best I can hope for is that we stay together. Anything else is a bonus. A 'white wedding' is pretty much beyond the realms of possibility. It feels somewhat like now the possibility of transition has come to the fore so much - possibility? Probability - even if I'm wrong again, if C can't get her head around me potentially becoming a woman, then we - I - may have dealt a fatal blow to our relationship. In a way, not being wrong could be better in this respect. Otherwise, there is the very real chance that whenever things get difficult, I may decide that 'this time' it's real. How many times could I call wolf before it's too many?

This week has been of the few times I've wished I was a 'normal', cis gender man. Reading it back, that entry confused me a bit. I think I was saying that if I was wrong about needing to transition and stayed as I was would it become a standard go-to position for whenever I was under stress. And, if that was the case, how many times could I do this before C just got totally pissed off and decided that whatever the truth of my gender was she couldn't live with the constant back and forth of 'yes I am'/'no I'm not'. At least, I think that's what I was saying.

The kitchen will continue to be a problem for some time to come. Although angsting about the lack of wine racks is potentially one of the most middle-class things I've ever done.

28th February 2015

Ellen Mellor

This has been one of the hardest, most unpleasant and distressing weeks I have ever experienced. Even in the throes of depression there were small bright spots, but I can't really see any at the moment. And, to make it worse, I can't talk about it to anyone. I feel pretty constantly on the verge of tears, but I have to hold it in because I don't want to - I can't - upset C and M.

I'm going to Pete's birthday party but really don't feel like it. For a start, C has asked that I go as [Deadname], which usually means that I spend quite a large part of it wishing I was in a skirt. People are going to ask how the week has been and I can't really tell them. I also can't ask C if it's okay to tell them because I know the answer. Even if she says okay, she wouldn't be happy about it.

A short entry but one that is really full of woe. I was unhappy and really going full on with the 'poor me' stuff. Looking back, there were bright spots - for a start I got to start transitioning! That's a pretty bloody major one right there. C may not have welcomed the change with open arms and told me that at long last I was going to become the person she always wanted me to be. But that wasn't exactly news to anyone. I may be being a bit harsh on me-from-five-years-ago but, bloody hell, get a grip woman.

1st March 2015

I didn't finish my thoughts last night, but it doesn't really matter.

The party was good last night apart from one loudmouthed twat who decided to spout forth bullshit as he tends to do. I didn't actually spend a lot of time wanting to be in a skirt, I guess at least partly because I spent a lot of time talking and catching up with Julie and Paul [two dear friends who I worked with at Waterstone's] whom I haven't seen in years. We had a good discussion about gender though. I did have a very strong urge though at several points to confide in Lesley and Pete and Julie [a different Julie] but didn't. Which is probably for the best as it wasn't really a good place to tell them. It was Pete's birthday party, and I couldn't really hijack it for my own purposes. It would have been selfish.

C and I talked about the interview I went for this morning, about which I should take if offered both. It does make sense to take the RSPB position and try to do something about building a web design business, but I am also worried about what happens if our marriage does break down. I would be left with only £4000 a year from the RSPB as a guaranteed income - and I have to contemplate the possibility that I may lose that because of transitioning. I do think that it would be a lot more interesting than the South Tyneside job. Of course, there is absolutely no guarantee that I'll get either one, so this falls into the realm of idle speculation. At least this week, I won't have to worry about the kitchen. Hopefully, with those two things out of the way, C and I will be able to think about the future a bit more.

This is an excellent example of something that I do on a regular basis - over-thinking stuff. In hindsight, of course I was going to have

a good time at Pete and Lesley's place. They are two of my favourite people and never fail to make me happy. The 'twat' wasn't going on about trans stuff or anything like that, rather he was getting at Lesley about feminism stuff. I think that was the last time he was ever invited to anything.

Another little spoiler alert and yet another example of over- thinking: I didn't get either job...

3rd March 2015

I told Katrina [a true and beloved friend despite only actually meeting her in person once] today and I also joined a couple of Facebook groups. As such, I'm feeling quite positive for the first time in quite a while. Support from Katrina and getting words of encouragement from the women on the FB groups has given me a stronger hope that C and I can work it out. It's going to be a very long, difficult journey, but I feel more confident that we'll get through it together.

I told Katrina without asking C. I just had to talk to someone else and she was someone that has no contact with my life other than through me. And I trust her implicitly. We have talked to each other so much over the years and shared a lot of things that I have not felt able to tell anyone else about. She truly is one of my closest (and yet simultaneously, most distant. She literally lives on the other side of the planet) friends, and I absolutely adore her. And I suspect that she is feeling a bit embarrassed but pleased at reading this bit.

11th March 2015

This last week has been just so busy with kitchen stuff that I don't really feel that I've had time to focus on the transition stuff. It's been a tough, stressful week and feels like anything that could have gone wrong actually went wrong. I know that's not true, and things could have been a lot worse (we may, for example, have had to build the whole thing ourselves) but it's how it felt at times. At least Kevin is here now doing the last big thing. After today, we basically have our kitchen, with the single exception of the wire racks.

C had a day off sick on Monday - she slept badly due to worry about GCSEs and her shoulder really hurting badly. She went to the doctor's and while there talked about how she felt about my transition. The doctor is referring her to Relate [The UK's largest relationship counselling group] which is a good thing, but it does remind me how in danger our marriage actually is.

We talked about how things were going, and C doesn't seem to have really made any progress towards acceptance. I know it's only been a couple of weeks and I have no reason to expect any sort of amazing change of heart but still it scares me. We also talked about how and when we are going to tell other people - especially M - but didn't really come to any conclusions other than it had to be done with both of us agreeing to it.

One of the things C said was that, although I viewed [Deadname] and Ellen as being the same person, she couldn't see it that way. I hope that when the time comes, she can find a way to care for Ellen as much, that she realises that there aren't many fundamental changes.

One of my biggest worries is that I am wrong, but I don't realise it until I've gone far enough down the road to really fuck everything up. That I will have done enough to screw up the lives of myself and everyone around me and then I'll have to go back to being who I was, but without the support from family and friends. C has said that whatever happens, she will support me, but what if it does get too much for her and she has to pull away from me for her own health. I can't expect her to stick around if it hurts her too much. It might be that for her happiness she needs to stop being around me at all. Do I have the strength to let her do that? To make her do that? I don't want us to go on being in pain, just because we can't break free from each other.

One high point of the week is that my diet seems to be working - I am lighter now than I have been in years. When I weighed myself on Monday, I was at 114.6kg.

This is the first example of real 'am I trans enough' worry that I have actually committed to paper. It's a constant worry for (I think) every single trans person I know - if it hadn't already been taken, another really great title for this memoir would have been *Am I Trans Enough?* It's really difficult to come to terms with and accept that you are the person you think you are rather than the person that society insists you should be. That by embracing your true gender you are somehow failing and that (trans women and feminine non-binary people who were assigned male at birth) are doing this because of some kind of perversion and kink. Even now, nearly a year after my surgery, I get the occasional worry that I am just a deluded crossdresser that has let the whole thing go just that bit too far. But you know what? It doesn't exactly make any difference whether I am or not. I love who I am now, and I wouldn't go back to my life as a male for anything.

13th March 2015

I had an excellent evening last night at the Tyne Trans group. I met several really lovely people, including my first ever non-binary people which was really interesting. I guess that coming to terms with the concept of people being non-binary is probably similar to how cis people feel about meeting [binary] trans people [for the first time]. Lex and Felix were both lovely though, so that certainly helped.

I also met Rachel, a cis woman and the wife of Amy - who wasn't there. They are about six months further down the road of transitioning and it sounds like they started from a similar basis as C and I - that Rachel had a lot of trouble coming to terms with her becoming a woman. However, she is now fully behind her wife and really happy. While I know that C and I are different, I can't help but take comfort from seeing that their relationship has survived (well, so far anyway) and Rachel is happy enough to come down to the group by herself.

I chatted to Rachel on Facebook this morning and she gave me her mobile number so C can get in touch with her if she wants. Hopefully, I can get C to come along next time and meet her in person.

I'm going to go and meet Tara (the organiser of Tyne Trans) next week for a coffee/chat which will probably involve catching the bus while dressed. This is something that scares me a bit as it is sitting somewhere enclosed for an extended period of time where people can get a good look at me. But, being scared of it kind of suggests that it is something I need to do.

I also rang up the Clinique counter in Debenhams and changed the name of the appointment from [Deadname] to Ellen which just seems right to do.

Another good thing about last night was that all the people I spoke to seemed to be geeks - which makes a great change from the usual. Maybe it's the difference between being a CD and being 'properly' trans - it just attracts the naturally geeky. We're already pretty marginalised so we are more open to accepting a new gender identity - or not 'new' but 'correct'.

I really wanted to gush to C last night about how good it was to meet Rachel and how much hope it gave to me, but I managed to hold back, mostly I think. I know I've got to hold back from doing that and give her the space she needs. She is away this weekend with Lesley and Julie and I kind of hope she says something to them. I doubt she will but if she did, I think she would get a lot of support.

C also got a letter yesterday asking her to ring for an appointment with Relate. That has got to help as well, hopefully. Well, it will do, one way or another. Relate's ultimate aim is to save marriages so they will put a positive spin on things, presumably. We'll see.

I also applied for some jobs and had a bit of paranoia applying as [Deadname] when I know I'm not going to be him for much longer. I got some good advice from Trans Rights UK on FB and I'm doing the right thing. I think I'm going to ask if people know how Relate deal with trans issues as well. It certainly can't hurt.

'Tyne Trans' was the name of the trans support group that has since become 'Be: Trans Support'. I had discovered them a couple of

years previously and had arranged to meet Tara but had had to cancel due to a bout of norovirus that meant that I was expelling nastiness from both ends rather than sitting in Costa drinking tea and I never managed to get around to re-arranging. It was probably a good thing that I didn't go then although if I had been able to make it maybe my transition would have started earlier than it did? Who is to say?

There are some pretty awful things in this bit. I seem to be implying that if Lex and Felix weren't lovely it would have made it more difficult to accept non-binary people? It sounds like the sort of thing some transphobes say - 'Oh, this trans person said something nasty to me and called me 'cis' (which is a slur*) and so now I totally hate all trans people'. *(*No. It isn't.)* I don't think I'm like that and I don't think that I would respond that way - I have often said that just being trans doesn't prevent you from being a dick although to be honest, I don't think I've ever met any non-binary people who haven't been anything but absolutely lovely. (Actually, that's not true. There is one - absolutely naming no names - who is a total pain in the arse, but they are definitely the exception to the rule).

Then there is the reference to the difference between being CD and being 'properly' trans which is just desperately problematic.

There is no hierarchy in which a crossdresser is a 'lesser' version of anything. Crossdressers are perfectly valid in and of themselves and although there may be some people who initially identify as crossdressers before realising they are transgender there is absolutely no judgement about those for which this is not the correct path. And talking about being 'properly' trans just makes me feel more than a little nauseous. There is a bunch of trans people referred to as either 'trutrans', 'truscum' or 'medicalists' who believe that you can only be 'properly' trans if you experience dysphoria, take hormones and have surgery. As such, if I chose, I would be accepted with open arms by them but on the other hand, fuck em. They're as bad in their own way as the TERFs and transphobes who spout anti-trans bigotry. There are no prerequisites for being trans apart from realising you are not the gender to which you were assigned at birth.

Meeting Rachel and Amy was wonderful. I love them both - Amy has become the sister of my heart if not of my blood and I can't imagine ever being without either one of them. Obviously, basing my hopes and dreams on someone else's relationship is more than a little foolish - and, looking back, their relationship was never really very similar to the one that C and I had - but seeing how much those two loved each other, I knew that there was no way that they were going to separate and it gave me a real ray of hope that C and I could do the same.

Ellen Mellor

I actually drove Rachel and Felix home that evening. Felix was fine because they lived quite close to me. Rachel told me that she lived in 'Shields' which I took to mean North Shields but was actually South. When I realised, it was kind of an 'oh fuck' moment. I mean, I don't mind going out of my way to drive people places but this was really a fair distance and not what I was expecting at all. However, it worked out as it did mean I got to meet Amy. Although I'm not sure how happy Amy was to meet me that night. She had really settled down for the night and didn't want to come out and meet me. She'd been sitting watching Muppets clips on YouTube all evening and really just wanted to keep on doing that. But she did and we immediately hit it off - we are definitely kindred spirits (apart from her utterly inexplicable liking for wrestling and motor sports), as her watching of Kermit and Co. amply illustrates. We have been there for each other, and we tell each other everything.

17th March 2015

It's ten to six, I've been awake since four 'o'clock and couldn't get to sleep until after midnight. I don't know if it's talking to C about trans issues that does this, but I talked to her last night about telling people and got a definite sense that she wasn't very happy about it. I also may have been overly harsh when discussing the rights of trans women to use a public lavatory. She said she could see why some [cis] women may be uncomfortable with trans women using them and I said "fuck 'em' - their discomfort doesn't mean I don't get to go for a pee." Which is true, but I could have found a better way to say it.

There were good things about yesterday as well though. I got my legs waxed and while I was talking to Kerrie, told her I was transitioning, and I had a good vent to her about everything. She is happy for me and happy to call me Ellen. There were two firsts while I was talking to her - I said to her 'I am a girl' and knew it was true and then I told her my full name - Ellen Stephanie Andrea Inman Mellor. Just writing that makes me happy, it makes my stomach turnover and my eyes prickle - but in a good way.

[There is a vague squiggle here which was the first time I signed my name as Ellen]

I'm going to have to practice my signature. That was the first time I signed my name. And it is my name - [Deadname] is now a temporary thing until the outside can catch up with the inside. Is this how brides feel in films when they sit and practice their new signature?

I also told C that I didn't think I could wait (I may have said 'couldn't wait') until I have my appointment at the GIC to go full time. Which undoubtedly didn't help with the insomnia.

Good thing today - I'm meeting Tara for a coffee. My first time as Ellen on a bus. Which is scary, but I'm sure it'll all go fine. I'm looking forward to meeting Tara properly, she seems - from her FB posts and the conversations I've had with her there - really nice. I guess that goes with the territory really.

Rather than finding a 'better way' of saying 'fuck em' in regard to cis women being uncomfortable with trans women using public toilets, I have actually grown harder about it. Cis women being uncomfortable is often a 'dog whistle' that is a cover for other 'gender critical' beliefs and a general starting point for removing rights from trans people. The worry that allowing trans women into public toilets will allow abusive men to wear a dress and claim to be a woman in order to gain access to these (and other) women's spaces is absolute rubbish. It has never happened. Trans women are much more likely to be abused in these areas than vice versa. If cis men did pretend to be trans women to gain access to these areas, then that would be an issue with cis men that needs to be tackled. By excluding trans women to prevent this happening then it is attacking a minority in order to prevent an entirely different group of people from doing something which they don't do anyway. If a cis man actually wanted to gain access to women's toilets, then all he would need to do would be to put on a hi-viz jacket and carry a clipboard. Shockingly, gender critical types who object to trans women in women's toilets have never objected to male cleaners. Which I think says it all.

I dropped the 'Andrea' before legally changing my name. It was just too much of a mouthful. My signature is still a barely legible squiggle and has actually barely changed from my original signature because it really doesn't bear much relation to the actual letter forms anyway.

That first bus ride was absolutely terrifying. I had not felt that nervous since I started clothes shopping back in the late '80s, feeling like everyone was staring at me and that it was all going to go horribly wrong. Of course, nothing happened and I met Tara and everything was lovely. That bus journey and talking to Tara that first time helped bolster my confidence greatly. Before the Covid-19 pandemic I was regularly taking public transport to and from work without any worry whatsoever. I admit that when I go on public transport I listen to my iPod (a wonderful 132GB iPod Classic that is at least ten years old and still going strong despite my (accidentally) throwing it across the room on several occasions) at least partly to ensure that I don't hear anything anyone might say to me. When I pass people in the street, I get paranoid if they start to laugh or talk to each other, convinced that they are laughing and talking about me which they almost undoubtedly aren't but that knowledge doesn't stop me worrying.

20th March 2015

I'm still having trouble with insomnia - three nights in a row. I don't know if it's because I've been doing things that have been very stimulating mentally but not physically or of it's the stress getting to me. I went for a bike ride this morning so maybe that'll help tonight.

Yesterday was my girly spa day with mum - my 'mother/daughter day'. It went really well - I was treated like a female client - even down to showering off in the women's changing rooms, which freaked me out a little when the woman said I need to do that. But I quickly realised I had to do it. It was actually completely fine - individual showers and no-one around either. I also felt a bit nervous afterwards with all my make-up taken off but again, no worries. No one seemed to take any notice.

Telling mum was on my mind all morning but I swear that I wasn't planning on telling her - I was actually intending to arrange going up to Amble next week to tell her then. But I may have steered things around to a point where she asked me. At one point when we were going through the children's department in Debenham's, I remarked how I had 'retroactive' jealousy over the clothes little girls had and how I would have liked to have been dressed like this. Mum asked if I wanted to be dressed like that all the time and I said that I did.

Over lunch - after our makeovers (another happy, joyous occasion when I just felt so good and so right) - mum came back to the subject and asked if I ever saw myself living as a woman. I said yes, I was doing it now (or words to that effect). She was surprised but not overly, she says that after the last time, she was half-expecting it to happen. She was a bit upset but more because she was going to lose [Deadname] rather than for any other reason. She is also worried about what is going to happen with C and M and I hate that I couldn't reassure her on that score.

However, I think she's happy for me and I know she will support me. She knows that this is something I have to do.

So really, it just leaves a couple of 'big ones' left - Dad and M. I worry a little how dad will take it He'll be upset but I think he will manage. I actually have very few worries about M, except for how he'll be treated at school but even there I know he'll be well looked after, so hopefully, that should work out alright as well.

After that I need to tell Sean and then our real-life friends and then pretty much out myself on Facebook and that will be it. Of course, it's a constant stream of outing yourself - especially if you want to be open and help the trans community (talking to Johanna-Alice Cooke on Facebook this morning and Tara on Wednesday really makes me want to be active and work for equality).

I changed out of my skirt today before M came home so as not to push things too far. I wish I didn't feel like I needed to do that, but I have to take C's feelings into account but Christ, I want to go full time now. Soon. It will happen soon. Just keep telling myself that and make opportunities to dress when I can - like I always have up until now.

I always feel a little uncomfortable talking about how I have 'retroactive jealousy' of the clothes that little girls can wear. I am aware that it's the sort of thing which could be taken out context and weaponised to make it sound terrible. One of the insults that 'gender critical' types throw at trans people is that we are paedophiles and we're 'transing' children (we are often being accused of forcing young gender non-conforming lesbians to transition. As if we're holding them down, injecting them with testosterone and making them have surgeries. As Amanda Jetté-Knox (amazing trans ally and author) says though 'I can't get my child to clean up her room. How am I supposed to make her change her gender?'). However, it's true. Little girl's clothes are so cute and compared to what I wore when I was growing up, they are absolutely perfect. I would have loved to have worn them. I mean, it was the 1970s so the clothes would have been vastly different, but I would still have rather been a little girl than the little boy everyone thought I was.

The whole concept of 'losing your son or daughter' when your child comes out as trans is one that I find hugely problematic. I do understand it and can sort of see where it's coming from but the idea that someone has to mourn the person that they thought they knew but is actually just a facade put in place over their true identity is quite upsetting. Transition should not be a time for mourning it should be one of celebration. The person is finally being true to themselves and it's a good thing - they will be happier, freer and an enormous burden will be lifted from their shoulders. Please don't be sad that the burden is no longer there but be joyful that we are 'blossoming'.

I feel that I may have insulted my big brother a little by saying that he wasn't one of the 'big ones'. I think it was rather more that I knew there wouldn't be any issues with his acceptance of having a sister rather than a brother and so while it was important it wasn't one that I had any concerns over. (Have I covered my arse enough there?). I don't think I out myself much now but that's at least partly because I am never 'in' enough to have to do so. Even so, it can become incredibly tiring being the 'token' trans person (more at work than anywhere else), the one who is always expected to show up and talk for the community and be visible. I admit, I volunteer for a lot of things - just this last week I took part in an online discussion around coming out stories which actually tied in quite nicely with writing this to be honest - but occasionally I wonder what it would be like to be totally cis normative and be hidden and able to just be a woman rather than a trans woman. I have been asked on more than one occasion whether or not I would ever drop the 'trans' part and just be a 'woman'. I don't think I will for a number of reasons - firstly, I am incredibly proud of who I am and where my life has taken me, and I would never want to forget that. Secondly, I feel that it's vital to be a loud, visible voice for the trans community in order to be supportive to my siblings and to fight for a future where we don't have to fight. Thirdly, I am 'just a woman' - my transness is just part of that. You would never ask a red-headed woman if she was ever going to drop the 'red-headed' part and just be a woman. I am trans because I have to be. I am working for a day when that doesn't matter, and everyone can just be who they say they are - when 'trans' is as non-descript an adjective as 'red-headed' - but there is an awfully long way to go before we get there and there are days when it feels like that it is getting further away rather than closer.

23rd March 2015

I am worried that I may have inadvertently outed myself to Lesley. I was responding to a comment and Lesley replied as well, saying that 'sometimes [she] can visibly see [me] breathe out as if [I] have been holding [my] breath for a long time'. It really sounds to me like she suspects this might be in the offing. I really want to tell her, but I just

Tea, Comics and Gender

can't do it. She's coming over for a cup of tea and, if she asks, I will tell her. I will try my absolute hardest not to just blurt it out to her, but I know it will be difficult. I've got to go along with C's desires in this but it's so hard.

The comment Lesley made actually made me cry - it was so sweet and touching and exactly what I need to hear. The fact that it was completely unsolicited and out of the blue made it even sweeter.

The post in question here was one made with regarding 'newly out people' thinking they are an authority on the subject. I replied:

I think I know what you are talking about. It is something I worry about doing - I am very aware that I have a tendency to immediately assume that I am an expert in whatever it is I am doing. I think - hope! - that I'm avoiding it when talking to other trans people and what I say is purely taken as encouragement (I admit that I'm self- centred enough that the first thing I thought when I saw this post is 'Oh shit, is it me she's talking about?'). I also hope that if it is something I am doing then people will call me on it. I think that all of it, from actually doing it to worrying that it's me you're talking about, is part of the cis-sexist, white, middle-class male privilege mindset that I really need to dump.

After being (sort of) reassured that it wasn't about me, Lesley said:

"Hey I'm jumping in here and I hope this is ok as I am neither trans or male so of course in this case I can only imagine rather than experience. But being a very good friend of [Deadname] and Ellen I need to comment on your struggle to try to stop you giving yourself such a hard time. I see you as a loving husband and a fabulous father, as a socialist and a feminist and now as someone who is finally (after waiting until your son was older enough to understand) spending more time as Ellen and I often think that sometimes I can visibly see you breathe out as if you have been holding your breath for a long time. Of course, you always think you know everything - we all do and we all take each other to task about it. I would also add that the men in our group of friends exercise their white, male, middle- class privilege less often than most and again we all challenge these behaviours all of the time. We can't all have the 'lived' experience, immediately or at everything in life. But I don't believe that makes us unable to offer insight and a certain level of understanding of what people are going through even if sometimes this is from a completely different perspective. Even if your over enthusiasm does come across to some people as if you think you know it all, we know that isn't what you mean and your heart is good and well meaning. I happen to love [Deadname] and Ellen and wish they both would stop worrying so much about what people think. Lxxxx"

It really made me cry back then that a close friend who didn't know the truth could show such insight and empathy and compassion for me when I truly needed it. To be honest, I can feel the tears pricking at my eyes a little as I write this now.

26th March 2015

It's been an interesting few days. On Tuesday, after I wrote the last entry, I had a total panic attack about what was going to happen when Lesley came over. My heart was racing, I was on the verge of tears, and I felt like I was going to throw up. Fortunately, Rachel was able to talk me through it and calm me down and advise me what to do. I felt bad about dumping on her, but she was utterly wonderful - sweet and caring and sensible which was exactly what I needed.

So, when Lesley came over, I was far more collected about it. She asked me if everything was okay, and I nearly burst into tears but I was able to hold it together. I told her that no, things weren't okay, but I couldn't talk to her about them. I still think she has to have a pretty good idea about what it is, and I promised I would tell her as soon as I could, but it was okay.

I talked about it with C in the evening and that's actually when the tears happened. She was completely understanding and said that, if it comes up again, it was okay to tell her, but I shouldn't force it. Which is great, although I think it's going to be difficult to keep the second part of that promise. But I will try.

On the Wednesday, I drove up to Amble to spend some more time with Mum and to be able to talk to her about it properly. It was really good with her and John trying really hard to call me Ellen and use the correct pronouns. It felt really good to be able to refer to myself as her daughter. It's a sort of jump in my tummy that makes me feel that it's the right thing. It's still quite strange obviously but I know that it's right and I know that I want to be the best daughter I can be.

When I was out cycling yesterday, I had another thought though. Is she actually ready to call me her daughter, is she comfortable with me saying it? I texted her when I got back from the ride and asked her, saying that I didn't want to make it harder than it already was and how I need her to tell me when I'm going too far. She replied that she thought she was okay with it, and she feels very comfortable with me as a woman. And that makes me want to cry again. I never, ever expected that immediate level of acceptance.

Two things I forgot to say - when I was talking to C, I made the comment that if this is what my emotions were doing now, I was totally fucked when the hormones start. She didn't get what I meant, and I explained that starting on female hormones would essentially be like going through puberty again, but this time as a girl. C said, 'Oh great, I'm going to have to deal with them at home as well as at school'. This made me very happy - it implies that she intends to be around for it, that she is being positive about it. It was exactly what I needed to hear.

Then, when I was at mum's, I was explaining about my panic attack and showed her the comment from Lesley that kicked it off. She cried as well but then said that she agreed entirely that I did seem so much happier and lighter.

Cycling this morning - cycling gives me lots of time to think - I realised why I am currently being so successful with the exercise and diet. It is absolutely no coincidence that I was able to start it and stick with it - and it's far stricter than any that I've ever done before and I'm not craving chocolate or cake or Greggs pasties or anything like that, which I have always done in the past. Finally admitting my trans status has given me an entirely new outlook. I need this now, it's part of the process of getting my body to conform to how I need it to be. Inside this overweight man, there is a healthier, slimmer woman waiting to get out. And I love that.

However, for the next couple of weeks, it's going to be [Deadname] all the way. Phillida is coming up today until next Wednesday and then we're going to Wales on the Thursday evening. I'm seeing Tara on the Thursday morning but that's going to have to keep me going. I have no idea how easy it's going to be, but I really don't like the idea, despite the fact that I'm really looking forward to Wales. I never for a moment thought that the dysphoria would actually bite this hard. I guess it's because I want it all and I want it now. I console myself with the thought that 'next year... I'll be Ellen when we go to Conference next year'. The Conference in question was the annual NASUWT (National Association of Schoolmasters/Union of Women Teachers) Conference which was in Cardiff that year. We had been going every year for several years and it was always good. I got a free weekend in a hotel and went places that I probably wouldn't go visit otherwise. That particular year was especially good because I took M to the Doctor Who Exhibition (Cardiff is where BBC Wales, the part of the Beeb that films *Doctor Who*, is based). The most memorable part of the whole Exhibition was when a Dalek approached us. It was dead silent (which I admit is unusual for a Dalek

Tea, Comics and Gender

but even so) and absolutely terrifying.

29th March 2015

This last few days has been pretty much as hard as I was anticipating it to be. I have dressed as femme as I have been able - girl jeans, a girly top etc. - but it just feels different now. It feels false. It's like trying to explain to C about why it feels wrong going to the Graphic Novel Group while they think I'm still a crossdressing man. It's no longer true and it feels like I'm being untrue to myself and to them. I understand entirely why C doesn't want me to tell them yet, but I also feel she doesn't understand my feelings. The little, paranoid, horrible part of my brain tries to tell me that she's not trying to understand either. But I know that is untrue. It's just the tension and the fear and stress talking. I just need to tell myself that it's a short-term pain and upset for a long term gain and happiness.

I received the letter from the GIC yesterday, saying that they had received my referral but that 'it could be many months' before I would be seen. I knew this but seeing it written down in black and white is hard to take. I need to focus on what I can do though. And that's the social transition. In my head, I've thought that my birthday would be a nice time to go full time. I haven't discussed this or mentioned it to anybody, but it feels like it would be quite good. It still gives C plenty of time to work things out - hopefully, by that point, she will be comfortable enough with the idea that we'll be able to take it to that level - and also gives me time to tell all the people who still need to know individually before giving a collective, overall coming out on Facebook and whatever. The list of people I need to tell seems to keep growing though:

[I've deleted the list because it was unnecessary and just took up space]

Ellen Mellor

Basically everyone. And some of them - family especially, I need to tell soon. I need to make a trip down to see Sean & Jane. I was hoping to tell Dad last week, but he didn't come over and I was too scared to go and see him, so now, it's going to have to wait until I come back from Wales. Unless I go and see him on Wednesday after I've dropped Phillida off at the station. I really think he is the one I am most worried about - not because I'm worried he'll reject me but that it will hurt him most and he'll have the hardest time accepting it.

This entry perfectly illustrates the difficulty of communicating with cis people as a trans person. C is and was fully accepting of who I am, but she didn't get why it felt more wrong to 'crossdress' as a woman rather than to present male. (Interestingly, when writing the original entry, I mis-wrote and said they 'think I'm a crossdressing woman'.) There are so many aspects of being transgender that cis people have no way of understanding. It's not that they don't want to understand it's just that they have absolutely no context for it. It is so difficult to put into words the visceral hatred of yourself that dysphoria brings and, while I am in no way denigrating or attempting any kind of 'oppression Olympics' thing, I really don't think there is any experience that cis people have that can compare. I honestly can't think of a single thing that annihilates cis people in the numbers that dysphoria does to trans people. The percentage of trans people who have attempted or successfully committed suicide because of their dysphoria is astronomical. And of those who have not done either of those things, I would wager that a fairly large proportion of them have contemplated it. I know that I have certainly done so at various points. This is a very heavy point to take from not wanting to lie to friends about who I am - especially when my alternative was to present male - but it is in a way all on a continuum. Going out 'en femme' while having people think I am still male just felt utterly wrong to me and ironically the thought of wearing a skirt only to be read as a crossdressing male made the dysphoria hit harder than the alternative of wearing jeans and a t-shirt. Whatever happened, I was going to be Deadnamed and referred to as he and him so leaning into it was probably easier than the alternative.

The NRGDS letter had a 'Client Information Questionnaire' enclosed with it that really needed a massive rewrite and extra guidance. I assume that it was the standard form that went along with these sorts of letters, but it didn't look like anyone had looked from a trans point of view. Firstly, it asked for my name. Which name? My legal one or the one I preferred to use? Then it asked for my gender - Male/Female/Not Specified/Other. This was awful for a couple of reasons - did they mean the gender to which I was assigned at birth or my true gender? And it also showed a deep lack of care and understanding of genders that existed outside the binary, it was literally othering them.

I sent NRGDS an email regarding the questionnaire - or at least, I wrote an email and then left it in my drafts folder for a few days because I forgot to send it - saying pretty much what I said in the previous paragraph (although with lots of wishy washy, apologetic 'I know it's just an oversight and you aren't being deliberately shitty' stuff added in order to not piss them off before I even saw them off. I assume that I did get a reply, but I can no longer find any trace of it.

Ellen Mellor

30th March 2015

I feel utterly shit. The insomnia is really fucking with me - I was awake before 4am again this morning. I wish C's mum wasn't here, so at least I could feel shit while dressed properly. Which makes me crap for thinking that.

Of course, what I wasn't saying there was the incredibly obvious 'if C's mum wasn't here, I could dress properly and probably wouldn't be suffering as badly from the insomnia'. It was quite amazing how rapidly the dysphoria around having to be 'him' escalated. While I had never had much interest in how I dressed before - jeans, a geeky t-shirt and a long-sleeved shirt over the top of that was pretty much the limits of my wardrobe, once I started my transition doing anything that could be conceived as 'male' rapidly became anathema to me. I hated my Deadname, I hated his clothes, and I hated having to be him. So even a few days of unremitting maleness was enough to send me into a spiral, especially when I wasn't able to talk about it openly.

2nd April 2014

Two pretty crappy comings out over the last couple of days. Firstly was [....] on Tuesday. I was pretty certain that she would be fine with it - she's one of my oldest friends and has known about my dressing for years and already has a trans friend. I don't know if she was just caught unawares or what, but she seemed to just withdraw from me. The only vaguely positive thing she said to me was 'Good Luck' which I know is meant to be positive and congratulatory but really didn't feel that way. Perhaps I'm being overly sensitive because it was so flat compared to all the other things people have said to me. I know she was surprised but it felt like she withdrew from me and reacted by pointing out negatives. Which shouldn't surprise me, it's what she does, but there was no suggestion of support or positivity - more like I'd lied to her (she actually brought up something I'd said in the past about not being TS ever as they just think that CDs/TVs are just TSs who haven't got there yet and so look down on us. Which I may have thought at one time, I don't remember saying it and, anyway, what does it matter? It's not about what I may or may not have thought at some point or about how other TSs may feel. It is about what is happening now, to me.) She also said 'I'm going to have to think about this' which is true but just made me feel like I was imposing on her and doing this just to make life harder for her.

Yesterday, I told dad and Molly. That was so difficult, it took me about an hour to get myself screwed up to say it. It just felt so hard, like I was disappointing him, and I was pretty quickly in tears. They said the right things though, about being there for me and helping me. It was strange, after telling them, dad called me 'son' and [Deadname] more than he usually does. Unless I was just being overly sensitive (again) and reacting to it. I do think it's going to take them longest to get used to my transition though.

I spoke to mum when I got home and told her about dad, and she called me 'her darling daughter' which had me in tears again.

C's mum went home yesterday and I'm going to have a cup of tea with Tara again this morning.

And, I've made contact with Natalie, an American trans woman who has just moved here. She is a Whovian comic book geek girl like me!

We're going to get on so well! It seems like all the trans geeks are coming out of the woodwork now that I've started to transition. Which is rather wonderful. I think Natalie will be coming to the Graphic

Novel Group with me as well, which is excellent. I need to meet up with her beforehand though and get to know her at least little bit better before then.

We're pretty much all set for Wales. I'm not taking and skirts or dresses, although some femme t-shirts are going, and I may go and look in town for a blouse I could wear as 'male' today as well. It's not enough but it's going to have to do. I'm worried that C is going to want to have sex with me and I really don't know if I'm going to be able to do anything. I've started to feel uncomfortable when my penis starts to react to things, and I haven't felt the urge to masturbate for a while. I don't know what I'll do if it comes to it, I really don't.

It was another early morning - about 4.15-4.30. It's going to make the drive to Wales loads of fun…

I still don't know exactly how that friend feels about me transitioning. Ever since then, we have seen each other far less often than we did beforehand although I admit that some of that is down to me feeling not entirely comfortable with seeing her because I don't feel like she is entirely comfortable around me. She's supportive and happy to see me when we do see each other but it's become one of those relationships that is all about saying to one another that we must see more of each other but never actually doing anything about it. Again, I know that I am at least partly to blame for this and if I made a bit more effort then we could perhaps get back to something approaching the old days but at the same time I feel somewhat like she was [Deadname]'s friend much more than she was Ellen's and with him departing and Ellen coming along properly and for good instead of just being a costume he wore occasionally, it just feels like she isn't too worried about having the relationship we once had.

Tea, Comics and Gender

Telling my father was really, really difficult. I went over to his place with every intention of just sitting him and his wife down and telling them but when it came down it, I very nearly chickened out. My attempt was chronicled in three brief Facebook posts in a Facebook group:

Well, I've got another Exciting Adventure in Coming Out now. I'm going to go and see my dad and tell him he has an unexpected daughter in the bagging area. It should be okay. But he's the one I'm probably most worried about.

1 Apr 2015, 12:04

Well, so far, I'm failing. I just can't get the words out.

1 Apr 2015, 13:14

Well, that was incredibly fucking horrible. I finally managed to get myself screwed up to say that the reason that I had been so depressed and suffering from insomnia was because I was going to be starting to live as a woman. He was fine with it. As much as he could be. Didn't freak out or anything, but it just upset me so much, talking about what was happening and what was going on between C and me.

So yeah. I now have Nirvana playing at maximum volume. Which always helps.

1 Apr 2015, 14:48

It's true that he's probably the person who has found it hardest to deal with my transition but he has been caring and here for me. He loves me as his daughter and while he may not fully understand what I'm going through recognises it for what it is and acknowledges that, on the whole, I have been happier since my transition than I was before.

Ellen Mellor

6th April 2015

On the whole, I've been having a really good time here in Cardiff. I haven't slept brilliantly but that's more to do with the bed than anything else and I've got some more gorgeous jewellery from Babazeka.

However, yesterday C and I started to get intimate. I'd spent ages caressing and undressing her and she was starting to do the same to me. She pulled my panties down and caressed my penis and I had a horrible, visceral reaction to it. I said 'no' and started to get really upset. She asked if it was discomfort from having my penis inside the panties or from it being touched. I told her it was having it touched and started to cry. I've been having discomfort and not liking when I've got hard and was a little worried how I would react to sex but I had no idea it would be that strongly. I thought there was a good chance that I wouldn't be able to actually have sex, but I did think that stroking each other would be do-able. But apparently not. I still find C sexy and desperately want to show her that, but I don't know if I'll be able to - if she will let me. I'm worried that this could be the final straw - especially as it indicates that I probably need to have GRS. If I have this level of dysphoria about my genitals now (even writing the word 'penis' makes me uncomfortable) how much worse is it going to be? I enjoy sex, I want to have more of it in the future. That's going to be difficult if I start crying when the woman I love touches me. I need to discuss with her how she feels about vibrators and other sex toys. Not expecting her to use them on me - at least not yet - but they could be good for her.

I feel really confused and unhappy at the moment. I really don't know or see how we're going to get past this hurdle. I feel like I've lied to her and betrayed her. I've just fucked everything up. At the moment I don't really see how things are going to get better.

Tea, Comics and Gender

In a lot of ways I think that, from that point on, we essentially

stopped being husband and wife and became best friends. Neither of us ever attempted to initiate sex again after that. Although we shared a bed right up until the day I moved out we pretty much became sisters. Our relationship was always about far more than sex but that was part of it and once that went it was the beginning of the end for our marriage.

That was the first time I really admitted to myself that I needed GRS. The dysphoria around my genitals (I still find it difficult to refer to the genitals I had before surgery and don't like thinking about ever having had them) was growing inexorably almost day by day. I think I had by this point started tucking everyday (pushing my penis back between my legs and testicles back into the inguinal canals in order to present a flat front in my underwear). Certainly, I found having a bulge in my panties upsetting and extremely ugly. Although, admittedly, it was never a large bulge. I was not hugely endowed for which I am truly grateful. And that's one way that you can tell a trans woman - she is grateful that doesn't have a huge cock. (NB. This is a joke and is absolutely not to be taken as an indication of transness.)

16th April 2015

The couple of weeks since I last wrote anything haven't been too bad. There are still a lot of rough patches and quite a lot of tears and I still worry constantly about what is going to happen me and C but I'm not feeling as terrible about it as I did.

That may be partly to do with that fact that I've been able to get out dressed a couple of times. Last Friday was Natalie and Robyn's housewarming. Unfortunately, I misjudged the level of formality and put on my polka-dot party dress and too much make-up while the others were just in jeans and t-shirts. I think it was that fact that I was wearing so much makeup and felt like I'd put it on pretty badly as well that made me feel a bit uncomfortable. Natalie, Robyn, Tara and the others were really pretty effortlessly feminine, even in just jeans and t-shirts and absolutely minimal make-up. I felt like a bad transvestite, a parody of femininity. I know they all had several years of transitioning on me - hormones, electrolysis, implants and the rest - and I just have false breasts and a ton of foundation but it really made me feel uncomfortable and desperate to get on with it.

At the moment, I am still just a crossdresser with delusions of girlhood and they are all women but it emphasised that to me. I think if I'd realised how the evening was going to be and gone more casual it would have been better. Whatever.

On Tuesday, I went to Readers of the Lost Art - again with Natalie and Robyn - as Ellen for the first time. It was really good, being accepted and treated as Ellen - or rather, not treated any differently (apart from being complimented on my outfit which is always good). My makeup was a lot better as well.

Dad is slowly getting better. We had another long conversation on Tuesday where he grilled me a bit. At the time, it felt like he was being a bit overly aggressive, demanding proof and trying to get me to 'see reason' but looking back I think he was really just trying to understand and didn't know the right way to phrase things so as to make it sound less transphobic. I asked him to stop calling me 'son' and 'bonny lad' and he failed miserably then but I spoke to him since and he did acknowledge my request but he didn't know what to say instead and didn't yet feel right calling me 'bonny lass'. We'll see how it goes.

Tea, Comics and Gender

A discussion on the Tyne Trans FB page led me to discover the existence of eflora, which is a cream designed to inhibit hair growth. It is used to help hirsute cis women but is also used to help trans women. I have got an appointment at the doctor's where I'm also going to ask about getting some therapy or maybe some anti- depressants to help me get through this period. The appointment is straight after I'm getting my legs waxed and I'm doing that in a skirt so I shall be visiting my doctor as Ellen. That'll show her how serious I am! But I really hate the necessity of wearing so much foundation and there is no way I can afford laser or anything yet so maybe it will help a bit. If it means I don't have to shave so often, I'll be happy.

C and I watched 'Boy Meets Girl' last night. It was really sweet and funny and it made me cry at the end - Ricki's video about why she wasn't going to commit suicide was utterly perfect and Michelle Handley is just so beautiful. I wish I could have looked like her when I was in my twenties.

I've been thinking for a while about drawing an auto-biographical comic and I think I'm going to try. I've decided on a title - "Badly Drawn Trans" - and I've been running through a few stories I could tell - including how desperately I wanted to be Kitty Pryde when I was younger. I'm mulling it over, I'll probably (might) start on it next week when M is back at school.

I'm going to do an interview for a woman who is doing research on 'Lived Experiences of Trans* in the North East' in a couple of weeks. She is writing a PhD on it and it sounds really worthwhile. Plus I get to talk about myself for an hour and a half!

C is meeting up with Rachel today for the first time. I'm confident this going to be a good thing but still a bit nervous about it. I hope they get on well and C sees some points of similarity.

There was some terrible misgendering going on in that bit - Tara is not a trans woman, they are non-binary and so lumping them in with the trans women was totally wrong of me and I apologise for it. All the rest was true though and to be honest is still true to a certain extent. A lot of my trans women friends somehow manage to be effortlessly feminine while wearing jeans and a t-shirt whereas I still wear a skirt or a dress nearly every single day. I wear a lot less makeup than I used to and have been known to go out without any on the odd occasion although this is often more to do with how much sleep I managed to get the night before and how long it takes me to drag myself out of bed on a work day than any actual desire to not wear makeup. I used the eflora (AKA eflornathine or Vaniqa) until relatively recently but I'm not entirely convinced that it did any good (not that I have a version of me who didn't use it to compare). I have had some laser and electrolysis but I still need to shave every day and I really don't know if the hair is any weaker or thinner than it would have otherwise been. Obviously there's no way of knowing at this point and all I can do is save up for more electrolysis. (The NHS only paid for a certain amount of facial hair removal which frankly wasn't anywhere near enough. I was able to afford a little bit myself but that was with a company who were really quite cheap but have now gone out of business. While most of my dark facial hair has gone there is still a lot of white hair which is not affected by laser treatment and needs electrolysis to get rid of it.)

That first time going to Readers of the Lost Art (the Graphic Novels reading group of which I am a member) as Ellen was absolutely lovely, I still remember it with a lot of happiness. It was always a very welcoming and open group and they have always been wonderfully supportive and accepting of who I am. The month after this first time I

Tea, Comics and Gender

wrote a Facebook post:

> Last night, after the graphic novel reading group, several of us went to the pub. Half way through the evening, I realised that, of the seven of us sitting around the table, there were three straight cis-males, one bisexual woman, a couple of lesbian trans women and me. I so felt like oppressing the guys...
> 13 May 2015, 10:48

I deliberately left a couple of sentences out of this part. They were talking about a woman who subsequently really hurt me emotionally at a time when I was in a very bad place. At the time, she was supportive and really 'there' for me but I had to completely cut her out of my life. I will talk more about her later on.

Amazingly enough, the webcomic thing didn't happen. I know. You're shocked. It was a nice idea and I really like the title it. I still mull it over every now and again but I think I have to finally admit to myself that I am far more suited to this kind of writing than I am to the sort that includes pictures. I have been berated by friends (but in a kind, loving way) for saying that I can't draw because it's literally just a matter of practice. In the same way that a writer has to write a 'million rubbish words' before you can start to write well, I am pretty sure that you have to draw a million rubbish lines before you can start to draw well. And to be perfectly honest, I don't have the patience to do that. I'm just too busy trying to get up to a million words.

Boy Meets Girl was the wonderful movie that came out in 2015 rather than the truly awful BBC 'comedy' that was broadcast shortly afterwards. I need to go back and rewatch the film at some point.

And I still really fancy Michelle Handley.

The interview with the woman for her PhD was the first of several pieces of research with which I have been involved. It seems a bit like being openly and actively trans involves a lot of taking part in research so the cis can try and understand our experiences. To be fair, the thesis was actually really well written and very interesting - especially the bits about me - but I do long for the days when we don't have to do this stuff. Academic research into why and how minorities are oppressed conducted by people who are not members of the group being researched are often just crutches for to show how supportive they are and very rarely actually of any use to the minorities in question. I guess that it all adds to the body of work we can point to when the 'gender critical' crowd try to attack us using their own twisted version of 'science' but considering trying to get a gender critter to listen is as much use as hoping for a giant to suddenly appear and tell me that 'You're a wizard, Ellen Mellor!' you have to wonder at the point of it all. 17th April 2015

C and Rachel meeting up yesterday went really well. They seemed to find that they had a lot in common.

C and I had another long conversation yesterday. C is still unable to talk about me going full-time without getting upset, although I don't think it's particularly a problem with me living like that, more it's about losing [Deadname]. Unfortunately, there is nothing I can do to reassure her, although I hope that when it happens that in itself helps her to see that it's okay.

22nd April 2015

Tea, Comics and Gender

I got interrupted yesterday as I was writing the entry and I didn't have a chance to finish it. I don't think there was a lot more to say about C meeting with Rachel or our conversation in the evening.

I went and saw Sean on Saturday. He said that he had guess what I was going to tell him. [Our conversation] did get a little heated at times in the way that our conversations tend to. He was trying to tell me how I should be accepting of other people not being accepting of my gender or my name. About how I should decide if the friendship or the gender stuff was more important. My reply was that if, after a sufficient amount of time had passed, they were still regularly calling me [Deadname] or 'him' or saying that it was too hard and they would just prefer to keep calling me [Deadname] then, to be honest, they are the ones who aren't trying to keep the relationship going. They obviously didn't respect me so it's not worth staying friends with them.

I was actually a little unsure of whether or not I was going to include this entry as it really doesn't show Sean in the best light. The

only reason I decided to do so was because he has since become one of my strongest allies. I don't see him or speak to him anywhere near as often as I would like but I know that he is completely, one hundred percent beside me and that he looks upon me as his little sister.

I realise that I have not mentioned Sean very much in this whole thing and I am doing him a great disservice. It's not that he is not important to me and has not been a huge player in my life, it's just that his presence is one that I have taken for granted in a lot of ways. Whatever our disagreements - and believe me we have had a hell of a lot of them over the years - I know that ultimately he will always be here for me and I truly can't imagine a life without him.

Having said that, I still stand firmly behind my belief that my friendship with someone has to be based on whether or not they are prepared to accept me as who I am. Using the correct name and pronouns is the absolute least I can expect. To do otherwise just shows that the other person is really not worth my time. I suspect that his saying that was due to him being unsure and worried about how long it would take him to come to terms with having a sister rather than a brother. In the event, he seemed to get used to it very quickly and, with a couple of exceptions, has been absolutely brilliant in not getting it wrong. I've actually been lucky that with one exception I have not had to make the choice between allowing a 'friend' to Deadname and misgender me. However, knowing how much it hurts me when it happens accidentally, I am pretty certain that I know how it would go.

30th May 2015

It's been over a month since I last wrote here and lots of things have happened in that time - most of them good.

I had a doctor's appointment at the beginning of May asking for eflora and to be referred to a therapist. Dr. MacBride was lovely. She said she had no problems with prescribing it but I had to see a dermatologist first. I'm still waiting for that to happen and if it gets to the end of the week then I will ring and find out what's happening. I had an initial phone conversation with the therapist where I said that I knew they couldn't help with the trans stuff but I wanted help coping with the stress and anxiety. Again, I'm still waiting for that. C is still waiting for her first proper appointment as well.

Tea, Comics and Gender

We spoke to M a couple of weeks ago and explained what was happening. His response was 'cool' and I had to do what I needed to do to be happy. And, he doesn't seem to be worried about it at all. He has remained as caring and loving as ever. He hasn't told any of his friends at school yet but it will happen - I suspect that he will probably tell Elizabeth - who has come out of nowhere to be his closest friend. They talk all the time on his iPad. She is not his girlfriend though, he insists. Just a girl who is a friend. Give it time…

C and M went to London last weekend and told her family. It seems like it went okay. Phillida came up for a few days and had no problem with me dressing in skirts.

C has told me that I should dress as Ellen all the time when I am at home. We are planning on me going full-time in September. I've got a job - just temp but it's something. The only drawback is that I have to go as [Deadname], which I am finding harder and harder to do. If I am still there in September, I will talk to them about transitioning at work.

I had a really bad day yesterday. I was feeling a bit odd in the morning and it just got worse through the day until I was standing in the shower hating myself, feeling fat and ugly and male and knowing that no-one was ever going to call me 'pretty'. I went to bed at about 8.30 but couldn't sleep and had a long, tearful conversation with C at about 11.30 - talking about how hard it was to talk to her and how scared I was (and am) that she is going to find a man who will be able to satisfy her. She promised me that she wouldn't but I replied that I had promised her that I would never transition into a woman.

I'm feeling better today, still a bit shaky, but happier. I had my legs waxed and I've been into town where I am treated like a woman in Travelling Man and at the library, where I changed my name and got a new library card. I think a few people may have had a bad reaction but I don't know for sure. Nor do I care.

In the end, I never saw a dermatologist. For some reason

I just never got an appointment and so after two or three months another doctor just prescribed it to me on the basis that cis women didn't need to see one to get it.

M's reaction was one of the most perfect moments of my life. Just that level of acceptance and love and care in one so young was a beautiful thing to see. It made me so proud that this was my child, along with a certain amount of back-patting that we had done such a good job as parents. I cried so much when M said that I just have to do what I need to do to be happy. I think it was then that I knew that things were going to be okay. None of M's friends have ever shown the slightest bit of difficulty with me being transgender. I suspect that the feeling of 'Oh no, an adult trying to be friendly. How embarrassing' far outweighs anything else.

When I wrote about C finding a man to 'satisfy her', I wasn't referring to sexually, although I admit that is exactly how it reads. Instead, I was worried that she would find someone who could fulfil all her needs - emotional and psychological as well as physical. That she would discover what she had been missing by being with me. I was being deeply selfish and insecure. I was not yet in a place where I could separate my need for support from C's need for the same thing. I felt that without her I wouldn't be able to get through it all. I have (I think) now come to the point where I do actually hope that she finds someone who can bring her happiness and we have both said that if we were ever to remarry the other one would be matron of honour. And, while it was a joke, it is an idea that I really like and if I ever get into another relationship which ends up getting to that point, I will more than likely broach the subject with C.

That entry was, apart from one I wrote a few years later,

the final one. You could already see how as time went on the entries got further and further apart. This was mostly because I had less to write about - all the initial things had happened and I was just waiting for the rest of the world to catch up and help me be the person I was but also because I was getting used to the situation and coming to accept it for what it was. Things were starting to crystallise and I could see my future path ahead of me. I wasn't yet out to friends but I knew it would be coming soon and I knew that my family all supported me and cared for me. There were still things that needed sorting out - not the least of which was what sort of relationship C and I were going to have going forwards but that was not the sort of thing that was going to be sorted out by keeping a journal. I was also using Facebook a lot more and a lot of the things I said in my journal actually went on there. Whether that was a good thing or not - do I really want Facebook to have all of my secrets? - is kind of a moot point by now. Facebook is bad, we all know that and yet for many of us it and Twitter/Instagram etc. are also valuable lifelines that allow us to connect with other trans people. Social Media has actually brought me some of my best and closest friends. I met Katrina through LiveJournal and there are other friends who I have yet to meet at this stage in my life who I only know through Facebook and Twitter and yet absolutely adore.

2
The Waiting Game

I have never really explained why I called myself Ellen, always saying that I couldn't remember why I had chosen that name.

Well, that's not entirely true. After settling on the name, I decided to keep the reason behind it secret, mainly because I didn't think that it was anyone else's business.

However, I made a pact with myself that if I ever wrote a memoir, I'd reveal the truth.

So here it is:

I was (and am) desperately in love with Sigourney Weaver. My favourite character of hers is, of course, Ellen Ripley. Although 'Dana' was in the running for a while there as well.

Up until this point, I had been writing *Ghostkin* with a straight, cis male protagonist. I quite liked him as a character, he was an absolute bastard but he was *my* absolute bastard. And then, I had a thought. What if this character was actually a trans woman? There are so few trans characters in genre fiction or indeed in any fiction that having a trans woman as the protagonist in a story that doesn't focus on and centre her transness was definitely worthwhile. And when she was written by a trans woman as well, it might make people (editors and agents) sit up and take notice. I did have another reason for doing it. This was the period when the 'Sad Puppies' - a group of right wing, cis, straight, white guys were making a noise about there being too much diversity in their science fiction. In 2015 and 2016 they chose to try and game the Hugo Awards in a way that meant all the decent sf was pushed out in place of their list of (objectively) very bad, 'real man' sci-fi. In 2016 especially, almost the whole list of nominations was from a slate put forward by the 'Angry Puppies' (an even more virulent, misogynist, racist, homophobic, transphobic bunch of men). My theory was that doing this - having a trans protagonist written by a trans woman - would really annoy them and if it upsets them then it has to be the right thing to do.

I didn't change very much. There were a few extra things added because of Rachael's transness but on the whole, I just changed pronouns and her name. I took to calling what I did as 'pulling a Ripley' in reference to Sigourney Weaver's character in *Alien* who had been written as male until they cast her in the role. Nothing in the script changed except for her pronouns. (Although I doubt there would have been the long, loving shot of a male actor in his underwear while changing into a spacesuit.) There were a couple of flashbacks to Rachael's pre-transition days and back then I chose to refer to her with her Deadname and male pronouns. It's only recently that I reconsidered my ideas and wished that I hadn't done that. I know she is a fictional character - obviously, I created her - but it still felt disrespectful and wrong. Lots of nasty things happen to Rachael - some of them overtly transphobic - but they are all done to her by unpleasant characters in the story. By deadnaming her, it was me directly doing something nasty to her. It felt to me like it was similar to cis men getting cast as trans women in films. By using her Deadname and referring to her as 'he' and 'him', I was suggesting that it was okay to misgender trans people. I know there are trans people who are fine with people knowing their Deadname and that's absolutely their choice and I am not for one moment suggesting that they are wrong but I'm not one of them. While it is relatively easy to find out my pre-transition name (just go on Amazon and read some of the reviews for *The Long Sleep* and *Down Among the Yla*, even if you already have a copy - but if you do that then you have to buy them. I'm sorry, that's the law. I don't make the rules, I just follow them...) I will not readily tell people what it is.

The job that I mentioned in the previous chapter was as a system administrator for a school just next to the Meadow Well Estate in North Tyneside. The Meadow Well was the site of a major riot in the early 90s after a couple of kids were killed when they crashed the car in which they were joyriding during a high speed chase with the police. It was very much a sink estate with a lot of very low and no income people being moved there along with other 'undesirables'. Once there they were essentially left to rot. By the time I started working at the school a lot of money had been spent on the estate and it actually looks really quite nice now but it is still not an area from where wealthy people originate. The school itself was at the time I worked there not doing very well. It was not quite under 'special measures' according to OFSTED but it was getting there. Morale among many of the staff was quite low and the behaviour of a lot of the pupils was somewhat less than exemplary. However, having said that, I had no issues while I was there. This was probably two fold - first, I rarely left the 'server room' and when I did it tended to be during lessons so the kids were in the classrooms and secondly, I was seen as male which does help with having some authority. Mainly though, I had very little to do with the pupils. It wasn't a bad job and I actually quite enjoyed it most of the time.

The important part though was that it was also reasonably well paid which meant that I could actually look into having some facial hair removal. I found a place called Pro:Skin which was cheap but really pretty good. I ended up having about a dozen sessions there which did help a lot with the amount of hair there was on my face. Laser treatment, for those who have never had it, is incredibly painful, especially the hairs on the chin and upper lip. The best way to describe it is that it's like having someone ping an extremely hot elastic band on your face repeatedly for twenty minutes. To make matters worse, it's necessary to grow your facial hair for a few days beforehand so there is enough for the laser to work on. And, of course, it doesn't work on white or grey hairs because it depends on the melanin in your hair to channel the laser down into its root to kill it, which is why it is less effective on Black people or those with blonde hair, the former because the melanin in their skin absorbs the laser radiation as well and the latter because they don't have enough melanin in their hair. So, for someone who is getting older whose hair is starting to get a bit 'salt and pepper', laser treatment can only ever be partially successful. It is probably the second most painful thing I have ever done - beaten only by the pain of electrolysis which is best described as being like someone sticking a needle into your skin and then giving you an electric shock through it because that is exactly what it is but it's also the only way to get rid of those annoying white hairs. The pain of my surgery barely registers when compared to either of these two treatments, but we'll come to that.

Tea, Comics and Gender

May 7th 2015 was the General Election. I was in absolute agony about my voting choices. I had pretty much lost faith in the Labour Party by that point. I felt like it had been almost entirely silent during the previous Parliament which had been controlled by a coalition of the Conservative and Liberal Democrats, the latter of whom seemed to be perfectly willing to go along with whatever vileness the Tories wanted to enact. This included dropping their manifesto pledge of scrapping tuition fees and supporting cuts to benefit payments in return for a 5p tax on plastic bags. For the first time ever I wasn't definitely planning on voting Labour. I am lucky enough that I know that I am able to do this - the Labour Party could pretty much stand a corpse and probably get voted in where I live. If I had been in an area which was less certain of returning a non-Tory candidate, I would have had to hold my nose and vote Labour in the hope that they didn't screw things up entirely.

In the weeks leading up to the election, I had written to all the candidates, including the standing MP, Labour's Mary Glindon, the Tories, Lib Dems, The Green Party and even UKIP and one or two other smaller ones. The only one I didn't write to was the National Front one because, you know, fuck them. My letter had asked if they would support the Trans Manifesto (www.transmanifesto.org.uk) which asked them to support three principles around the rights and welfare of trans people. I wasn't expecting a response from the Tories or UKIP and no matter what their response I wouldn't have voted for them anyway but I was hoping for something from the others. In the end, I only got two responses. One from the 'Trade Unionist and Socialist Coalition', a party of which I was previously unaware. He was also the only candidate who actually did any canvassing

- at least around where I lived. He seemed like a really nice guy and the Party had lots of policies with which I agreed entirely and he said that he was happy to sign up to support the Trans Manifesto. Obviously, being a candidate for a party that had very little hope of actually getting into power, he could say whatever he wanted but he still replied to me putting his support in writing.

The only other reply I got was from Mary Glindon. Or rather, from Mary Glindon's Junior Secretary. In it, he said that Mary condemned the misrepresentation and harassment of trans people by the media and supported an immediate end to that misrepresentation. What she very blatantly did not say was that she was supportive of the Trans Manifesto which doesn't directly talk about the misrepresentation in the media but instead 'encourage(s) diverse, representative, realistic and positive portrayals of trans individuals'. I was already dubious of Mary's views as I knew that she had voted against equal marriage rights and felt that her reply was somewhat disingenuous and read very much a like a politician's response. It read like she didn't want to be supportive at all but at the same time she didn't want to say anything directly negative. I had done a little bit of research around Mary's views and had discovered that she had signed a petition against gay marriage created by the 'Coalition for Marriage' - an allegedly Christian organisation that holds views that are decidedly homophobic and transphobic - firstly that marriage must be between a man and a woman and also allowing trans people to legally change their gender will undermine what it means to have a 'traditional marriage'.

So, by the morning of May 7th I was in complete turmoil. There was obviously no way I was ever going to vote for a right wing party; the Lib Dems had proven themselves to be utterly without morals in the previous Parliament and the Labour Party was proving itself to be barely more left wing than the Tories and were represented by someone who arguably hated me. And yet, if I voted for TUSC or The Green Party I was in danger of letting the Tories or even UKIP in. I was confident that Mary would win (see my previous comment about a corpse. Actually, I would have preferred a corpse as candidate over Mary) but at the same time, if UKIP won by a tiny margin then I would be blaming myself for the next five years. I was awake at 4.30 in the morning worrying about how I was going to vote. I was desperately hoping that the end of the day would produce a hung Parliament in which the Labour Party and the Scottish National Party (and y'know, maybe the LibDems - they had proven themselves to be slippery so I'm sure they could have contorted themselves into something vaguely left wing) would work together to produce a government. My angst lasted right up until I got into the polling booth and I was standing there with my pencil poised over the ballot paper, trying to work out where my 'X' was going to go. Ultimately, I ended up voting for The Green Party. It felt very odd at the time but I was pretty sure that I had made the right decision. All that I needed to worry about now was the result. And we all know how that turned out. The Lib Dem voters apparently decided to punish their party for going into coalition with the Tories by... voting Tory? I was very confused and more than a little depressed by the following morning. The only high point in the whole thing was Nigel Farage (then leader of UKIP) losing in South Thanet. Which, considering he lost to a Tory was pretty a pretty depressing high point really.

Mary Glindon won as well that day - she got 55% of the vote, although the Tories and UKIP came second and third with 19% and 16% respectively which I found worrying then and still do today. The Green Party came fifth with 3% (only 1% behind the LibDems) and the TUSC candidate came sixth with 0.7%, fortunately beating the NF candidate which is a definite plus point.

May 7th was also a day that proved to be something of a watershed moment in my transition. On that day I applied for a job with New Writing North actually as Ellen. I had been thinking about it for a while and considering what to do. Even if I had got the job as 'him', I would have been transitioning pretty quickly and so would have to disclose my trans status basically in the interview. Instead, I decided that the best way to go about it was by being up front about who I was from the start. I asked for advice from the trans support group on Facebook and got two entirely different points of view - one of which was 'don't disclose in the application form but go to the interview as Ellen', the other being 'tell them'. While I could appreciate the former point of view, I ultimately decided to be open about it - I'd rather be turned down earlier because of my transness instead of having to go through an interview process for someone's bigotry to be revealed. Their point was that by saying something I would be perpetuating the idea that being trans 'is an issue'. Looking back now, I think that what I did was correct. The argument could just as easily have been reversed - by not saying something I would be pre-judging the person who was reading the application form and assuming that they were going to be discriminatory and that by not disclosing I was essentially hiding myself away which in and of itself is implying that there is something wrong with being trans.

Ultimately though, it didn't matter because I didn't get an interview. I don't know why - I suspect that I just wasn't a strong enough candidate - but if it was because I told them I was trans then I had a very lucky escape.

One of the things that transition had done for me in the months since I had started was to make me become louder and more political. I had always been a Socialist - being brought up by two kind, caring and wonderful people who were at the same time staunch left-wingers (and I'm not saying that the two things are related but they totally are) started me down that road but seeing what the right wing of the country had done to the less-well off people of the country (the Miners' Strike, Poll Tax, Section 28 and on and on and on) had only strengthened my resolve. It seemed that in direct opposition to the tenet that people become more right wing as they got older, I was actually moving more to the left. Discovering that I was a member of one of the more under-represented and under-privileged groups made my commitment even stronger. Essentially, I became one of those 'strident women'. And one of the things I got strident about was the time trans people had to wait to get an appointment at one of the NHS gender identity clinics. 2015 was one of the last times that waiting times for the GICs was actually made available to the public and the figures were appalling. People were being forced to wait for years for their first appointments and it was having a deep and profound effect on their mental health. The now sadly defunct group, UK Trans Info, regularly made Freedom of Information requests to the various GICs about their waiting times. The report they published in July 2015 was particularly damning. In it, they stated that if nothing changed then trans people who had been referred to the Northern Region Gender Dysphoria Service in Newcastle (the one to which I had been referred) could end up with a wait of twelve and a half years. I had been waiting for nearly six months by this point and had only had one letter telling me that I was in for a long wait. I had not however anticipated that it could be that long. And, even if it wasn't going to be for me, the prospect of it

being that long for others was just as awful. If I was going to be someone who stood up for my trans and non-binary siblings then this was going to be somewhere I could start.

So I wrote a letter. I know. Much wow. Such revolution. Elect her now. But, it was the first step and what else was I going to do? I was worried enough that by doing this I was already sticking my head above the parapet and making myself a target for the GIC. I had heard horror stories about how people got treated if they didn't conform to their expectations and being a bolshy, strident woman could potentially be seen as an attack which could cause problems for me down the line. But something needed to be said by as many people as possible and I had to be one of those voices.

So I wrote a letter to the GIC. And I cc'd it to Mary Glindon, my local councillor (a lovely woman called Janet Hunter), Jude Kirton- Darling MEP and NHS England. I didn't know what sort of response I would get but I needed to say something:

Dear sir or madam,

Tea, Comics and Gender

I am writing to express my concern and distress at the report published by UK Trans Info on current waiting times and patient population for NHS England Gender Identity Clinics from February to April 2015. I am especially concerned with the data given by the Northern Region Gender Dysphoria Clinic stating that no patients

had their first appointments in those three months. As someone who was initially referred to you in February 2015, I am obviously extremely worried about what this means for the length of time I am going to have to wait before I am offered an appointment.

I appreciate that, having only been referred in February, I am a long way down the waiting list and I am in no way asking for special dispensation or prioritisation, but I feel that making my concerns known at this point is important to ensure that you are aware of them as things continue. However if, as appears to be the case, the Northern Region Gender Dysphoria Clinic has stalled when it comes to dealing with new patients then it does not really matter if I have been waiting five weeks, five months or five years, the result is the same. I am not receiving the care that I feel I need.

Despite the love and support I have received over the last few months from family and friends, my dysphoria has been increasing quite rapidly, leading to greatly increased feelings of stress and anxiety, prolonged periods of insomnia and panic attacks and emotional meltdowns. One of the things that worries me, not just for myself, but for others in similar situations who are not as lucky as I am and don't have people they can turn to in times of stress, is that the situation with the GDC is going to inevitably lead to people harming themselves, either through self-medication of hormones or worse, attempting (and perhaps succeeding at) suicide. I feel that this neglect of the situation directly contravenes the Hippocratic Oath: "First, do no harm." By allowing the situation to get to this point – which has to be, by anyone's measure, a crisis point – the GDC is failing in its remit.

I am aware that there are many reasons for this crisis to have occurred, not the least of which is the constant hacking of budgets by the current government's austerity measures. However, this does not excuse the failure to keep in contact with your patients. When the only communication that I have had since being referred to you is one stating that my first appointment will not be for 'many months', I have to wonder what measures are being put in place to reassure and inform your patients. When all I hear are the horror stories about having been on the waiting list since 2013, it does not help my peace of mind during this period of my life which is already stressful enough. I feel that the Gender Dysphoria Clinic needs to look at its remit once again and decide if what it is doing is truly in the best interests of its patients - if acting as a gatekeeper to care and then locking those gates is really what the trans community in Northern England needs, especially at a time when the world is embracing the trans community in a way it never has done before. I hope that you are able to come to the same conclusion that I have done and realise that you need to change your focus and start to act to enable the community to push forward rather than holding it back. I believe that the only way to overcome these problems is to refocus your service and shift the paradigm when it comes to care. A new care model based around decentralised GP-led care with specialist support would not only help the waiting list but would free up a lot more time and money within the GDC to focus on patients who really need a greater degree of care rather than spend too much time, energy and money on those who are relatively 'simple' cases.

As you can see, I am forwarding this letter on to my local MP, my local councillor, my MEP and to NHS England. This is not intended as any sort of censure or threat, but in the hopes that they may be able assist in affecting some sort of change which will alleviate the pressures on Gender Identity Services nationwide.

I would like to close in saying that I truly believe the NHS is still the best health service in the world and that many, if not most, of the problems that the clinic is experiencing are due to external pressures that have been placed upon you. I truly have faith that you want the best for those people in your care and you are as frustrated with the problems as we are. If we work together, we can overcome them and make the Gender Identity Service better than it has ever been.

Yours sincerely,

Ellen Mellor.

I received a reply from North East Labour on behalf of Jude the following day. It didn't say much, just that they had sent my letter onto colleagues in Brussels. They did say that they had been in touch with the Beaumont Society (who style themselves as the longest running Trans support group in the country although they aren't exactly at the forefront anymore - their website still refers to people being 'transgendered' and describes trans women as 'mtf' and trans men as 'ftm'. All of which are terms that are really pretty outdated and frowned upon now) and they recommended GIRES but failed to mention Tyne Trans (as it was then). They also told me that I had somehow managed to get in touch with an MEP who was part of the European Parliament's LGBTI rights group which really cheered me up. It felt like I had found someone who was definitely going to be on my side.

That July was also the first time I went to Northern Pride, Newcastle's pride march and festival. While I was aware of it and knew it was important I was someone who identified as a straight, cis male, even if he did wear women's clothes on a regular basis, so it never felt relevant to me, that going along would have been co- opting something that wasn't mine. But that year, I knew that I

Ellen Mellor

wanted to be part of it. I wanted to be in a group of friends who were there supporting each other and showing the world that we exist and are proud. The march itself was great. Being surrounded by lots of queers making lots of noise was wonderful and something I can highly recommend (with one or two caveats which I'll come to later). The actual Pride festival itself though. Well, it was very definitely a festival, crowded, loud and full of people doing their best to get as pissed as possible as quickly as possible. It was very much part of the 'scene', which meant that it was aimed at a particular type of cis gay guy - the hi-energy dance and house music, the over the top campness and the partying as hard as possible were front and centre and it felt very alienating to me. I've never found those things attractive. I'm an indie girl - give me the Pixies and REM and Nirvana over... I dunno. I have no interest or knowledge in the artists who produce modern R'n'B or house or whatever. I did think about googling it but then decided that it didn't matter. I know that I can't use the 'it's not music, it's noise' excuse because frankly, have you listened to early Pixies? It's excellent but, yeah, it's got a lot of noise going on there. But, I just don't get it. But that's my cross to bear. I'll just console myself by playing *Debaser* at full volume. On top of that, the bouncers were forcing people to discard food and drink before they came in so the concession stands and bars inside the venue area (a fenced off part of the Town Moor) were free to sell their specially-over-priced offerings. I witnessed parent's being forced to discard baby food and people with diabetes having to throw away their water bottles and snacks. The bins at the entrance were full of it and it was disgusting.

I also heard reports from friends who said that they were

verbally abused inside the grounds by cis gay guys. They were told that they were ugly t*****s (I've censored that word as it is a slur thrown at trans people and I really don't like it. Nor do most other trans people.) and bad drag queens with no right to be there.

All that being said, there were aspects of it that I very much enjoyed. That year there were various different 'zones' including a women's zone and a health zone (although the concept of having to have a separate women's zone and, the following year, a trans zone, more than highlighted for me how the rest of it was intended for the cis men). The health zone was excellent - lots of stalls with lots of support and information, including one being staffed by people from the Northern Region Gender Dysphoria Service. I spent a while talking to Helen Greener who is a consultant there telling her about the letter I had sent. She told me that it was a good thing, that people writing letters was needed and helped get things done. She also said that the waiting list was not as long as the report made out but still couldn't actually give me an idea of when I would get an appointment which was not ideal but made me feel more hopeful than before.

The women's zone made me feel very uncomfortable but it was purely my reaction to being in somewhere intended purely for women. I still had so much internalised transphobia and transmisogyny that I didn't feel like I belonged, that I wasn't woman enough and everyone saw me as an intruder. There may well have been one or two who did think like that, although back then the trans-exclusionary crowd were far less obvious than they are now, but I am certain that the vast majority of people in that zone didn't give a damn and, if asked, would probably have been welcoming. But, I was still only presenting female on a part-time basis and I wasn't doing anything more than wearing a dress and makeup. Being in that space made me very aware that underneath that I was still a 'fully-functional male'.

I have been to Northern Pride most years since although after the second year I gave up actually going to the festival part as it became more overtly trans-exclusionary. There were vague attempts to pretend they were being inclusive without listen to anyone in the trans community. One year the only thing they were actually considering offering was a 'dressing service'. When people in the trans community protested and said how appalled this was they cancelled it and didn't bother with anything. For several years, the compère for the main stage show was a drag queen, part of whose act was to make transphobic, lesbophobic and biphobic jokes. The official programme made more mention of drag queens than it did of trans people. Hell, it made more mention of dogs (they had decided that one of the major events for that year was going to be a dog show) than it did of trans people.

Fortunately, the people who run the event seem to have changed in the last couple of years and things are getting much better.

Although I make a point of marching, I've had some problems there as well. In 2018, when anti-trans campaigners seemed to be getting braver, a small group (which is a bit of a pointless thing to say. It's *always* a small group of anti-trans campaigners. There aren't enough of them to make a big group) hijacked the start of London Pride by just walking at the front. They weren't stopped or removed or anything. There was a massive backlash - just one of many cases when these bigots have managed to shoot themselves in the foot by giving a focus to the majority who support trans people - and Pride marches that came afterwards made a point of focusing on trans people to show their support. Northern Pride was no different and asked trans people to walk at the head of the march. This really felt like a great honour and for about the first third of it, I felt proud. Unfortunately, the march organisation was fumbled quite badly and the trans contingent went off far faster than the rest who were following and getting farther behind.

One of the problems with walking through the main shopping street in Newcastle on a Saturday afternoon in the middle of summer is that it's very busy. The march was hemmed in very closely on either side by onlookers - some of who were supportive and waved rainbow flags and clapped and cheered while others just gawked at the queers. They seemed to get closer and closer, pressing in more and more, squeezing the trans contingent together which set off a major panic attack in me. I'm not claustrophobic but it hit me hard and I had to get out of there. It felt like I was being eyed up like a piece of meat and at any moment they were going to pounce and tear me apart . Breaking away, I pushed through the ranks of on- lookers until I got out into the clear area beyond, allowing me to calm down and get my breath back, before re-joining the march when C came past with the NASUWT. I don't have panic attacks often and that was one of the worst, leaving me feeling trapped and certain that everyone was staring, judging and hating. I got to the end of the march but didn't go into the festival itself because it was just so crowded, the queues to get in were so long and I still felt very shaky. I had done the important thing and I probably wouldn't have been inside very long anyway.

That August was the first time I spent an extended period as Ellen when we went down to the New Forest when my friends Rachel and Tim married without a single item of masculine clothing. They had asked me to do a reading from a Pratchett meaning that I was exposing myself to a bunch of people - in a church no less - that I had never met and only knew that they were friends and family of the happy couple. I was confident this meant they'd be good people (or at least well behaved enough to not cause a fuss) and I was right. The reading went well, the ceremony went well. Rachel looked radiant, Tim looked handsome and slightly embarrassed by all the fuss being made (I love Tim but he is one of the most 'proper' English people I have ever met.) Someone compared me to Kate Middleton! Although I think it was for the style of dress I was wearing (a gorgeous deep blue, lacy retro number) and the fascinator than for any actual physical resemblance. But still, it was one of the nicest compliments I had ever had.

September and October were particularly momentous months for me. I had my first job interview as Ellen - which I totally messed up and didn't get. I officially came out on Facebook, although I don't think there were many people who were especially surprised. While I hadn't specifically said that I was trans, I had also shared a lot of trans information since starting my Ellen account, been pretty obvious about wearing women's clothes far more often than I had ever done and had spoken about transitioning Rachel, the protagonist of *Ghostkin*. As expected, everyone was supportive, which made me very happy.

Tea, Comics and Gender

To help celebrate my official coming out, my friend Lesley, who had invited us all over to eat scones, made me a special one all of my own. A vagina shaped scone. A *scogina*, if you will. And this is one of the strongest arguments yet for me including pictures in this book.

Friday the twenty fifth of September was the last day of my job at the school and the last day of ever having to be him. After cycling home and showering I put a skirt on and that was it. There would never be any good reason for anyone to refer to me by my Deadname ever again. From that point on it was all Ellen, all the time. And being all Ellen meant skirts and dresses. In fact, in the (as of the day I'm writing this) nearly five years since I stopped ever having to pretend I was male, I have not worn trousers. I wear leggings on a reasonably regular basis but never anything else. In fact, I no longer own any pairs of trousers. Some people have found that hard to believe, even going so far as to suggest that I'm doing it wrong because 'normal' women don't do that. Which is of course absolute bullshit. It may not be something done by the majority of cis women (or indeed trans women) but I do know some women who I've never seen wearing trousers. And some women who I've never seen wearing anything other than trousers. It makes no difference to who they are. I used to say that I had worn trousers for the first forty three years of my life and I was sick of them. But, to be honest, that excuse is probably a bit old now. The truth is, I prefer skirts and dresses. I have a particular style that I love - retro styles from the forties and fifties and that's what I want to wear. My absolute style icon is a beautiful, queer, chronically ill, deaf Youtuber called Jessica Kellgren-Fozard. I adore everything about her. When I went to Brighton with Dylan (who has yet to enter my narrative), we actually spotted her (Dylan adores her as well and is actually the person who first told me of her existence) and she was even more mesmerisingly beautiful in real life than she is on YouTube. But yes, that's why I don't wear trousers. I don't wanna. And that's all the reason I need.

Once I was 'full time' there was one thing I really needed to do basically immediately which was to get my name changed legally. Fortunately, I am a clever girl and I had already prepared for this.

The Monday after I had finished both my job and old gender I went to a solicitor and had him witness a statutory declaration stating that I was changing my name and 'renounce, relinquish and abandon' my old name in favour of my new one. So, on the 28th September, I legally became Ellen Stephanie Inman Mellor.

One of the things that nobody tells you about transitioning is how much of it is based in admin. There were so many things that I had to do once I had my stat dec. Immediately after the change I went to the bank, presented them with the stat dec and changed the name and gender marker on my bank account. That was easy. But I also had to change one or both of them on my driver's licence, my passport, my various pieces of insurance, National Insurance number, my GP, pensions (actually that's one of the things I haven't done properly - over the years I picked up several different pension plans, none of which will actually give me enough money to live on when I retire), TV Licence, Amazon account, PayPal account and on and on. And not all of them are as straight forward as going into the branch and flashing a piece of paper at them. When changing my details with my life insurance company they were happy with the name change bit but they demanded a birth certificate in my new gender or a doctor's letter confirming my gender change. That set off all kinds of alarm bells. Demanding a new birth certificate just seemed especially dodgy to me - implying that I needed a gender recognition certificate to do so. Demanding to see a GRC is in and of itself against the law - the Gender Recognition Act 2004 specifically states that it can't be done. There was the additional question of whether or not a cis person needed to prove their gender. I could understand that a life insurance company may need to know that I was AMAB (Assigned Male At Birth) but a new birth certificate wouldn't do that. It just all felt very much like a cis-sexist attempt to make trans people into second class citizens.

When I rang the company I was told that a birth certificate was one of the pieces of proof that can be given for a change of name. I specifically asked if cis people were required to prove their gender and was told that they weren't. At this point, I suggested that what they were doing could be seen as potentially discriminatory and as gender identity is one of the protected characteristics under the Equality Act 2010 this could be very dodgy ground for the company. Just to make matters that teeny bit more fun, the woman I was talking to called me 'sir' twice during the phone call.

The phone call was followed up by a letter:

Dear sir or madam,

Ellen Mellor

This morning, I received a letter from you confirming that you have updated the records on my life insurance policy to show my new name. However, the letter also said that if I wished to change my gender, I would be required to provide a birth certificate or letter from my doctor.

I rang your customer services department and spoke to [...] at the Cardiff offices and she enquired as to the reason why this is a policy. She told me that it would be necessary for anybody - i.e. a woman changing their name due to getting married or something similar. However, she confirmed that nobody else would be asked to prove their gender at any point. This suggests to me that this policy is specifically aimed at transgender people and is, at the very least, bordering on being discriminatory. When you consider that gender reassignment is one of the protected characteristics in the Equality Act 2010, I would think that this would be quite difficult territory for Legal and General to get into.

For a trans person to be given a new birth certificate involves a long and quite complicated process, which includes living 'in role' as your correct gender for two years, providing a lot of documentation as proof and then paying a £140 fee. Not everyone is able to do this - trans people are very often unable to find well-paid stable work due to their trans status. So expecting this when this level of proof is not expected of cis-gender people is, frankly, a disgrace.

I hope that you are able to see the sense of my argument and change your policy forthwith.

I would also like to recommend that your staff in the call centres have some training around transgender issues. While [...] was pleasant and efficient, she also called me 'sir' during the course of our conversation. Considering the subject we were discussing, this absolutely should not have happened. Please understand, I do not want [...] disciplined or anything bad to happen to her, but I would like to see some sort of training happen for her and her colleagues so it does not happen again.

Yours sincerely,

Ellen Mellor.

It took a while after that, but the company did finally come back to me with an apology, an offer of compensation and a confirmation that my marker had been changed. I hope that they changed their policy on this - when I first posted about this on Facebook another trans woman said that she had had the same problem with the same company - but I don't know if they did or not.

It's very rare to make any money out of changing your identity like this. In fact, it can be really bloody expensive. Changing your name and marker on your driver's licence is free unless you want to change your photograph as well (which most trans people would want to do) in which case it will cost £17. To change your details on your passport costs £75. Getting new qualification certificates so you don't have to out yourself every time you apply for a job starts at £50 for a single certificate from the university I went to but then there is the cost of changing all the certificates for my other qualifications - my O and A-Levels were done with various different exam boards (some of which no longer exist) and they all cost money. And then there is the cost of getting your birth certificate changed. This can only be done with a Gender Recognition Certificate which at that time cost £140 plus the costs of various doctor's letters and the time and effort to pull together as much proof as possible. If you're married then you need to pay for a statutory declaration which states that your spouse is happy for this to go ahead (and if your spouse is for whatever reason unable or unwilling to do this then you're screwed and your only option is to divorce them). And then you have to put all of that in a big envelope and send it off to a group of cis people, most of whom are anonymous, who get to decide whether or not to accept your application. If they decide that you haven't sufficiently proven that you are trans enough then they can (and do) reject you with no explanation and no recourse to appeal. You'll need to start again and pay another £140. Surprisingly, I haven't yet done this nor have the majority of other trans people in the country.

(A brief update as I'm editing this in May 2021. The government recently dropped the price of the application to £5 - the only positive outcome from the recent GRA Reform consultation. It's still as humiliating and invasive as it ever was though.)

To jump back for a moment, the day I legally changed my name was an absolutely wonderful day. I was on an amazing high, like I had done something positive for myself. Minutes after coming out of the solicitor's office I bumped into someone I knew and got a huge hug (the fact that this person later turned out to be a huge dick and I cut off all contact with them is neither here nor there. At the time, they were lovely.). And then the ease with which I was able to change my name and gender marker at the bank made me feel that it was all going so well and I was on top of the world. Until I was walking down Northumberland Street and a young woman decided to shout at me telling me that she thought I was a freak. Frankly, there's nothing like a taste of good old-fashioned transphobia to really put you in your place. This reminded me that, despite everything else, there are people who would rather see me dead either by my own hand or otherwise than happy and content. During my transition I have only been subjected to transphobic abuse a handful of times. It's always been verbal rather than physical and the fact that I am actively trying to think of ways to talk about this without describing myself as 'lucky' is extremely telling. I have been 'lucky' that people haven't physically attacked me. I have been 'lucky' that I am supported my friends and family. I have been 'lucky' that I am apparently cis-normative enough that I don't get challenged more often and feel like I am able to (for example) use the women's toilets when I'm out and about - even though I still feel nervous about it, especially if I have to wait in a queue. There are days when I even feel nervous about going outside my front door. I am white, middle-class, neurotypical and 'lucky' enough to have a job that pays me a reasonable salary. In the community of trans people I have immense privilege. I am standing at the top of the pile. And yet, people still feel that it's okay to call me a freak and to verbally abuse me because of who I am. I know that there are black and/or poor and/or mentally ill trans people (most notably trans women) who are dying purely because of who they are and/or who are forced into sex work in order to survive (not that I think there is anything wrong with sex work but when you are doing it because you have no other choice, then it becomes a problem). Being called names is an extremely minor irritant but it is the thin end of the wedge that leads to women being murdered because a guy got a hard-on when they saw her and then discovered that she is trans so being attracted to her must have meant that the guy was gay in some way. And so the only way to prove his manliness was to inflict violence on her. I know that despite my privilege I am potentially endangering my life every single time I go out there. Even writing that sounds like hyperbole but it's really not. Being trans is an excellent way of shortening your life. 'Freak' was probably one of the mildest insults I've received. It was just a random comment from a passing stranger who chose not to go into any greater depth. A man driving past me once decided to tell me that he thought I looked ridiculous. Another shouted the t-slur while also calling me a slut. Another - I believe he was a homeless man - followed me through the centre of Newcastle while shouting that I was a bloke in a dress.

Then there was the guy who followed me off the bus one dark winter evening and asked me 'what I was in to'. He was less than attractive - dressed in really scruffy tracksuit bottoms and a t-shirt, unshaven and just generally unkempt (a word that I shall come back to later on). Even if I was into men there is no chance that this one with his unsubtle come on would have revved my engine. Except possibly into reverse. Feigning ignorance I said that didn't understand to which he replied was 'for sex'. I don't quite remember what I said, but it was something along the lines of 'I'm not interested' - I don't think I said anything directly against him, at least partly because I was so scared of what he might do. Fortunately, he walked off and just shouted at me that it was 'A pity, because [I] was quite pretty for a bloke.' I was very careful walking the rest of the way home in case he decided to follow me and I was very aware of where he was going.

Another decided that having the temerity to be on the London Underground wearing a dress while with my child was child abuse.

This one went on for some time as I was trapped there. I tried to ignore him to begin with but he just kept going on and on. Eventually, I turned to him and tried to argue but he told me I was disgusting and a paedophile. He backed up his statement by claiming that he had been abused as a child so he was allowed to say these things. I feel great pity for the abuse he suffered but at the same time, he can totally fuck off. He completely ruined my day out leaving me shaking and very upset. One of the things that really gets to me about this incident though is the fact that nobody else on the Tube (and it was quite full) said or did anything. They just acted like it wasn't happening. I'm sure some of them will have tutted and may have said something about it to their friends and family when they got home but when it came to it, not a single person came to my defence. Obviously, I don't include C and M in this. C is deaf in one ear and didn't realise there was anything going on until it was too late and M was twelve. But every other adult who was there - if any of them have the temerity to claim to be allies after that then they should be thoroughly ashamed of themselves. Allyship isn't just about 'liking' things on Facebook and retweeting things saying 'This is terrible'. It's about being there for the people for which you claim to be an ally. It's about placing yourself between the target and the aggressor and saying 'to get to them you have to go through me'. It's about being a voice for the rights of those people even when there aren't any of them around. It's NOT about shoving your nose deeper into your copy of the *Evening Standard* and saying 'tsk tsk' but quietly so as not to draw attention to yourself. Obviously, I am still angry and upset about this. One of my biggest fears in this whole thing was that I would be hurting M in some way. And so for someone to target that very fear and weaponise it against me is, in itself, abusive. To vocalise it in front of my child is abusing him. And all of those people who didn't say anything, who chose to turn away, were complicit in that man's abuse.

So, yeah, that last one was pretty bad. But it's not the worst. The worst abuse I received came from an entirely unexpected angle, from someone who had, up until that point, been one of my closest friends and who had been entirely supportive of me when I identified as a crossdresser and indeed for about the first eighteen months of my transition. Suddenly, she decided to reveal her previously unknown transphobic views and unleash them all on me.

The reason she decided to do this? I had come across a Facebook post from a friend describing how she was constantly being cat-called. I (perhaps naively) asked if this was a regular occurrence for cis women. Obviously, I got lots of replies saying that it was. This woman (who I have taken to calling my Own Personal Transphobe - OPT for short - as for some reason that I don't quite understand I don't want to name her) chose to use this post as proof that I wasn't and never would be a woman. That I was just a bloke in a dress and I was trying to invade women's spaces. Several cis women stood up for me and argued with her. OPT essentially accused them of being men as well.

Not content with that, she wrote me an email, cc'ing several of our closest mutual 'real life' friends in an obvious attempt to recruit them to her side. The email (which she delightfully headed 'Meaningless Fucking Cunt (again)') stated that 'a (former) male friend' had left her in a 'state of utter emotional distress' because 'his theorising as to what a woman is' negated her experiences of being a woman. She referred to me as 'he' throughout the email and described me as a 'man in a frock'.

I replied politely. Her next email to me was a long, bizarre rant which went through her life describing every single time she had been attacked and abused by men (and on a few occasions by cis women which I think rather confused matters) which meant that she was within her rights to dismiss me as just another man trying to put her in her place (which reminds me a lot of the guy on the Tube). She spoke approvingly of Germaine Greer who not long before had described trans women as "lop[ping] off their dicks and wear[ing] a dress" and argued that being trans is the same as having a doctor give her liver spots and long ears and wearing a brown coat to become a cocker spaniel. After I replied again, she told me that I was being patronising, which she said was apt as it has its roots in the ward 'patron' which is a derivative of the Latin word *pater* meaning 'father'. I realised that there was no coming back from this, she had closed off any avenue for discussion. The last thing I wrote was to say that I no longer wanted to hear from her, blocked her email address and her phone number and told our mutual friends that while I understood it if they wanted to remain friends with this person, I expected them not to tell her anything about me or vice versa. They have mostly kept to this although there have been a couple of occasions where my request was ignored. To be honest, I'm not sure why I said that I was okay with them remaining friends with OPT. I now think that I was being too nice but, at the time, I was too scared of losing them as well. Looking back, I was being unfair to myself. If a black person knew that other people were friends with a white supremacist who had directly attacked them would it be reasonable to demand that these friends cut the white supremacist from their lives? For them not to do so just shows that they think that being a white supremacist is a reasonable thing to expect in a friend. If equating transphobia to white supremacy feels like too much of a reach, if it feels too much like hyperbole then, firstly, you have to ask yourself why you feel that it's okay to be against someone because of their gender identity but not because of the colour of their skin? Secondly, you have to put this book down and get the fuck away from me. Transphobia is the same as racism. It is bigotry and it is violent and it is unacceptable. Anything less is telling me that I am less. That my existence means less to you than having a drinking buddy. And if that is the case then I don't want to know you.

I realise that this section has come across as extremely ranty and less than fun. Unfortunately, this is what society has done to me. I am living in a country - in a world - which elevates the voices of transphobes, giving them newspaper columns and television interviews where they get to spout their lies and their bigotry and claim that the 'Trans Lobby' is silencing them without any comeback. Any other bunch of bigots who seem able to conjure up large chunks of cash from apparently nowhere would be the focus of a major journalistic investigation but instead they are able to do this with impunity. There has been an informal investigation into this and, unsurprisingly, it appears that the vast majority of it comes from far right, American, 'Christian' fundamentalist groups who have an explicit aim of splitting the 'T' away from the 'LGB' in order to weaken both groups and make it easier to eradicate us all. But, the investigation was conducted by a trans woman so of course hasn't been picked up. There isn't a single mainstream news outlet that I feel able to trust anymore. Obviously, the Murdoch papers and the Daily Mail are right out. But The Guardian is just as bad. The BBC is just as bad. Channel 4 is just as bad. There is nowhere I can turn to in order to keep myself informed of the news without worrying that I am going to see some 'think piece' about how trans women are forcing gender non-conforming young lesbians into becoming trans men, filling their bodies up with testosterone, cutting out their wombs and lopping off their breasts. (That last sentence is unfortunately not hyperbolic at all. It is a regular argument that the 'Gender Critical' crowd use.)

Ironically, I have subsequently received exactly the sort of sexist behaviour to which the original post referred. While shopping in the local supermarket, one of a pair of guys started talking to me. They weren't threatening or unpleasant and in that moment I felt a certain amount of validation as I don't think they clocked me as being trans.

I was polite to them and thought that was it but then, as I was going home and rounded a corner into the street upon which I lived it turned from being kind of okay into something scary when they pulled up next to me in their work van. One of them started to tell me about how his mate fancied me and asked me for my phone number. When I said I was married (I didn't say that I was lesbian or married to a woman, just that I was married) he asked if his mate could give me his phone number in case I became single again. I declined politely and they drove off again. Once again, I had to be very careful of going up to my door just in case they decided to circle back again. These men to whom I had given no hint that I was interested in either one of them decided that it was okay to try and pick me up on the street - even worse that it was the street on which I lived. If they decided to come back, it would have really narrowed down their search for me.

I mentioned that the first part of the encounter gave me a feeling of validation. Which is, I know, weird. But early in my transition - and I know this is not unique to me as other trans women have said the same thing - when I encountered sexist behaviour being directed towards me, I felt a weird disconnect. There was part of me thinking 'Yay, this person sees me as a woman' while another part of me was thinking 'fuck off, you sexist arsehole'. It's a very difficult dichotomy to navigate and I don't think I've managed to completely understand it even now.

I reported most of these occurrences to the police (the ones which I didn't were, ironically, the two which were definite cases of sexual harassment - the guy following me off the bus and the two men in the van - and my OPT. Although if she had continued, I would have taken that one further). As far as I know nothing ever came from any of them. Certainly there is only one of which I know the outcome. The police were unable to spot the homeless guy at the Monument who followed me, even though I had a bright, hot pink coat on so I should have stood out quite nicely. The man on the Tube was reported to British Transport Police with no follow up from them so I have to assume that nothing came of that either. I don't think I have heard of a single consequence of these 'minor' infractions and, arguably, it isn't worth the time and the effort to follow them up properly. After all, nobody was physically hurt. There have been consequences for long-term harassment -

the once-relevant comedy writer, Graham Linehan, was visited by the police on several occasions for his constant attacks on the trans community on Twitter - and for physical attacks but for one-off, purely verbal attacks which make up for the vast majority of abuse that trans people receive, absolutely nothing. All it does is make another tick mark on the hate crime statistics table. As I said, I understand why the police don't feel they can follow up all of these incidents but that is to treat these things as individual, discrete instances without taking into account the corrosive effect that these things have. I have had half a dozen odd instances of it in the last five years and I am very much towards the bottom end of the list. I am reasonably cis-normative in my appearance and have a certain amount of 'passing privilege' so that most people probably don't realise that I'm trans for good or ill. Most of those who do recognise me for what I am probably don't care or, if asked, would say that they support my right to be who I am - and a large part of that will be because of how I look. If a trans woman is unfortunate enough to have been cursed with a particularly masculine set of genetics to the extent that passing is that much harder for them, then they are much more likely to be a target and much more likely to be attacked both verbally and physically. For those women, the likelihood of them reporting all of these instances to the police is much lower because in some cases they would spend all of their time talking to the police. The vast majority of transphobic hate crimes don't get reported to the police - often because they have no faith that the police will take any interest and nothing will come of it. And there really isn't a lot of evidence to the contrary.

So yeah. Being trans is all fun and games and I did it

because I woke up one morning and decided that I was bored of being a bloke.

To counter all the transphobic shittiness of the last few thousand words, here's something nice. The day after getting my name changed and being called a freak, a woman that I vaguely knew (she lived over the road from me and we occasionally shared a bus to work when I worked for the Council) stopped me in the street to congratulate me on my transition and to tell me how good I looked and how happy she was for me.

After the joy of going full time, I thought that I would have a few weeks of getting used to being Ellen all the time and doing some of the admin around it before getting another temp job. I was looking for permanent work but hadn't even succeeded at getting an interview for most of the jobs to which I had applied. I wanted to relax a bit and maybe focus on getting *Ghostkin* properly edited and finished - especially as I had seen an invitation from one of the mid-size genre publishers for submissions from 'diverse backgrounds and lived experiences'.

However, on the Tuesday of that week, I got a phone call from a guy in a temp agency who had a job for which he thought I would be ideal. I filled in a ton of paperwork, updating him about my name and gender as I did so and then he rang me back on the Wednesday saying that they wanted me to start on the following Monday - the only time I've ever managed to get a job without having to go through some kind of interview process. All I knew about the job was that it was based at the University and was some kind of IT based thing. But, it was a job and it meant that I would be able to 'pop my cherry' as a trans woman in the world of employment.

That Monday morning I arrived at the university just before nine 'o'clock, dressed in a smart skirt and blouse, sitting in reception surrounded by students and waiting for meet my new line manager. My head was swimming with fearful, paranoid thoughts. Would he accept me? Laugh at me? Tell me to fuck off? I was pretty certain the latter wouldn't happen but I couldn't stop the scenario from playing.

The one thing I hadn't anticipated was that he would come out of the office, look around and then call out my Deadname.

I panicked and sat frozen in place for a few seconds, terrified and with no idea about what to do. A huge part of me screamed out that I just needed to get the fuck out of there as quickly as possible. Instead, I shakily stood and went over to him. I don't remember what I said to him, I think I was running in autopilot but I did manage to explain that I was the person they were expecting, that I was no longer going by that name and the agency should have informed him. He apologised profusely and adjusted really well but I was very deeply upset. After my initial introduction to the rest of the team, I went and hid in the toilets for a while in order to get my breath and composure back. That was the first time I cried in the toilets at work but it was, unfortunately, far from the last.

When I rang the agency, I was extremely polite. Extremely. Polite. Devastatingly so. They in their turn apologised and assured me that it was an oversight and they would make sure their records were updated properly and so on... I believed them because there was no point in doing otherwise. I just took it as another example of cis people not realising how important this stuff was. Names have power and Deadnames especially so. Telling someone your Deadname is a symbol of trust that is very rarely given. Deliberately using a someone's Deadname is tantamount to telling them that you don't believe that they are who they say they are which is why using it as a weapon against us can be so devastating.

After that things went somewhat quiet for a while. I got on with my job - which was not exactly strenuous (I made one Facebook post about actually having some work to do one day: copying names from a piece of paper into a spreadsheet). Life continued much the same way as before except now in a dress, heels and makeup. I completed my work on *Ghostkin* and started to look for a publisher; read lots of comics and books; I joined the Labour Party; and did a Counselling course.

Before the Covid-19 Apocalypse, I would regularly go to a comic book reading group - The Readers of the Lost Art. After the group we would go to a pub to continue geeking together and then I would catch the bus home. The first time I went there after going full time was in mid-October and by the time I left the pub it was dark. The route I took from the pub to the bus stop took me through a short tunnel and that night, the lights were off and it was very dark.

Despite the fact that I was still, physically, a nearly six foot tall male, I felt very nervous and incredibly vulnerable in a way that I had never felt before which prompted me to buy a personal alarm and to find a different route to the bus stop.

Until I started going to Be, I had not heard of the

Tea, Comics and Gender

Transgender Day of Remembrance. While it has a massive presence in the transgender community, it has almost none outside of it. I knew that trans people were killed just for being trans - watching *Boys Don't Cry* when it was released in the cinema taught me that but I had no idea of its extent. This is what I wrote on Facebook to commemorate the day that year:

> Today is #TDoR. The Transgender Day of Remembrance. For this year. There's been one every year since 2007. It's intended to commemorate and memorialise the many trans people around the world who have died purely because they are trans. The official list (at http://tdor.info/) only lists those who have been murdered, not those who have committed suicide - purely because there are so many of them. And there was another one in the news today - Vicky Thompson, another woman sent to an all-male prison (http://www.theguardian.com/society/2015/nov/19/transgender-woman-found-dead-in-all-male-prison).
>
> I have been transitioning since February of this year. Living mostly as a woman since about July and full-time since the end of September. Before that, I crossdressed on a regular basis since I was aged 13. My first time going out was when I was 18. And, since that day, I have been nervous and worried every time I step outside. In all that time, I have only ever had one single moment of abuse. I don't know how or why I have been so lucky, because I'm damned sure it's not because I am totally 'convincing' and can pass perfectly as a cis-woman, but I am so thankful for it. It doesn't stop the nervousness though. When I'm out, I'm constantly on the look out, wondering if that person is going to point and laugh, or if that person is going to call me a freak, or if that person is going to hit me.
>
> I am a white, middle-class, socialist trans woman in a fairly easy-going city. I'm not one of the people who is most targeted. I'm not a trans woman of colour. I'm not Brazilian. I'm not working the streets. In many ways, I have had the easiest transition possible - supported and loved by all my friends and family. I have privilege that many others

don't but I still get scared. I don't let it stop me, but it's always there.

But. Today is also a day to be thankful.

It's a day to draw strength from friends and family, to come together and say no. To remember and support those who are still here and who are working to make sure that the lives of trans people is that little bit easier. I want to say thank you to everyone that I have met at Be:Trans. I absolutely want to say thank you to all of my friends who knew me before transitioning and have shown love and support for me at every step and I know will be there for me as I keep going. To my mother and father, my brother and all the rest of my relatives who have been happy for me, even when it hasn't been easy for them. And, most of all, although they don't use Facebook and probably won't see this, I need to say thank you - every single day - to C and M.

I don't really know what I want to say in this post, it's just a rambling jumble of thoughts and feelings. I nearly didn't write anything, but seeing all the other posts from my friends spurred me to do this. I don't have any conclusions. I don't have any answers. But I do know two things, I don't want to be scared any more. And, more than anything else, I don't want anyone else to die for trying to find happiness for following their heart and becoming the person they need to be - the person they really are.

Please, whether you are cis or trans, please spread the word about TDoR. It's only by working together that we can make sure that we'll have a November 20th that isn't a day of remembrance. We need to make sure that it's sooner rather than later.

Updated 20 Nov 2015, 13:50

One of the unexpected side effects of my transition was seeing my confidence in myself and my abilities grow. For the first time ever, I stood in front of an audience and read one of my stories. This was at a trans book reading event, headlined by Imogen Binney and Casey Plett - if you haven't read any of their work I highly recommend it. As well as these two, local trans writers had also been invited to read.

Tea, Comics and Gender

Talking to Imogen and Casey while buying their books, they asked if I was a writer. When I told them I was they pretty much insisted on me getting up and reading something. Despite my nerves screaming at me, I went for it, reading 'Bonnie' from *Stories From the Corner of the Room* which was warmly received. Casey then told me about the book she was putting together - an anthology of science fiction stories written by trans people and suggested I submit something for it. I knew that I had to do something but had no idea what. Then, while sitting watching the other performers, I came up with a first line: "You'd have thought that transitioning in this fucked up science-fiction future we're living in would be a doddle. There'd be amazing body changers where you go in rough and hairy and masculine and come out smooth and curvy and girly – or, y'know, vice versa. Or neither. Or both. But apparently fucking not." There was just one slight problem. The closing date for submissions was four days away. I spent almost all my waking moments in that time sat in front of my computer trying to work out the story and get it down. And I did it. I managed to write a story in less than four days. The one problem with writing a story in four days can often be that it reads like you had written it in four days and this was very much the case for 'Goddess On The Mountaintop', meaning that it got rejected. When I was re-reading and re-editing it for inclusion in *All The Books of Earth* I could see why it had been rejected. Hopefully the version that will appear in there is somewhat better. The anthology to which I had submitted was published in 2017. It's called *Meanwhile, Elsewhere* and I recommend it wholeheartedly.

All this time, I had of course been waiting for my first appointment with the Gender Identity Clinic. I had been referred to the Northern Region Gender Dysphoria Clinic but discovered that the wait to be seen by the clinic in Northampton was only two or three months. After some back and forth trying to persuade the CCG (Clinical Commissioning Group, the people who hold the purse strings for local health care) that I was allowed to go to any clinic, my GP referred me there. Talking to a friend had been referred there after my initial referral to NRGDS and had already been prescribed hormones, I found out that she had been required to write a no- more-than-four page essay on her life. While I understood the necessity for it - it saves the need to constantly repeat things over and over again - I was also a little taken aback by this latest example of gatekeeping and the naivety in asking for it. Were they really expecting it to be honest? Anything that was written was going to be twisted to present the best story possible and by 'best' I mean the one that is most consistent with the narrative needed to ensure that the trans person is accepted as trans by the clinic. Even worse, it was desperately ableist and elitist. If someone presented with dyslexia or was unable to produce a coherent essay for some reason, was this going to be used as a reason to refuse them treatment? Obviously, that wasn't going to be an issue for me - my problem would be keeping it down to four pages (for proof, see this book. Originally intended to be no longer than 10,000 words, it is currently - at the time of writing these words - 55,326 words long. Not counting anything after the last hyphen) - but my ability does not make me any more or less trans than anyone else.

Of course, the fact that Northampton had such a short waiting list meant that everyone else in the country who was seeking help to transition had exactly the same idea, so it quickly ballooned out of control and meant that it wasn't until a long time after I had been seen by NRGDS that I heard anything from them.

Waiting for either one to come back to me was not a fun time. At one point, I had a dream that I had an appointment. It had a specific date as well - March 16th, although it didn't state the year. The dream consisted of me sitting in a waiting room. There are times when my subconscious can be decidedly unsubtle.

3
Girl Cooties

I have never really explained why I called myself Ellen, always saying that I couldn't remember why I had chosen that name.

Well, that's not entirely true. After settling on the name, I decided to keep the reason behind it secret, mainly because I didn't think that it was anyone else's business.

However, I made a pact with myself that if I ever wrote a memoir, I'd reveal the truth.

So here it is:

I love Will Eisner's work and especially his female characters in The Spirit *who always seemed like they were five steps ahead of the male characters. I didn't feel like 'Sand Sarif' was a name I could get away with, so I took the one belonging to The Spirit's girlfriend, Ellen Dolan.*

My first appointment with the Northern Regional Gender Dysphoria Service - NRGDS or, more generically, 'the GIC' (Gender Identity Clinic) - was on June 8th, 2016, 1 year, 3 months and 16 days since I asked to be referred. While I was really happy and excited and nervous to finally get there, I was very much aware that this was another step on the road towards C and I separating. I already knew that the changes I had made meant that she was no longer attracted to me and as I went further down the medical path of hormones and potentially surgery that lack of attraction was only going to get stronger. However, at the same time, I knew that I needed someone who was able to love me for my femininity. I wanted someone to want to touch the breasts I was going to grow. Someone who found the idea that I was probably going to have a vulva a good thing and something to which they looked forward. None of this was C. I didn't and don't blame her for that. I was unlucky enough to fall head over heels in love with a straight woman. And she was unlucky enough to fall for a lesbian trans woman. Life can be imperfect sometimes.

I ended up not needing the essay I wrote, but it still helped as that first appointment consisted of the Nurse Practitioner asking me a lot of very personal questions about my life, including my experiences of sex and masturbation. To say it was uncomfortable would be understating things but the Nurse Practitioner helped as much as she could to reduce the embarrassment a bit.

A few weeks later, I received a copy of the letter that been sent to my GP. I knew it was coming and would include all the details I had disclosed in that appointment but to know it intellectually and to see it laid out in stark black and white was really quite unsettling. It was one thing to talk to someone at the GIC about masturbation and sex but to have that sent out to my GP just felt invasive. It's not that I don't trust my doctor, but I also feel that this is not something they actually need to know. Being aware that I used to get turned on by wearing lingerie and that I never considered myself very good at heterosexual sex has absolutely no bearing on my life now. A few things in the letter stood out including being described as 'well kempt'. I don't think I have ever been described as having any level of 'kemptness' before. I know it means, at least in part, that I appeared to be able to look after myself to the extent that I can keep myself and my clothes clean, but I also wonder whether or not it would have been different if I had turned up in jeans and a t-shirt without any makeup. The GICs are better now than they used to be but there are still a load of assumptions around how trans people should appear - trans women are expected to be feminine and trans men masculine. Non-binary people still cause a certain amount of confusion and difficulty when it comes to getting help and I am aware of trans masculine non-binary people who were assigned female at birth being advised to just say that they are trans men in order to ease their treatment path.

Reading the letter again for writing about it, I noticed an interesting typo. In the section about my sexuality, it refers to the fact that I 'fanaticised about being feminine'. Which, you know, okay, it's true up to a point but damn, that's harsh... The letter also said that in her opinion, I meet the 'criteria of Transsexualism' (ICD 10, F.64.0). This is a reference to the *International Classification of Diseases v.10*. Up until 2019, 'Transsexualism' was categorised as a mental disorder, described as "A desire to live and be accepted as a member of the opposite sex, usually accompanied by a sense of discomfort with, or inappropriateness of, one's anatomic sex, and a wish to have surgery and hormonal treatment to make one's body as congruent as possible with one's preferred sex." (ICD-10 Version:2019). The previous sub-section included pyromania and kleptomania and the subsequent one, fetishism, voyeurism and paedophilia. Not only did it contribute to the medicalisation of being transgender, it also gave transphobic bigots a boost to their argument that 'all trans people are insane perverts'. In May 2019, the World Health Organisation updated the ICD, removing the terms 'Transsexualism' and 'gender identity disorder of children' and replaced them with 'gender incongruence of adolescence and adulthood' and 'gender incongruence of childhood'. At the same time, they were moved out of the 'Mental and behavioural disorders' chapter into a newly- created 'Conditions related to sexual health' one. Which is great but was obviously four years too late for me. I have been diagnosed as being mentally ill because of my gender and that won't change. Which is fun.

The referendum on whether or not to remain in the EU happened a couple of weeks after that. Even before the vote I was concerned that there would be consequences for LGBT+ people being able to live freely and openly if the Leave Campaign won. Admittedly, the Remain Campaign were really pretty rubbish in actually explaining why we should remain while the Leave Campaign had two very strong messages: "£350m for the NHS" and "Ugh. Brown people" but I was still utterly shocked by how dense some of the people who were voting Leave could be. One woman I worked with said that she was voting Leave to honour what her grandparents did in the war because they didn't fight for 'this'. Which kind of made my head explode with the sheer failure to understand why the EU had been created. It was at that point that I got really scared about the result.

On the morning of the 24th June, soon after the results had been announced and Nigel Farage had said that he thought it had been a mistake for the Leave Campaign to say that the country could save £350m a week from leaving the country which would go to the NHS, I wrote the following:

I feel scared.

I am scared I'm never going to be able to find a job now because businesses are going to pull back while the economy is fucked.

Tea, Comics and Gender

I am scared this is going to make transitioning that much harder as the NHS gets screwed over even more by the government.

I am scared that my son's future is in jeopardy.

I am scared that when I go out into my local community I'm going to be going out into a place where more than half of the people are either racist or idiots who got suckered into believing a lie which is already being revealed for the lie it is.

Fuck, I'm scared what this is going to do to the prices of the comic books I buy.

This is not the country I want to live in.

Ultimately, I personally have done reasonably well. Neither my employment nor my transition have been impeded too much by the ongoing attempts to 'Get Brexit Done' but at the same time it has become harder for trans people to live in this country. Waiting times have shot up and are currently somewhere in the region of three-four years for the first appointment and then another year or eighteen months for the second. I managed to get into the system before it got too bad, but I don't consider that a cause for celebration. It was hard enough waiting for the 14 months it took to get my first appointment and I had regular appointments after that but the NHS has been constantly and chronically underfunded for years and as part of this - combined with the constant attacks from 'Gender Critical' people - the Gender Identity Clinics have failed to receive the funds they need to keep going on an even keel, even ignoring the rise in the number of trans people seeking treatment in the last few years. I am not the first to make this observation, but the success of the Leave Campaign allowed all of the unpleasant, right wing, bigoted tendencies of this country which is still smarting from no longer having an empire to rise to the surface. In the four years since the referendum my fear has grown to the extent that I am contemplating the possibility of having to leave the country, although I don't know where I would go or how I would get there if I did decide that I had to get out of here. At the same time, my anger has only increased.

Time and again since the referendum, the British (or more rightly, the English) public have shown that they only care about themselves and that they will believe anything. There has been a constant stream of lies and propaganda by the right blaming everyone and everything else for any problems that have occurred. Lies that would be revealed as such if people had the nous to do even the barest amount of research. Instead, though, they swallow anything the Murdoch papers and the Daily Mail shove down their throats. As long as it doesn't affect them personally then they don't care.

One of the services the GIC offer is voice training. While I didn't hate my voice as much as other people do, it still bothered me and there were times it sounded far too masculine for my own comfort. Just before my first session, I saw a document which was apparently handed out by NHS SALT (Speech and Language Therapists). It was awful - for a start a large part of it was written in comic sans. I'm not going to get into my hatred of comic sans right now. Suffice it to say I loathe it and think it should never be used - especially not in a formal document. Then it talked about the differences between the way that men and women speak. It was not good. The best examples are that "It is said that men speak in a more aggressive blunt authoritarian manner [the lack of commas was in the original document], but women speak with a clearer enunciation, correct grammar and politeness and tend to talk about trivial topics", "Men demonstrate a greater sense of humour in speech" and "Men have a predominance to discuss subjects such as sport, politics and business. Women are more concerned with people, relationships and clothes."

Not only did this really annoy me with its appalling generalisations and sexism but it also really worried me when it came to what they were going to try and teach me in the sessions. I'm not exactly subtle or a shy, retiring wallflower. I make jokes - many of them utterly inappropriate. I swear - often when I shouldn't. I talk about politics, people and clothes. And comics and books and TV and, of course, tea. I suspect if anyone had tried to suggest that I stop making the jokes or expressing myself when it came to matters other than who is dating who and how nice Megan Markle looked on telly last night, I'd have told them exactly where to go. Pretty much all my closest cis women friends are at least as bad at me at being inappropriate, swearing and talking politics. And I can pretty much guarantee that not a single one has any interest in transitioning.

However, when it came to the actual sessions, I found that the document was somewhat outdated. It seems likely that it had been used by one of the Speech Therapists who had recently retired but I don't know for sure. My practitioner - Naz - was supportive and understanding. She had no interest in changing what I said, rather she was interested in helping me find a voice that sounded more like I wanted it to sound. In my first appointment, I did some speaking tests to ascertain my vocal range and found that it was in mid-high masculine range and would be reasonably easy to train to sound more gender neutral or feminine.

Over the next several months, Naz gave me more tests and exercises to do and in between appointments I practised at home. My voice definitely improved over the months I was seeing her, to the point where I did actually sound really quite feminine. It's still a lot better than it used to be but I know that it would be even better if I kept practising the exercises, but I am, unfortunately, essentially lazy and I don't remember the last time I practised.

I did recently download a voice analyser app and it says that my voice has pretty much reverted to what it was before I started seeing Naz, if a little more into the neutral/feminine range. People with whom I've discussed it (including some of the Speech and Language Therapists who work in the same office) are all of the opinion that my voice still sounds feminine and, while part of me is paranoid and telling me that they're just saying what I want to hear, the rest of me is willing to accept their professional opinion at face value. Which is, let's face it, far and away the most sensible option.

The same day I had my first Speech Therapy appointment, I also had the first of two job interviews in quick succession. This one was for a position in an NHS Trust, and I was really hoping to get it. The second was the following week at Tyne Met College. This is the direct competition to the college where I was working when I had attempted my first transition (although opinions vary about whether or not they are any competition at all. Those who work or study at Newcastle are adamant that they are the better college, Tyne Met firmly believe the opposite. The truth is that Gateshead College, just over the river, probably beats them both). In both interviews I was entirely open and honest about being trans and told them that there was a strong possibility that at some point in the, hopefully not too distant future, I would be undergoing bottom surgery.

As it turned out, I didn't get the NHS job although I was their 'second choice' and they were actively trying to get another post approved. If it was then I would be offered that one. So, I had to wait and worry and angst about that and about the second interview. I think I interview pretty well - I am (usually) reasonably knowledgeable and the jobs I had been going for up until that point have all been very much ones of which I was capable of doing but I never seemed to get them and had spent several years bouncing from temp job to temp job, being told over and over again that 'it's easier to get a new job if you already have a job' which, to be honest, is a logic I've never quite understood. But now, I was starting to get desperate. One of the things that transitioning did was to finally give me a sense of ambition. I had always been 'okay' with just rolling along the bottom of the employment ocean doing dead- end, no hope jobs and not bothering about trying to find a better position. But now, I was looking at these jobs a gateways to bigger and better things. So, while failing to get jobs in the past had been annoying, now it was starting to get frustrating as well. I wanted to start earning a decent salary and stop having to rely on C so much - at least in part because I was worried that I may not be able to rely on her for much longer.

The day after the Tyne Met interview, I was offered the second NHS job. I had a brief period of happiness, tempered with the knowledge that I was second choice and the fact that I could potentially have to make a choice between the two jobs. I was, as so often happens, totally over-thinking the entire situation and getting myself in a tizzy before I had anything to actually tizz about. In the end, Tyne Met turned me down anyway.

I had had other jobs as Ellen (as I have previously said) but this was going to be my first permanent position. And that thought really terrified me. The knowledge that if I encountered transphobia in a temp job, it would be relatively easy to leave and pick something else up had been a buffer for my nerves. But this was permanent. I had no plans to go stealth - partly because I was pretty much certain that there was no way I would actually pass as cis but also because I refuse to hide who I am. It went without saying that I would join a union as soon as I started which would help if there were problems but the possibility of low level micro-aggressions which are hard to prove and even harder to stop was very much in my thoughts. Once again, I was over-thinking, I hadn't even started and I was angsting.

However, the possibility of micro-aggressions and other more overt transphobia was not something that was entirely improbable.

Transphobic attitudes were still very much the flavour of the month. For example, at the same time as I got my job, the comic book *2000AD* was running a *Judge Dredd* storyline featuring the return of PJ Maybe, a mass murderer who always managed to escape Dredd's grasp before. This time, he was back but in a shock twist, he had been through a magical sci-fi body changer and was presenting as a woman. The entire story was utterly awful and prompted me to write my first letter of complaint to a comic book - I'd written a few positive letters in the past, but this was my first entirely negative letter. During the entire story, Maybe is shown living as a woman - even her droid servant referred to her as 'madam', but Dredd's (and I'd argue that of the writer, Pat Mills, who had co-created Dredd in 1977) position exposed the usual prurience for a trans person's genitals. Dredd described his old nemesis as being 'disguised as a woman' but how 'he' won't have had 'the operation' and so 'a quick scan will identify if you've got your man'. On the very next page, a trans woman was arrested with the line 'this lady ain't all lady'. Essentially, Mills had decided to recycle the 'trans psycho' trope which was old when *Silence of The Lambs* did it. This wasn't the first time there has been a trans character in *2000AD* - nor even the first time there had been one in *Judge Dredd* but those story-lines (though deeply flawed in their own way) treated the trans characters better than they were being treated here: Nobody in *Halo Jones* (by Alan Moore) was sad and pathetic; Metamaid in *Zenith* (by Grant Morrison) was a joke; and Bennett Beeny in 'America' (by John Wagner, another of Dredd's creators) was torturing themself by shoving his brain into her body (er... spoiler). But none of these stories denied they were who they said they were. Everything about 'Lady Killer' (I mean, seriously, even the title is clichéd) is saying that trans women are 'really' men and they are deceiving 'normal' people. I didn't cancel my subscription to the comic at this point, but it was very much the beginning of the end.

While I was waiting to start my job, things kept on moving with my transition. I had a blood test to check my hormone levels with the results showing that my testosterone levels were a little low for a cis male although nowhere near as low I would have liked them to be. My brother got married in a beautiful ceremony with all of the decorations hand made by him and Jane (his wife-to-be).

Sean looked great in his kilt and M, who was usher, looked wonderful in his outfit. It was also the first time that many of my relatives had met me as Ellen. Once again, I was very worried, but it turned out (once again) that I was worrying over nothing. My Scottish uncle, aunt and cousins were so warm, loving and accepting. They were just really pleased to see me, and it was as if nothing had really changed which, apart from the outfit I was wearing (a gorgeous flowered dress with a lace overlay) and the name, it hadn't. I was hoping that this lack of change would in itself change in the very near future. (The one bad note for the day was that I received the second email from my Own Personal Transphobe where she recounted her own life of abuse and insults from cis men as a reason for her transphobia. I obviously didn't read it immediately because I was busy and refused to allow her into the rejoicing but seeing it ping up on my phone certainly put a shadow over the day).

My second appointment with the GIC - actually with a doctor this time rather than the nurse practitioner - happened the following Monday. I went hoping to be approved for hormones but discovered that there was one more obstacle to overcome. My case needed to be discussed with the other doctors in the clinic who had to agree to allow me to take hormones. She said that she it was just formality and booked me in for another appointment a fortnight later for 'The Hormone Talk' but, even so, it was so frustrating. I had been a good girl, not gone the self-medding route and done everything I was supposed to do and still they made me wait while yet more cis people that I had never met would discuss me and decide on my life.

When I finally had 'The Hormone Talk' it was pretty much as expected. The changes that would occur were explained - breast development, fat redistribution, reduced erectile functioning, genital atrophy and infertility - none of which were news to me and it was all positive as far as I was concerned - especially the breast development and the 'failure to launch' of my bits. And, since I had already had a vasectomy, the infertility wasn't a concern either. I was starting with a very low dose of oestrogen and wouldn't have the testosterone blocker until after the next appointment to help deal with any potential side effects from either one which was disappointing. I was still having to wait but, I suppose I understood her concerns. However, just because the GIC had said I should get them didn't mean that I skipped out of there with a box of HRT patches in my hot little hand. The GIC has no prescribing budget so it has to go through the GP which involved sending snail mail (because apparently there's no such thing as email or even faxes) to them. One of the major issues with the GIC was (and probably still is) their pretty awful admin. Letters take forever to be sent out, phone calls are often not returned, emails take a long time to be acknowledged. And so, I had to deal with yet another delay. If this memoir hadn't already been called *Tea, Comics and Gender* it could just have easily been called *Delay*.

While I was dealing with one delay, another finally came to the end. At the end of September 2016, I finally started working for the NHS, after being offered the job at the end of July. I was incredibly nervous for all the usual reasons and had been awake since 3.30am - neither the first nor the last time that would happen. Of course, everything went very well. I met the man who had been offered the first iteration of the job who started on the same day and we got on well, although of course I had to tell him off for taking 'my job', All in all, nearly everyone I was working with seemed to be really nice. And yes, I do mean 'nearly'. There was one person - and there's always one - who rubbed me up the wrong way pretty much from day one. They were self-righteous and snotty when, really, they didn't have the ability or the status to be either, as evidenced by the fact that they had been there for years and had never progressed past a Band 3 position. I was starting at a Band 2 so technically they were higher up the ladder than me but not by much and, frankly, they were only my superior in salary. (Does that sound self-righteous and snobby in itself? I can't help it. The other day I was talking about them to a different colleague, and he could tell that they had really managed to get under my skin because he said he could see my blood pressure rising as I was talking about them. And I hadn't seen them for nearly a year. People don't usually get under my skin like that but somehow they have managed to be like the splinters in the little boy's heart in the *Snow Queen*. They really bring out a side of me that I do not like very much.)

It was finally time to start properly trying to get fit. At least, in part, because I wanted to lose weight in order to be ready for my surgery whenever it was going to happen. So, while I didn't cycle that first day, I did for the second and subsequent ones. Having a bike which was really quite old and heavy made the nine and a half mile ride harder than it really needed to be so I immediately applied for a loan for a new one through the Cyclescheme which would let me repay it via a salary sacrifice scheme. The attractive thing about it is that the money comes off before tax is calculated so you end up paying quite a bit less than the actual purchase price for it.

Tea, Comics and Gender

That second day was also the day that I received the last email from my Own Personal Transphobe (after I had asked her to delete all my contact details and never get in touch with me again). I was very tempted to write back saying 'Dear {OTP}, Fuck right off, love Ellen' but instead chose to be the bigger woman and just blocked her email and phone number to ensure that she would be forced to abide by my wishes.

Starting my new job meant that I had an excellent excuse to meet up with my 'sister', Amy, in town for tea and cakes on the way home from work. She lives south and works north of the river while I am the other way around. And really, who can argue with the idea of tea and cakes with a person you adore?

After about a week of working for the Trust, I had my Corporate Induction - normally people started at the beginning of the month with their induction and then went on to their proper job after that but, ironically after all the delays, they wanted me to start as quickly as possible. Corporate Inductions are, on the whole, not exciting affairs and this one was no different: A series of PowerPoint presentations about different aspects of the Trust and its policies. One of the presentations was from an HR representative talking about equality and diversity. There was a - very - brief mention of trans people, in the form of mentioning 'gender reassignment' as being one of the protected characteristics in the Equality Act 2010. She elucidated by explaining that there were two genders - male and female. I remember clearly emitting a really quite audible hiss of annoyance. Immediately afterwards, I wrote an email to the head of HR gently pointing out the error which, I think, shows how I intended to behave in my new job. While legally there are only two genders in the UK (because apparently legal recognition of non-binary people is 'too complicated'), I suggested that being part of the NHS should mean that we are endeavouring to go beyond the legal minimum requirements and to make our work environment as inclusive, welcoming and accessible as we possibly can. And we could start by giving better information at the induction.

It was lucky that I had decided to get a new bike because after a couple of weeks I managed to kill my old one. Somehow, the rear tire got completely buggered and the inner tube was literally shredded.

On top of that, I had to walk the last couple of miles to work, pushing the bloody thing and repeatedly catching my legs on the pedals. By the time I got there my calf was scratched to bits. It wasn't a pretty sight at all - thank god for opaque tights is all I can say!

Around this time the enormity of everything I was doing - and the fact that after all the delays it all seemed to be happening at once - really got to me. I had a massive anxiety attack but at the same time didn't feel like I could really discuss it with anyone in my immediate circle. I'm not sure why but it just didn't seem right. I couldn't even discuss it with C. I wrote the following in a private Facebook group on the ninth of October 2016:

I've not said anything like this before but I'm really scared. I'm scared that I'm going to hate my new job as much as I ended up hating my other jobs. I'm scared that my hormone treatment is going to be the thing that finally causes C and I to separate. I'm scared that hormones are the wrong thing.

Tea, Comics and Gender

One of the results of the blood tests I had to get a baseline for taking hormones was the discovery that I have chronic kidney disease stage 3 and I'm scared that it is going to mean I can't take hormones. I'm scared that if I choose to have bottom surgery it's going to be a terrible mistake. But at the same time, I'm scared to keep what I have. I'm scared that no one will ever love me and desire me as a woman. I'm scared.

There's not a lot I can say about it. I had a huge amount of things going on - so much so that the kidney disease almost entirely passed by unnoticed and was forgotten about for a few years. Despite my fears, I knew that I had to forge on. I had to find out what was going to happen because reversing course and de-transitioning was never an option, nor was quitting my job. The whole thing was too intricately intertwined. If C and I did separate then I needed a permanent position and some route to getting a better job with more money which wasn't going to happen if I went back to temping. I also knew that even if it turned out that I was actually unable to take hormones it wasn't going to stop me from moving on and living as a woman as authentically as I could. I just had to tough out the panic attack and keep going. It was truly 'big girl panties' time. Especially as three days after writing the above I got my copy of the letter from the GIC to the GP with the official request for me to be prescribed oestrogen. I wrote on Facebook that 'I think I just have to rub the letter on my skin now and I'll have c-cup breasts by next Friday' but, annoyingly it doesn't seem to work like that.

It took a week - another delay but only a relatively short one - before the prescription for hormones was finally filled. There are a few different types of patch that are available and initially I was prescribed 'Evorel'. To begin with, I only had to use one, changing it twice a week but when my dosage increased and I started to use more patches they really started to take up real estate on my hips. One of the real problems with patches is that the edges have a tendency to pick up muck so, even though I only have them on for three or four days each, by the time it comes to replace them, my skin has a black, sticky outline that it is really difficult to get off. It took me several months before I discovered the secret to cleaning it off by putting baby oil on a cotton wool pad and then rubbing hard. My only problem then would be remembering to change them. Even now, four and half years later, I often end up in the shower on a Wednesday or a Saturday morning, starting to wash myself down and feel the old patches still on my hip. By then it's too late to do anything with the oil as the wet skin means that the oily pad just slides over the marks and doesn't actually do anything. It's really very annoying.

But I digress. Again. That Wednesday, at about 6.30 in the morning, when I opened that first box with the express intention of sticking a patch full of girl cooties on my skin was a real mix of emotions. Mostly elation that I was finally able to do this, that I had reached this point. My social transition had been incredibly successful and now I was finally able to start my medical transition. But I was also really scared. Intellectually, I knew what this meant and what it would do. Emotionally, I had no idea. I knew that as well as the physical changes there would be emotional ones as well. I was deliberately putting myself through a second puberty. To say that I felt 'somewhat shaky' (which is how I described it on Facebook) was a massive understatement. I was close to tears and shaking almost uncontrollably.

Tea, Comics and Gender

Changing my name, getting rid of all my male clothes, all of the stuff I had done previously could be undone. What I was doing now, that led down a path that would make irreversible changes to my body. If I was to follow it to its logical conclusion - and by this point I was pretty certain that I would be doing so - I would be allowing a surgeon to practice their craft on what was essentially a perfectly healthy body. Part of me could see - and still can - why some people might think that what I was doing was a sign of mental instability. To do this, to do any of this - especially in a society where it's okay for people to judge you so harshly for doing it - is in and of itself, madness. Or at least, it is from a cisgender point of view. Why couldn't I just learn to live with being male? Doesn't it say something that my hatred for my genitals grew massively *after* I started to transition? The only answer is that there is no way a cisgender person can understand. It wasn't a sexual thing. The idea of having breasts and a vulva didn't turn me on. Instead, it brought me peace. Imagining that my external features matched my internal self-image made me happy and quietened the anxiety and depression. I started to hate my genitals more because transitioning meant demolishing the walls I had built up in order to function. Being that person had been a lie and the person being lied to the most was myself. And if I believed it, how could other people not fail to do so as well? The necessity of getting rid of the testosterone that had been poisoning me and turning my body into a form that it wasn't intended to take was absolutely, completely vital. And, if it turns out that someone proves that being transgender is a form of mental illness then I will embrace it. Mental illness is nothing to be ashamed of and it turns out that there is actually a reasonably simple method of treating this particular form:

hormones, surgery and acceptance from your peers (or hormone blockers and acceptance for trans kids). Which, surprisingly enough, is what is needed now when we know that trans people aren't insane. Or at least, some may have mental health problems but being trans isn't one of them.

Although I knew that there was no way I would feel anything from them in such a short time, I realised after only a few days that I was feeling far happier than I had been in a very long time. Undoubtedly, it was just a placebo effect, but I certainly wasn't going to dispute it. I had experienced something similar the first time I went on anti-depressants. Within days of starting them, I felt the depression lift a little not due to any physical changes the drug had made but it was because I was actually doing something about the problem. And this was exactly the same, something that I had wanted and needed for literally years (I had, for example, long wished I had breasts, even before I had admitted to myself who I was) was finally happening. Just putting on that patch (or taking that little happy pill) was enough to allow me to start letting go of the stress and anxiety. Although, I rapidly discovered the downside of the girl cooties - walking through town at about half past nine in the morning, I was accosted by a man who certainly seemed very drunk who started to shout me, calling me a bloke in a dress and telling me that I was a man. This would of course always upset me - I was terrified that he would decide to something more than verbally abuse me - but it took hours to stop feeling upset, shaky and very close to tears. Again, whether this was the start of the hormones affecting my mood or not, I don't know, although I suspect it probably wasn't. Rather, it was more likely the balloon of confidence that had been inflated by the patches being rudely and viciously punctured. Essentially, some people are complete cunts.

Although social media is, mostly, a horrible and toxic place to reside, it is also a place where you can find support and friendship if you look in the right places. I joined several Facebook trans support groups where I got lots of support and advice that I wouldn't have been able to find anywhere else without a lot of searching. I also joined the 'Unofficial AFP Patreon Patrons' group, where fans of Amanda Fucking Palmer congregate. AFP is a 'punk cabaret' singer/songwriter and one half of the Dresden Dolls. I discovered her through Neil Gaiman to whom she is married and quite quickly became more than a little obsessed. Her fans are, on the whole, a wonderful, kind and caring bunch of people and, despite never having met most of them in real life, consider a great many of them to be true friends upon who I know I can rely. I have a plan (plan is perhaps too strong a word to use here. I have a desire) to tour the United States and Canada, couch-surfing my way around from Sloth to Sloth (AFP Fans refer to themselves as 'Sloths' because of something that Amanda once said which was before I discovered her and can no longer remember). While T***P was in power it was on hold but now that he has been ousted and replaced by Biden who actually seems to be pro-LGBT rights it may happen sooner. It basically depends on money.

I had already been to one small AFP event in London but that October, I was actually going to my first 'proper' gig in Edinburgh. This was also going to be the first time that I would properly meet Dylan, another sloth and a non-binary person who very quickly became part of my chosen trans family. We came to refer to each other as 'trans mama'

Ellen Mellor

(that's me) and 'trans child' (Dyl). Dylan themself has an 'adopted' daughter, Annie - a beautiful, fun and ever-so-sweet cis woman - who refers to me as 'Granny Ellen' which I really rather adore. The gig itself was wonderful - Amanda is a charismatic and exciting performer and she has an amazing rapport with her audience. I have never actually been a part of something that defines itself so completely by its fandom. I've not even found it in the hard-core of comics geeks. There are times when being a Sloth seemed to take on aspects of a cult. It wasn't necessarily a bad thing, especially as much of the philosophy that came from Amanda was based around the idea of asking and giving and acceptance of others. There were occasions when it isn't perfect - a furore around people taking advantage of asking for help or (as seems to be more often the case) people perceiving others of taking advantage seems to crop up from time to time and, because it seems to some that the object of their ire has fallen short of the 'ideals of Slothdom' it can turn very ugly, very quickly. Fortunately, the Facebook group has some excellent moderators (and, let me reiterate, the vast majority of Sloths are lovely, caring and giving people who would give up their last penny if they thought it would help someone in need), so these flare ups are only ever intermittent and quickly dealt with. Perhaps to be expected in this sort of situation, the other major bone of contention is Amanda herself. There are times when she herself fails to reach the heights that some expect of her, saying or doing something that is really less than ideal (although it has to be said, her misdemeanours are relatively minor in comparison to those committed by some male rock stars who somehow seem to carry on regardless). When she reveals herself to be human, some Sloths have been known to totally lose it and recant entirely, refusing to ever speak of her again. I am not saying that this is necessarily a bad thing. There are things she has done recently that have made me uncomfortable enough and tarnished my love for all things Amanda. I'm certainly not in any hurry to go to another AFP gig but I haven't forsworn her entirely.

That all being said, the 'Unofficial' Facebook group (there is an Official page as well but, for some reason I could never quite put my finger on, it never seemed as welcoming) is still full of some of the loveliest people I have ever met who I truly adore, even if I have never met them in real life (yet). It is also one of the queerest groups of people I have ever come across with individuals from all across all the different sexual and gender spectra there - I have met people who describe themselves as pansexual, polyamorous, ace, domme and sub as well as the 'standard' flavours of LGBTQI. There are a lot of straight, cis people there as well, obviously, but (nearly) every single one of them has proven to be the most amazing ally. I started a small offshoot of the Unofficial group called the 'Trans Sloths' which is a wonderful, tight knit community of trans lovelies (with a few special cis allies in there as well) and felt able to share things with them that I have never shared with anyone else (although most of it is coming out in these pages - sorry my Trans Sloth loves, you aren't as special anymore!) and received unequivocal support from them all, as well as being able to offer care and support myself.

While all this was going on, other things weren't going quite as well. Within about six weeks of starting my new job I had reached a position of absolute 'can't be arsed'ness. It was tedious, thankless and never-ending. I had quite quickly come to the realisation that my line manager was not the best manager in the world. He was excellent at the technical aspects of the job and knew pretty much all the intricacies of making the system jump up and do as it was told. But really, he should have been stuck in a cupboard somewhere and left to do that. Allowing him to be in charge of human beings was a definite mistake as he had no social skills whatsoever. One of the methods used by HR in order to categorise staff was called 'Insights' - after answering a long questionnaire about your thoughts, feelings and what you would do in a certain circumstances, you were categorised as having a certain personality type and given a percentage result of four different areas which were categorised as colours - simply put, someone who is very 'Blue' is a problem solver, someone who is 'Green' is a carer. My line manager was very, very 'Blue' and 'Red' (self-discipline and a go-getter) with very little in the way of 'Green' or 'Yellow' (creative and perceptive). (I'm Yellow and Green with low Blue and Red, apparently). However, rather than this being used as a method of helping someone work with and improve their weaknesses, it was often used as a justification for their behaviour. There were many, many times that my line manager was excused something he had done because "it's just him, he's so very Blue". Of course, being the absolute sceptic I am, I pretty much don't believe a word of any of this. The whole thing seemed to me to be just a form of cold reading, coming up with answers and justifications that were sufficiently vague enough to allow people to read whatever they want into it. The positives were always far more positive than the negatives were negative so people could feel good while fooling themselves into thinking that there were just a couple of tiny places that needed improving before they could achieve perfection and nirvana.

Tea, Comics and Gender

Despite the bloom fading from the rose in my new job, I didn't look for anything new. I wanted to make a go of it. I wanted to succeed and move upwards and onwards. This was only ever a stepping stone to better things. I took on extra responsibilities, including completely revamping the administration of the induction process. Up until I took over it had involved printing out a massive spreadsheet of everyone who was attending, what they had to do and when. It took up a dozen or more pages which were then taped together, hand-adjusted and then those adjustments entered back on to the electronic version. Just printing out everything that was 'needed' for the session took up an entire day. It wasn't the fault of the people who were doing the induction before me. Rather it was a failure of the system which had been allowed to grow out of control, combined with a lack of knowledge and training about how to actually use a spreadsheet. It was ripe for a revamp, and I took it apart entirely and re-built it from the ground up. This sounds like I did all by myself. I did a lot of it, but I was helped by a colleague who was an apprentice at the time meaning that the entire edifice of the Trust's induction process and policy was based on the work of two of the lowest paid people in the entire place. I did it because by doing so it meant that I was making myself indispensable and diverting me from the tedium of my actual job. I also started to push for more trans inclusion. One of my own personal goals was to show that the Trust was inclusive and welcoming and a safe place for trans people to be themselves. The office in which I worked was actually an old converted ward, meaning that the toilets for the office were three individual rooms - male, female and disabled. I tried my hardest to persuade the department heads that they should be converted to gender neutral toilets - not for myself as I was quite happy using the women's toilet - but because it was the right thing to do. There was no way of knowing if a non-binary person was working there unless they chose to out themselves and by doing this tiny thing it would help show that our enby colleagues were accepted. I tried for three years and failed to get anywhere with it. While the department heads were outwardly supportive of the concept, they would never do anything that would ever advance it beyond discussing it. At one point I was told that they needed to talk to the rest of the staff in the office in case any of them felt uncomfortable with the idea of gender neutral toilets. Once again, cis privilege reared its extremely ugly head. There was no suggestion that non-binary people, or even non- passing binary trans people (of which I was one at the time and, to a certain extent still am. Not least because I don't make any real attempt to pass and go on about it all the time - after all, I'm writing a whole bloody book about being trans) might feel uncomfortable

going into a gendered space. But, no, cis people might feel uncomfortable going into a toilet that had previously been occupied by someone with a different set of genitalia. Which, of course, ignored entirely the fact that disabled people were already using a gender neutral toilet at work and everyone did so at home. It was frustrating to say the least.

It wasn't all doom, gloom and cis privilege though. There was also really fun comics. Ryan North, creator of the webcomic *Dinosaur Comics* (which, if you haven't read is something you should really get on to) was the writer on *The Unbeatable Squirrel Girl* (along with Erica Henderson on art duties) for Marvel. During its run it was one of the most positive, upbeat and happy comics being published and I utterly loved it. So, when Ryan came to Travelling Man in Newcastle to sign copies of the graphic novel *Squirrel Girl Beats up the Marvel Universe* I was of course in the queue. My copy of the book, as well as being signed, has a little sketch of Doreen (Squirrel Girl's real name) saying 'To Ellen! The Coolest'. Being called 'the Coolest' by the coolest character in the entire Marvel Universe gives me a small, happy glow inside whenever I think about it. And Ryan is a really nice guy as well, as you would hope the writer of those comics would be.

I had said that I was going to put off making an actual decision about whether or not I was going to have GRS (Genital Reconfiguration Surgery AKA Gender Reassignment Surgery AKA SRS - Sex Reassignment Surgery AKA The Op (Capital 'T', Capital 'O')) but one night, late in 2016 I was provided with absolute proof - if it were required - that I definitely needed, never mind wanted, exactly that when I dreamt about having a vagina. I don't often have sexual dreams or even dreams where my gender has any bearing on the story but in this one, I was masturbating and my finger went inside. It felt right and good and really, really erotic. Unfortunately, upon waking and discovering that it had just been a dream kicked off a massive surge of gender dysphoria, especially as my physical body reacted in the way that bodies with penises do when something erotic happens. I have no doubt that if I talked about this widely by, for instance, writing it in a book, it would be taken by the Gender Critters as proof that I was an 'autogynephilic transsexual' - a man who was sexually aroused at the idea of having a female body. I'm not going to get into all the ins and outs (as it were) of how and why the 'AGP' theory is so utterly rubbish. Many have done it before far better than I could do in a short aside. (If you are interested, I'd recommend searching out Julia Serano's writing on the subject in her various books or on her website www.juliaserano.com). Suffice it to say that the tests for AGP in trans women that proves that they are basically fetishists who get turned on by having a fanny give broadly the same results when applied to cis women. The thought of being sexually active in a body that correctly fits your self-image is a sexy one. And, having been on the hormones for about six weeks at that point, I would suggest that they may have been kicking in and starting my second puberty. Not that puberty is a major cause of sexual thought and feelings or anything.

Although I don't have many sex dreams, I do have vivid dreams with a strong narrative, even if that narrative has a certain amount of dream logic. They do, however, sometimes provide fodder for my writing. *Ghostkin* was the result of a dream as is one of the projects that is on the cards for when I have completed writing this - a sit com (or maybe a drama because the idea of writing a comedy scares the crap out of me) about a trans woman who buys a down-on-its luck football club (and, if you're going to freak out about me dreaming about something weird then I'd highly recommend getting concerned about me dreaming about football... Seriously. That was the bit that made me go 'WTF?!?' after I woke up). My dreams are often so vivid that images sit in my brain for days afterwards - one from the trans woman football dream that has stayed with me was her having to escape down a fire escape except the escape was a really long slide of the sort you find in a playground. I have this image of a woman in a smart skirt suit and heels sliding down this interminable slide from the top floor of a building and getting stuck half-way (as always happened with slides like this) and having to shuffle her bum forwards until she could get going again. As I said, dream logic - it's not going to get used when I write it up, or at least not in that way, but it is just sitting there in my brain taking up space that could, theoretically, go to something more useful. Like remembering which issue of the Avengers gave us the first appearance of The Vision (#57 in October 1968, by the way. And yes, I had to Google it because I couldn't remember because there was this ridiculous image from a dream stuck in my head).

Anyway, once I had managed to get over the upset from waking up from that lovely dream to discover the unpleasant reality, I quickly came to the conclusion that suggesting that I was equivocating about surgery was just denying reality again and, as I'd spent forty three years doing that, I really needed to stop.

Once I had decided, I started to discuss it with others, choosing to use the term GRS meaning 'Genital Reconfiguration Surgery' to describe what I wanted. For me the process focused more on changing my genitals to their 'correct' layout rather than changing my sex or my gender which have, arguably always been female. It also meant that I could come up with my own meaning for the acronym and, in what is possibly 'the most me thing ever', I decided that it meant 'Genital Regeneration Shenanigans'. I had visions of a massive burst of orange energy exploding from my nether regions and then someone seeing me naked and saying 'hmmm. You've redecorated. I don't like it.' And if you don't get those references then you clearly haven't watched anywhere near enough *Doctor Who*.

Ellen Mellor

After the disastrous General Election of 2015, the subsequent election of Jeremy Corbyn as leader of the Labour Party and the way that the media portrayed and victimised him, I decided that it was time to join the Party which I did in early 2016. The local constituency party was a very white, cis, straight institution and I did my best to try and introduce a bit of diversity to the proceedings although it was not an easy task. While people may not have been openly transphobic, there was a lot of unconscious bias needing to be addressed. At one meeting, we had a request for a female delegate to attend the local area AGM. One member commented that if there were no women who were prepared to put their names forward then a man could just put on a dress and go. While I volunteered, there was a part of me that worried that people did just see me as 'a man just putting on a dress'. Joining the Party made it a lot easier to meet with and talk to my local MP, Mary Glindon. At one point, I asked her to speak at a debate on Transgender Equality. She agreed and subsequently made an 'intervention' in the debate to say "The right hon. Lady (Maria Miller, then chair of the Women and Equalities Committee) mentions health, and the constituents who have contacted me felt that was an area of great inequality. Does she think it is a disgrace and very worrying that 54% of trans people have been told by their GP that they do not know enough about trans-related healthcare to even provide it?" I note this specifically because it was the very last time that Mary was in anyway positive or supportive of trans people and even then she couched her question in neutral terms that didn't denote her own feelings on the subject.

Back at work, one of my regular tasks was to transfer information about new starters from hand-written documents onto the computer. Most new starters were transferred into the system automatically but, more often than I liked, the system failed and their details didn't get entered properly or something was missed and I had to correct it manually. I mention this purely because while doing it, I came to realise exactly how hetero-normative society really is. I mean, yes, I know that it is totally built for the straights but when the vast majority of them seem unable to actually spell the word 'heterosexual' it really drives it home. Straight people rarely have to come out or describe their sexuality except when it comes to this sort of data collection. It's a small thing but seeing the exact same error of missing out the second 'e' over and over again really got to me. This is only one small example, there were many others - for example, the employee data system I worked on did (eventually) have the option of using the non-binary form of address, 'Mx'. However, it still forced you to choose either male or female for the person's gender.

The relationship between C and I became more and more complicated as all of this went on. She was always completely supportive but there were things that we needed to talk about which we didn't, on top of which she kept having to deal with things happening for which she wasn't prepared and hadn't signed up to do.

An example of the former: Leading up to Valentine's Day 2017 I didn't know if we were in a place where we could celebrate it and I was far too scared to ask. As a result, I was basically paralysed and didn't do anything. So, when C came home from work with dinner, a cake and card and I had nothing to give her in return I was devastated because by failing to say anything I had made it worse. She was, of course completely fine about it and I got her something afterwards, but it upset me that I felt that way.

And another example, this time of the latter: Shortly after I started on hormones it seemed like I was having days when I was feeling unhappy and dysphoric on a regular basis - essentially every four weeks. I did a little bit of research into it and turns out that a lot of trans women report having something similar to a menstrual cycle which imitates a lot of the effects of a cis woman's cycle - cramps, mood swings and the like (although without bleeding). I only had cramps a couple of times but the mood swings definitely happened. Of course, there is no actual research into this because nobody really believes us when we say this. When I worked out what seemed to be happening, I told C that I thought I may be having a period and she laughed. It wasn't that she found it funny, it was rather a laugh of surprise but as I was already feeling very low, her laughter really upset me.

This seems like a good opening to talk about the effects of the hormones. For example: boobs! I love my boobs. They aren't huge but they are perfectly formed, and I love how they look and how they feel and how they move. Wearing a bra is a bit of a pain but it's all part of the package. I have curves and a bum now because of the redistribution of fat. At one point, relatively early on, while out shopping, C told me that I had a real 'arse wiggle' going on. It's still not perfect but there isn't any sort of surgery that can give me a 'female' pelvis. (According to one genius on Twitter I'd need to have a spine transplant as well. After all, this particular 'Transvestigator' - a believer in the conspiracy theory that 99% of women in politics and the media are actually transgender - claims that it was easy to see Marilyn Monroe's 'male spine' if you watch *Some Like It Hot*.

Seriously.) My skin is smoother, and my hair is thicker and grows a lot faster - the hair, not my skin. I also rapidly lost muscle mass - there are things that I am absolutely unable to lift now that I would have been able to pick up without any problems before. I first noticed this when trying to pick up a packed suitcase only to discover that I could barely lift it, despite it being only about two thirds full.

It's not all bread and roses though. My libido is pretty much dead at the moment and, when I first started on the 'mones the mood swings could be vicious, even when I wasn't having my 'period'. There were times I behaved like a stereotypical teenage girl - slammed doors and everything - over the most minor of mishaps. I would throw myself onto my bed in a fit of rage and weeping while part of me looked down saying 'what the fuck! Pull yourself together, woman. You're forty seven for fuck's sake' to which the rest of me replied 'fuck off! You're not the boss of me!' It was an absolute joy. Now that I've stabilised, I am still far more emotional than I ever was pre-cooties. I cry far more easily than I ever did and have found myself sitting in the toilets at work in tears more often than I care to mention. Although there are other reasons why this is the case which I'll get to later.

As I mentioned, one of the definite positives of transitioning was that it gave me some much needed confidence in myself In early 2017 I applied for another job in the same department in which I was already working - it was in a different section of the department and three grades higher and I didn't think I had much chance of even getting an interview considering I had only been in post for about six months. But I thought it was worth doing to keep reminding them that I existed and wasn't just an interchangeable peon. As I suspected, I didn't get an interview, but it did result in a long conversation with the head of the department where she said how pleased she had been that I had applied and how, although I didn't have the skills that were needed for that job, the second in command of the team in which I worked was retiring the following year and she wanted me to work on getting leadership experience so I would be able to apply when the role came along. She had discussed me with my line manager who said that he liked me because I challenged him. This discussion

really made me reflect on how far I had come in the previous couple of years and, despite the fact that I wasn't enjoying the job, it was definitely going to lead to better things. I just had to keep working towards them.

Over the last few years, I have involved myself in quite a few different research projects that revolve around transgender identities.

I've always tried to do this sort of thing. When I was in my twenties and thirties, I did several asthma research projects to try to find new, more effective ways of treating it but since transitioning, I've really sort of thrown myself into being a guinea pig. I've been interviewed several times for different projects ranging from a PhD student's thesis on trans lives in the North East of England to a psychologist's work on a new model for gender dysphoria to a study by the Centre for Family Research at Cambridge University on the effect that having a trans parent has on a family. That last one actually involved all three of us. C and I were interviewed together, and M was taken off to have a private interview so he could say anything he wanted without worrying that we would hear. At the time, the main thing I

Tea, Comics and Gender

got out of it was how very proud I was of M and how much I loved C. I cried again when I retold the story of how I came out to M and the perfect response I got in reply. Obviously, I don't know exactly what M said but I have to assume that it was positive. The research that was done actually ended up in a book - *We Are Family* by Susan Golombok. The research didn't just cover trans parents but also gay and lesbian parents, surrogates and more. We have a couple of pages in the trans parents chapter although obviously our names have been changed. However, I would have thought that it's not exactly difficult to spot us. For a start, C and I are described as 'a teacher' and a 'trans woman and a writer'. Also, I was allowed to choose our pseudonyms so of course I went all in on the geek references... Books are a major part of my life. To which the entire assembled audience replies 'no shit!' But, yes they are. And one of the things I do when I find something in which I'm seriously interested is to get as many books about the subject as I can. There have been two real areas where this has been true, and they are two thirds of the title of this book. I have a reasonably decent collection of books about comic books, as well as the 12,000 strong collection of actual comics - histories of companies, biographies of people both real and imagined, academic texts about comics and art books. I even managed to find a nice reprint of Frederic Wertham's *Seduction of the Innocent* which started the paranoia about comics leading to juvenile delinquency in the 1950s - it's hilarious. There's a panel of art from (I think) an issue of *Sheena* which has been cropped to show only someone's shoulder. If you are determined to see it, the shading sort of vaguely looks like a pair of women's legs with either a very skimpy pair of panties or a full bodied hairy 'Map of Tasmania'. The text that goes along with it is "In ordinary comic books, there are pictures within pictures for children who know how to look." The book doesn't actually make explicit reference to an actual child who 'knows how to look' (just as there aren't children who turned queer because Batman and Robin lived in the same house) but just the inference was enough and led to mass burnings of comic books all across America.

But anyway, unsurprisingly, the other third of the title about which I have somewhat obsessively built up a library is not tea. I do have a couple of books about it but there don't seem to be a vast number available. I wish there was. I'd like to read more. I do, however, have a reasonably large collection of books about trans issues and by trans authors. The majority are memoirs (hence the subtitle to this one), ranging from the fascinating (the two written by Janet Mock) to the unreadable (which I won't name because I'm nice like that). But I also have a reasonable number of academic titles. I want to know about it all. Knowing this stuff doesn't make me a better trans (or a better geek, for that matter), I just feel better for having the knowledge. It gives me a sense of connection to the larger community and where it came from. Arguably, it helps me to at least dimly see where we might be going. Although I'd challenge anyone who predicted the extent of the anti-trans movement that currently exists in this country. I also have a lot of prose fiction and comic books written by trans people - the number of trans women involved in producing printed comics - and doing so really quite successfully - is both really quite astounding and extremely gratifying (there are, as far as I am aware, no trans masculine people producing comic books professionally). And that's not to mention the number of really successful webcomics created by trans people. There were some trans books that I had for quite a while before I was actually able to read them. I mean, there are books that I got when I worked in Waterstone's more than twenty years ago that I haven't read yet but that's not what I meant. In particular, there was one book of transgender erotica (which differed massively from what people usually think of when it comes to trans porn because it was written by and for trans people) which I tried to read quite early on in my medical transition. Just reading the introduction scared me - I wasn't ready for what it was offering, not least because I wasn't going to be able to deal with the physical consequences of reading erotica that was actually aimed at me. Just the thought of anything happening 'down there' made me blanch - it still does when I think back to the sexual responses I had pre-surgery. I mean, it's probably pretty obvious that I'm going all around the houses to actually write the word 'erection'. And it's not because I'm shy. Writing that word just then, in connection with my body made me feel a little bit nauseous. I had read a certain amount of 'standard' trans porn in the past because it was pretty much all that was available. Most of it wasn't good - badly written, objectifying, written for a cis het male gaze and by someone who obviously had no idea what it meant to be trans. This promised to be something else. I did eventually read it and it was very different to the usual stuff - as with any anthology some of it was very good, some not so good. Some of it was right up my street and some not so much - and that didn't necessarily correlate with what was well written or not. I'm not deliberately avoiding naming the book, but I've just spent the last half hour scouring through my e-book collection and I can't find the damn thing, nor do I appear to have mentioned it on Goodreads. Perhaps I was too embarrassed to mention it at the time. Obviously, if I turn it up later, I'll edit this bit but, if you're reading these words then you can assume that I either didn't find it or found it but forgot about editing this bit. Hopefully the former because if it's the latter then you have to wonder how well edited the rest of the book was.

(Actually, as soon as I finished writing that bit, I did a Google search for 'transgender erotica written by trans people' and the fourth result was a review of the book in Bitch magazine - it's called *Nerve Endings: The New Trans Erotic* edited by Tobi Hill-Meyer and it's in both my Goodreads list and on my Kindle. I have no idea why it hid from me. But I'm going to go with the third option that I didn't mention. I'm not going to delete the previous bit, I'm just adding this bit on the end. Keep the word count going!)

The next page shows a picture of my vulva immediately after surgery. If this is not something you want to see I'd recommend skipping two pages to where there are some much nicer and far more wholesome pictures.

Tea, Comics and Gender

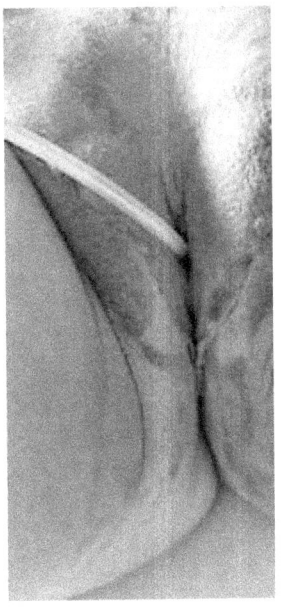

The first picture I took of my new vulva.

Tea, Comics and Gender

Me and my mum from the Mother & Daughter photoshoot

Some sloths!
(Back: Ali and Karen
Front: Me and Dylan)

The Readers of the Lost Art at Rachel and Tim's wedding
(left to right: Alex, Aaron, Louise, Rachel, Tim, Me, Simon and Sofia)

M the Steampunk Pirate for Prom

Being a proper author at the *Ghostkin* book launch.

Christmas 2018.
Dead inside.

My first post-surgery selfie.
I was still pretty stoned.

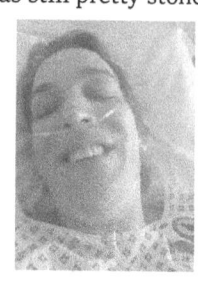

Me and Joanne at Plessey Woods

Me and Amy on top of
Northumberlandia

4
The Waiting Game (Part Infinity)

I have never really explained why I called myself Ellen, always saying that I couldn't remember why I had chosen that name.

Well, that's not entirely true. After settling on the name, I decided to keep the reason behind it secret, mainly because I didn't think that it was anyone else's business.

However, I made a pact with myself that if I ever wrote a memoir, I'd reveal the truth.

So here it is:

For years, I suffered from the worst ear-worm imaginable. The chorus of 'Nelly the Elephant' would just go round and round and round in my head. Just like it's doing with you now. You're welcome, by the way. I finally seemed rid of it for ever at about the same time that I was choosing a new name. Although the song was gone, the name just kept hanging around in my head. 'Nelly' is really not a name that worked though. Initially, I thought about just dropping the 'N' and going with 'Elly' which is a lovely name but didn't fit. Finally, I moved the 'N' the end to make 'Ellyn' which then became Ellen. Although I later realised that the Y spelling is just as valid, and I could have stuck with it.

As I became more confident with who I was I started to put myself out there more. I had already started to a certain extent by speaking at my friends' wedding and not dying, being beaten or struck by lightning for daring to set foot in a church and also by marching alongside C with the NASUWT (The Teacher's Union) at the Durham Miners' Gala. But in 2017 I took another step. May 17th is IDAHOBIT

Ellen Mellor

- the International Day Against Homophobia, Biphobia and Transphobia - and an event to celebrate the day had been organised at Newcastle Civic Centre. Hearing what other people said was extremely moving and I was very proud of being there, standing up both for myself and for trans people in general. I planned what I was going to say beforehand and wrote it out but when it came to actually speaking, I extemporised and riffed on the subject, so the text I am reproducing below doesn't quite match what I said, but it's close enough:

My name is Ellen. I'm a trans woman. I started to 'officially' transition just over two years ago now and, in that time, I have been lucky enough to receive the support of almost all of my friends and family. I started working here at the Trust last September and have been surrounded by colleagues who have been behind me all the way — they are the very soul of kindness and understanding (which I know can be difficult when my hormones are raging!) Wednesday 17th May is the International Day Against Homophobia, Transphobia and Biphobia. And it's a day which is important because these things are very real. I can't really speak about homophobia and biphobia because, although I am lesbian, it is my transgender identity which is most obvious.

In reality, I have actually been really lucky and suffered from very few incidents of transphobic abuse. But they have happened. And it really, really hurts. Whether it is being called a 'freak' while walking down the street; someone that I thought was a friend purposely misgendering and deadnaming me (that is referring to me as 'he' and 'him' and using my old, male name); or having someone accuse me of child abuse because I dare to be openly transgender while also having a son.

This stuff hurts. This stuff kills. I know how lucky I am — I have an awful lot of support, I have a job where I can be my authentic self and I have access to healthcare. But lots and lots of trans people don't have any of these things. Nearly half of young trans people have tried to commit suicide, Hundreds of trans people (especially trans women of colour) are murdered purely for the 'crime' of being themselves. Last year, 317 trans people were murdered which was the highest number ever recorded and it is looking likely that 2017 will meet or even exceed that figure. (In 2015, it was estimated that transgender people in the US have a 1-in-12 chance of being murdered. The average person has a 1-in-18,000 chance.) It is still legal in several states of the USA to use 'trans panic' (the 'terror' that is caused by discovering that the woman that you are planning to sleep with is transgender) as a defence in assault and murder trials. In this country, if decide to apply for a Gender Recognition Certificate — which I currently need to be fully recognised as a woman under law — my wife has the power to veto my application and make me choose between my gender and my marriage. Fortunately, I know she would not do this to me, but it's still something that needs to be taken into account. And let's not get into the problems that non-binary people have. And it's all due to transphobia. It is due to cis people (people who are comfortable with the gender to which they were assigned at birth) refusing to accept trans people as their gender.

So please, if there is one thing I could ask you to do, it is this: remember that trans people - Trans men, trans women and non- binary people - ARE real and their identities are valid.

One of the real problems that I have as a trans woman (have I mentioned that I'm transgender? I've been looking for a way to mention it subtly) is the fear that any media I try to consume is suddenly going to turn around and hit me in the face with transphobia. Obviously, the most obvious example of this is JK Rowling and her decision to come down hard on the side of the Gender Critters. Apart from the influence she wields as a billionaire who lives in a castle and has written the most successful franchise in the world, she doesn't affect me too much as I am really not a Potter fan but she is the most obvious example. However, over the last few years it has become more and more obvious that trans people - and especially trans women - are often used as the butt of a joke. The number of Specials on Netflix which have transphobic 'humour' as part of the act is incredible - I once started to watch a Kathryn Ryan special and five minutes in she came out with something transphobic which, of course, caused the audience to absolutely piss themselves laughing. Then there was a scene in the *Gilmore Girls* reboot where Rory was 'taken away from it all' with Logan and The Life and Death Brigade. They end up in a salsa club where of course the guys all end up dancing with the women. It is at this point that one of the boys says to another 'isn't that a man you are dancing with?' The response: 'Only until next Tuesday.' Ha. Fucking. Ha. This person has got a cock and therefore is a man, but they are having surgery next week after which it will be okay to call them a woman. Fuck. Right. Off. This was the season where they finally admitted that gay people exist in Stars Hollow. But apparently trans people are still jokes. I know it was only two lines passed between two people who are more than a little reprehensible and therefore not indicative of anything. But it was the only reference to trans people in the whole thing and it was a crass, pointless joke that stated that a person's genitalia was the ultimate arbiter of their gender. It rather soured the experience for me. And of course, I was watching it on Transgender Day of Visibility.

Then there's the news media. As well as the usual suspects - the Daily Mail and the Murdoch papers -

transphobia is rampant across much of the rest of the area with both The Guardian and The Morning Star having a particularly transphobic editorial stance. And then there's the BBC. Good old Aunty Beeb. I have a t-shirt which reprints the lyrics of Mitch Benn's song 'I'm Proud of the BBC'. It's not a shirt I can wear anymore because I'm really not. As well as their slow drift to the right, they have also embraced the concept of 'balance' as meaning 'we have to get someone who disagrees with this stance to argue against it' which, more often than not means that a trans person is confronted by Gender Critters who throw ridiculous claims and insults at them. The other alternative is that a member of one of the rabid transphobic cult groups - LGB Alliance, Fair Play for Women or the like - is asked for a quote without bothering to get one from a trans-supportive organisation. In one particularly egregious example, an article in 2020 written by the BBC's LGBT+ correspondent (who is actually pretty supportive) had a transphobic quote added by the editorial team. Not to mention the fact that they removed links to trans support groups from their website and gave JK Rowling an award for her essay about why she is anti-trans.

Other outlets like Channel 4 and The Independent aren't as bad but they still regularly give a platform to transphobic opinions (usually to allow them to complain loudly about how they are being 'silenced'). It's hardly a surprise that I have cancelled my Television Licence and no longer read The Guardian (which means that for the first time ever I will not be able to see *Doctor Who* as it's broadcast). I cannot and will not support any organisation that so actively works against my right to exist. Although, to be fair and balanced to the BBC, it's not just transphobes who get a platform. On the day of Joe Biden's inauguration, I decided to watch a little bit of the BBC's *Six-o-Clock News* as I had been at work all day and they have historically usually been pretty good at these big events. However, they chose to follow the roughly two minutes of actual coverage of the ceremony with an interview with a Texan militia member who believed that Biden had stolen the election. He was then shown standing in front of the Texas Capitol building with his heavily armed buddies without any comment from the reporter about how they were doing this only days after the Capitol Building in Washington DC had been stormed by fascists egged on by their fascist leader. That sickened me and convinced me that I had made the right decision about cancelling my licence.

So, all that makes it really pleasant when I come across something that has the potential to be awful and avoids it. In the last few years, I did a complete re-read of my Terry Pratchett collection.

In *The Last Continent* there is a scene with a group of Drag Queens. I read it, terrified that Sir Pterry was going to make a transphobic joke. I was happy because he didn't but also really quite annoyed because it's something I had to worry about. I last read this book pre-transition when I was so far in denial that I'd have probably found it funny if he had. (GNU Terry Pratchett. "A man is not dead while his name is still spoken" - *Going Postal*, Chapter 4 Prologue.)

Part of my job was (and still is) talking to people on the phone. I have never liked having to do it but, since my transition I hate it even more. Knowing that my voice sounds more masculine than it does feminine means that when people are speaking to me without the visual cues they get from actually seeing me, they are for more inclined to misgender me. I have never managed to work out which is worse - being referred to by my Deadname or as 'Allen'. It can be really difficult to know what to do and when it happens I still have a tendency to freeze. Should I interrupt and correct them? How do I interrupt without seeming rude? And, even when I do try it doesn't always work. There have been times when I have said that it's 'Ellen with an E' or even spelt it and they have continued to refer to me as Allen. When I'm having a bad day and the dysphoria is biting, making me feel fat, ugly and masculine, having someone call me 'Allen' or 'he' over the phone is bad and makes me even more dysphoric and more sensitive. I have had days when having it happen a few times in quick succession has driven me to tears. Most of the time, if people do catch what I'm telling them they will apologise and correct themselves. Most of the time. Once I rang a ward and spoke to one of the male healthcare assistants. Talking to his colleagues to relay the message I had for them, he referred to me as 'he'. I corrected him which he apparently found hilarious and then - while I could still hear him - started to call me 'this person'. Even with the distortion caused by the technology, I could still here the suppressed laughter in his voice. Fortunately for me a large part of my job involves talking to the sisters and matrons in the hospital which means that I have a good relationship with most of them. As soon as I put the phone down on the prick I sent off a quick email to the ward sister telling her about the incident and asking her to have a word. Fortunately, it seems to happen less often now although that in itself means that when it does happen it catches me even more off guard and I still haven't worked out how to deal with it smoothly. There is one positive though - when I get spam callers ringing up asking to speak to 'Mr Mellor' I can quite honestly tell them that he isn't here anymore and leave it to them to draw their own conclusions from that statement. I feel that I'm fairly safe in the assumption that if they're using a name that was defunct more than five years ago then whatever they are trying to sell me is not something I want. There's always one though. BT even now, after telling them several times (and changing the name on the account) text and email my Deadname.

My job did improve a little when I got a temporary secondment to take over as Team Leader for my team. However, that meant working closer with my line manager which did absolutely nothing for our relationship. The secondment lasted for around about six months at the end of which we were barely on speaking terms. This happened in large part because of his reaction when I decided the time had come to discuss how the Trust would handle my situation when I eventually had a date for bottom surgery. This came up because I was needing to take a day off in order to travel to Edinburgh to see another doctor for a second opinion on whether or not I was really trans. While it was essentially a formality and a rubber-stamp, I still had to go through it before I could be referred onwards for surgery.

His first response was to ask if GRS was elective or not meaning that his first thought was to look for a loophole to get out of paying me while I was recovering. After our discussion, he spoke with the department head who asked for a meeting with both of us. When I did so, the first thing out of her was the very same question. I tried to keep my emotions under control but when she asked me that, my face told her exactly what I felt. Technically, it could be argued that it is elective. After all, I had a healthy body and if I didn't have the surgery my physical health wouldn't be affected. However, my mental health was a different matter. If I didn't have the surgery there was every possibility that the dysphoria would just increase until, eventually, it would get too much for me. It would not be beyond the bounds of possibility that without surgery I could end up as another statistic. I didn't actually say any of that, maybe I should have. I just told them that it wasn't. I tried not to blame them for asking this, telling myself that I was the first trans person they knew so they didn't know the answer but that is just giving them an easy escape. The truth is that this being the first thing that leapt to mind demonstrated exactly how they thought - they both had their eye on the bottom line and the employees were just a line on the ledger. It wasn't necessarily transphobia, it was just plain old greed. After that, I knew I could not trust either one of them.

When the permanent position was advertised, I applied for it purely because I thought I should and if I got it my salary would be increased permanently. I mean, it was still not a great salary, but it was a couple of thousand pounds a year more than I got in my actual position. Ultimately, although I got an interview, I didn't actually get the job, being told that I had not had enough experience which pissed me off hugely. I vowed that I would try not to blame the woman who did get the position and went out of my way to be nice and welcoming to her. Unfortunately, the week after she started the line manager went off sick for several weeks meaning that she was put in charge of the whole thing straight away. I was asked to back her up which I agreed to do only if they extended my increased salary for the period. Working closely with her was a breath of fresh air compared to what I had dealt with before. She was open, honest and actually listened when you came to her with questions and problems. She allowed people to contribute and shared knowledge which is not something I had previously experienced in this job. Even when I had been Team Leader, I had not been able to effectively do my job because the line manager jealously guarded the information and refused to allow anyone else access to a lot of it. How much he had done this was highlighted when he went off sick because there were reports and tasks that needed completing but couldn't be done because nobody else knew how to do them - in some cases nobody else even knew of their existence. It was the perfect example of why businesses should never let one person become a single point of failure. We spent six weeks only being able to do half a job because we were literally incapable of doing the rest. I very quickly came to realise how close a shave I had had and how lucky I was not to have got the job. Of course, I helped the new Team Leader as much as I could and, to be honest, would have done so even if I hadn't managed to get the agreement to continue with my increased salary. I liked her a lot, even to the extent that I felt able to tell her about how worried I had been about my reaction to her getting the job instead of me.

At around the same time as I got the secondment, I also submitted *Ghostkin* to another publisher. Double Dragon Press were a small Canadian company that specialised mostly in e-books but, by making use of Amazon's Print-on-Demand programme, also produced paperback copies. I had submitted it to publishers and agents before and had had as much luck as I had with the other three books. This was going to be my final shot at persuading someone else to take it on before I took the self-publishing route again. Editing the book for what felt like the fiftieth time was difficult. It had reached the point where I was getting bored with the words on the page and was reading what I thought was there rather than what was actually there. Although it was useful as I found a 'your' where there should have been a 'you're'. Even with an English degree, a teaching qualification and three books under my belt, I was still making basic grammatical mistakes. And, to be honest, I still do. Not often, but certainly far more than I would like. I submitted *Ghostkin* to Double Dragon because they (or rather he - it was basically a one man operation) had published *Wolves of Dacia* by my good friend and author-sis, Eleanor Burns. (*Wolves* is an excellent book, by the way - werewolves and vampires in World War II era Transylvania - you should buy a copy.) So, I emailed it off to him and waited.

Deren (Double Dragon's publisher) got back to me quite quickly saying that he liked *Ghostkin* and wanted to publish it. While this was, of course, very exciting, it was also just the start of another long wait. Having someone else publish your book is entirely different from self-publishing. It has to go through a process - editing, cover art design and placing on their schedule. That being said, I'm not completely certain how much editing actually went on before it was published but the cover art was absolutely beautiful - a manipulated photograph of a city street at night with a monochrome picture of the bottom half of a woman's head superimposed over the top. When Deren sent the first version of the design for me to approve, I noticed that the only legible shop sign was for Snappy Snaps. Which I thought detracted from the overall image a bit.

Ghostkin wasn't the only writing I had done, although to be honest, I was really not feeling in the right head space in order to do much. I'd written a few short stories and tried to start writing a couple of novels. One of my short stories was called "Freeing The Bitch". I'm proud of this one in particular because it's the first piece of my writing accepted for publication by a 'real' publisher. *Maiden, Mother, Crone: Fantastical Trans Femmes* is an anthology of fantasy written by trans feminine people (i.e. Trans women and feminine non-binary people) and included stories by a few big names in the trans publishing world such as Casey Plett (whose book *A Safe Girl to Love* is one of the modern trans classics), Lilah Sturges, an award- winning comic book writer (check out her *Lumberjanes* graphic novels, they're wonderful) and Gwen Benaway (a seriously accomplished trans poet and the editor of the book). I was so proud to be in this crowd and finally felt like I could call myself an author. Actually, to say it's the first story to be accepted for publication is not entirely true, *I Wish I Could Be Like* which is included in my *Stories From the Corner of the Room* was actually accepted by two publications - one a magazine which failed to get beyond the first issue and then by a talking books service for local hospitals which I assume never happened because I didn't hear anything more from them after they read my story. Perhaps it was a bit too sweary. I think that it's the only story I've written which has the 'C Word' in it. (Apart from this one.)

After a fairly long period of not giving blood, I finally started again in June 2017. Before I went, I checked if I would be able to donate due to being on hormones and t-blockers and was happy to discover that it wasn't a barrier. When I arrived, I was handed a copy of the welcome booklet which they expect you to read every time which gives a long list of reasons why you aren't allowed to give blood. One of them being if you are a man who has sex with other men - although more recently the rule has changed from being totally disqualified to having to be celibate for three months before giving blood (and will change again in the summer of 2021 to those who have been in a relationship with the same partner for three months or more). Despite the appalling, close-minded homophobia this portrays, it's also desperately cis-sexist language making the assumption that everyone who has a penis is a man and that all men have penises. I challenged them on this, explaining how they were non-inclusive, and the wording would actively discourage trans people from feeling like they could donate. I was pleasantly surprised to find the Blood Donation service actually engaged with me and I had a long conversation with a woman who worked there. It wasn't especially a productive conversation and didn't actually bring about any change to the language, but it did show that they were pretending to listen. However, their website still talks about men who have sex with men and a search for the word 'transgender' on the site has zero results. I haven't actually given blood for a couple of years now because I got a letter from them stating that women with my blood type were not needed due to issues around women (especially those who have been pregnant) potentially developing antibodies that can be dangerous to patients infused with their plasma. Whether this means trans women or not I don't know and, to be honest, I don't feel particularly inclined to find out. That letter was enough to cause some dysphoria - being reminded that I will never be pregnant is not a fun time - and so following it up and being activist about it just didn't seem like something I could do at the time.

One of the major issues with the whole medical transition process as it was (and presumably still is) conducted by the NHS is that it can seem desperately unfair at times. When I first came out to C, she asked that I don't self-medicate (that is to self-administer hormones, usually sourced from the grey market). It seemed like quite a small concession for what I was putting her through, and I wasn't confident enough in myself to chance the possible dangers of taking un-regulated hormones. However, that was at the very beginning when I didn't realise how hard it would be when the dysphoria was fairly mild. A year into my hormone regime, still waiting for the go-ahead before I could take the next step, I discovered that another woman who had been self-medding prior to her first appointment which had been literally half an hour after mine had managed to jump so far ahead of me that she had been waiting for a referral to see a surgeon for about four months. While I in no way begrudged her having this, I was desperately upset and frustrated. It felt like I was being punished for following the rules. The NHS were quite firm in their guidance that one absolutely shouldn't self-med but then it seemed like they took it as further proof that someone who did do so was 'really trans'. I, on the other hand, still had to prove it - even though I had by this point been living full-time as the real me for two years - with a legal name change and a job where nobody knew me as anything else. As the year went on, the depression and dysphoria slowly increased. I found that I was spending entire weekends hating myself and dreading having to return to work on the Monday. My sleep pattern deteriorated and my worries about where things were going with C increased. After all, not only was she having to deal with me as a trans woman, I was blatantly failing to be happier because of it. What was the point of going through all of this if it wasn't helping?

The dysphoria didn't quite increase on a daily basis. Instead, I had sudden sharp attacks that hit hard increasing how bad I felt and then when the attack receded it didn't go back down to the level it had been before. When it was bad it all felt completely pointless and I had no idea why I was doing any of it. I felt fat and ugly and like a man in bad drag. I was certain that nobody would ever find me attractive - sexually or otherwise. The 'thing' between my legs was the most horrific part but, even when I got rid of it, I was just going to look like a fat bloke without a penis.

I was never actively suicidal. Instead, I would describe myself as 'actively non-suicidal' as in I would try to focus on the reasons why killing myself would be a bad idea and what I had to look forward to. I did recognise that this wasn't massively healthier than the other thing, but it seemed to be what I needed in order to keep going although it didn't exactly help my stress levels. My insomnia really started to act up again - I would have runs of nights when I would wake up at two or three in the morning. During most of December 2017, I barely managed five hours a night which was combined with a period when work became much busier than usual. I was pushing myself to just get through until Christmas when I would be off for a fortnight and could recover. Unfortunately, I fell ill with a really bad cold two days before I my holiday began. While I don't have bad asthma, it flares up in cold weather and, when I catch a cold it invariably ends up on my chest. Every winter for the last few years, I've managed to end up with a chest infection that has required antibiotics to treat. This time, it took advantage of how run down I was to hit me early. I had been feeling unwell for most of the week but that Wednesday it got really bad - a pounding headache, shivering, aching, dizziness and nausea. I managed to stay at work until the end of the day but went to bed as soon as I got home. The fun thing about my insomnia is that it doesn't give a toss what time I go to bed. It gives me a few hours and then bang! That's it, I'm awake. So, that Wednesday, after going to bed just after seven in the evening, I was awake again at midnight. After lying there for a few hours, I posted on Facebook about it, saying that "unless the co- codamol kicks in quickly and I sleep solidly for the next five hours, I don't see myself going to work today". And, indeed I didn't. I was actually off from that day until I went back after New Year.

At the beginning of the following year, I was really, seriously starting to think about the future and what it held. Namely, surgery.

While I definitely wanted it, it was only really then that it started to sink in that it was actually going to happen at some point. I had two main thoughts concerning it. Firstly, when is it going to happen? A large part of me wanted it as soon as possible, obviously. But another part thought that I should wait until the summer of 2019.

That way, it would allow M to finish his GCSE exams and C would be able to come to Brighton as it would be the summer holidays.

The second thought re-occurred on a regular basis. What if I wake up after surgery, look down and think 'what the fuck have I done?' I mean, I was pretty certain that I wouldn't, especially considering my feelings about what was down there but I was also certain that I had no intention of expressing my fears to anyone who could potentially hear them and decide that it meant that I wasn't really trans. I did discuss it with other trans women both in the lead up to their own surgery and afterwards and was reassured when pretty much every single one of them said that they had the same or similar fears. Looking back, I see that my nervousness was a sensible reaction to having major, life-altering surgery. People have regrets about these sorts of things. Although, despite the brouhaha about 'detransition' (when someone decides to return to the gender to which they were assigned at birth), the number of people who decide that they made a mistake after gender confirmation surgery is startlingly small, especially compared to other surgeries. Research has shown that breast reconstruction after surgery has a regret rate of 47%. People who undergo prostate surgery to treat cancer were found to have a regret rate of 20%. For hip replacement surgery it's 3%. For gender confirmation surgery? 1-2%. I had no reason to think that I would be one of the two people in a hundred who realised they had made a mistake, but it certainly didn't stop me - or, apparently anyone else in the same boat as me - from thinking about it. On the whole, I choose to see it as a positive. Having those worries meant that I thought about what I was doing and had a reasonable idea about what was going to happen. If I had been entirely blasé about it and absolutely dead certain then I think that would have been more worrying. As I said, this was major surgery that would irrevocably change everything. If I wasn't worried, then I hope that someone else would have been concerned that I hadn't fully taken it on board. Although, saying that, it's very much like having a baby. Everyone tells you that it's going to change your life, and everything is going to be different afterwards but there is absolutely no way to understand it until it actually happens to you.

Going back to work in the New Year after being ill was… interesting. Apparently, someone had told the management about my 1am post. This was taken as me pre-emptively deciding I wasn't going to work, and I should therefore be disciplined for it. I know what you're thinking. I thought the same thing and still do. What the Actual, Ever-living, Fuck? Apparently, talking about my intention to be off sick before I had rung and told them was a breach of the rules and that it was possible that I had made that Facebook post from a nightclub or some such. Initially, I thought they were joking. But no, they were serious. Even now, I can remember my astonishment at my line manager sitting across the table from me, telling me that he thought I may have been making it up. This, combined with the discussion about whether or not my surgery was elective were the two points that totally screwed my relationship with him. I was still acting up as Team Leader and his 'second in command' at this point and, while I had found it difficult due to his habit of jealously guarding information and his lack of interpersonal skills, finding myself absolutely unwilling to talk to him made the entire thing basically impossible and unworkable. I'm probably being paranoid but I'm pretty certain that if this hadn't happened, this secondment would have been made permanent. To be honest though, it was a very lucky escape.

Shortly after all this shit happened, I found myself in the position of becoming a writer-in-residence for a local charity working to enable and empower marginalised groups. The plan was for me to run writing groups, which was something I wanted to do anyway. However, at that point, the charity had only just started and wasn't set up to accommodate those plans so essentially it became somewhere I could go to write. I was offered the position purely because I knew the woman who ran it. We had a mutual interest in comic books and had met at the local graphic novels reading group before my transition. She suffers badly from fibromyalgia and at the time I did what I could to help her - driving her around, especially to and from the graphic novels group and just trying to be there for her as a friendly ear and shoulder should she need one. We lost touch for a couple of years when she lashed out at me for offering to return a book to the library for her that had been taken out on my ticket. It was just before I started my transition and was feeling really fragile and decided that I didn't need that in my life at that point.

We met up again after my social transition at the wedding of mutual friends and immediately got on really well again. Neither of us spoke about the previous incident and just kind of swept it under the rug. All seemed to be forgiven and forgotten.

I went to her office after work on a nearly weekly basis for several months until she said that she wasn't able to keep things going because her fibro was flaring up and she had started a degree on which she needed to focus. This was fine by me, if a little disappointing, especially as I had been planning on having the book launch for *Ghostkin* there. It had been a productive few months although, ultimately, the book I had been working on - a fantasy called *The Divide* which I had been attempting to make work for about ten years by that point - failed to come to fruition. But she needed to focus on herself something I could understand entirely.

So, I stopped going, hoping to re-start when she was feeling better.

The appointment for the second opinion on my transness happened in Edinburgh in early 2018. Although any excuse to go to Edinburgh and see Dylan is welcome, this one was more than a little infuriating. Yet more gatekeeping nonsense and delay for absolutely no reason. It had been more than two years this since I last presented as male, and I had spent more than a year on hormones and testosterone blockers so having another bloody cis person who met me once for an hour make a decision upon which my entire

future lay felt ridiculous and insulting. The fact that I would have had to do something pretty extreme for her not to sign off on it just added to the feeling of hoop-jumping for the sake of it. Dr Myskow was nice, and it was a pleasant conversation but it really didn't need to happen. However, one needs to follow the rules if one wants to get anywhere so I did what I needed to do and got a nice letter saying that she agreed with the diagnosis and that I was ready for surgery. Which meant that another hurdle had been overcome. Now I just had to wait for a referral to see the surgeon.

There are two hospitals in the United Kingdom that perform vaginoplasty (the technical term for trans-feminine genital reassignment surgery), Charing Cross hospital in London and the Nuffield in Brighton. Obviously, for a girl living in the north of England (or worse, in Scotland) neither of these were especially suitable. However, those were the choices, so I had to decide which one to go for. While I am firmly against the notion of privatised healthcare and would never willingly sign up for medical insurance, I chose to go to the Nuffield. The procedure was still being performed under the auspices of the NHS but in an environment that was rather nicer than the average NHS hospital - not that I'm dissing NHS hospitals in any way, but they are incredibly underfunded and do sometimes border on the 'lack of real comfort' side of things. I had heard that this was especially true of Charing Cross, although I do know people who had their surgery there and found it absolutely fine. However, people who had been to the Nuffield made it sound like a hotel which just happened to do medical stuff as well. Private rooms with an en- suite bathroom, beautiful surroundings looking over grassland towards the English Channel... why would I choose to go anywhere else?

While I was happily (or y'know, begrudgingly) jumping through all these hoops, the rest of the world just got on with becoming steadily more transphobic. The anti-trans children lobby group 'Transgender Trend' published a deeply vile document which they (I say 'they', although it seems to be mostly one woman getting lots of money from somewhere) distributed to every school in the country explaining how and why schools should not support trans kids. More and more American states produced 'Bathroom Bills' trying to ensure that trans people were forced into public toilets depending on the sex to which they were assigned at birth but actually having more impact on butch cis women (who were described as acceptable collateral damage by some in the 'Gender Critical' crowd. How's that for feminism?). British Media continued to be shitty. The Guardian newspaper published an editorial on the Gender Recognition Act Reform consultation that was so horrendous the American arm of the paper felt compelled to publish a response to it, distancing themselves from their UK counterparts. The Sunday Times seemed to take great delight in publishing lies about trans people most weeks while the Daily Mail continued its own merry way down the path towards hardcore fascism.

Eight weeks after initially being put on a disciplinary for posting about being ill and not going to work, I had a second meeting. Back in January, I had been told that if I wasn't off sick in that period, the disciplinary action would then be lifted. When I had the meeting, my line manager - nearly apologetically - told me that he had made a mistake and it had to be in place for six months. While I had fundamentally disagreed with the notion of being put on a disciplinary due to an illness caused in large part by the stresses of the job, I had been prepared to go along with it for a couple of months. To then be told that, due to an error on his part, it was being extended, left me feeling like I was being punished for talking about my mental health, which was ironic because the office was plastered with 'Time to Talk' posters encouraging you to be frank, open and honest about your mental health issues.

I hadn't spoken to my union about it back in January, thinking that it would blow over quickly and wasn't worth making a fuss about.

However, this second meeting and the way that it had been conducted made me change my mind about that. My union rep was very pleasingly annoyed on my behalf and immediately started planning on how she could tear large strips off several people. Maria (my rep and the Association Secretary) is a lovely woman but she can be fierce when she is roused. I am very glad that I have only ever seen that side of her when she has been standing in front of me. I'd hate to be on the receiving end.

In the same week that I didn't get the permanent Team Leader position (which, as I said, I'm really quite glad about, although I was less happy about it then), I did have a short story accepted for a trans feminine fantasy anthology, called *Maiden, Mother, Crone: Fantastic Trans Femmes*. I was so happy as it was yet more affirmation that I was a 'real' writer which in many ways was as difficult for me to accept as being 'really' transgender. I knew I could write, and I was getting better all the time but having professionals agree with me was incredibly affirming.

That exact same day, however, I had an appointment with my doctor for her to check on how I was doing on the anti-depression meds. She doubled my dosage and told me to arrange a blood test within the next couple of weeks. This was, in itself, mildly alarming as I had no idea what could be so important that I needed to have one so quickly when normally it's usually three or four weeks before an appointment is available. My mild alarm jumped to terror when she rang me almost as soon as I got to work to say that she had been thinking and wanted me to have the blood test immediately. The next available slot was at 11.00, she had rung me at 9.55 and it took around an hour to get from work to home, depending on how well the public transport system is working.

My blood test had obviously been expedited because it usually takes a minimum of 48 hours to get the results back, but she rang me that evening to tell me that everything was fine which was good although I was still curious to know why it had been such a rush. I don't think I ever found out to be honest. It's just one of those mysteries.

One of the proudest moments of my life happened in April 2018 when I decided to tell all my friends that I had written 'A Novel' and wanted to share it with them. For various reasons, it's never been published anywhere else, but I want to share it with everyone who has slogged through nearly 78000 words of me pontificating about my life. So, if you go to bit.ly/novelEM you can read A Novel that I wrote.

That April I also got official notification that I had been referred to Mr Thomas in Brighton for surgery, which made me very, very happy. At my next GIC appointment I discussed whether or not I could or should hang on until the August 2019 (18 months away) for surgery. Their argument was that because the dysphoria was increasing so much there was no telling what state I would be in by then and it would, in theory, be easier for C to care for me post- surgery rather than have to care for me while I was going through months of intense dysphoria related breakdown. My concerns around M's exams could be mitigated by the knowledge that for the time I was recovering, I would actually be more available to help. It all sounded sensible and, when I discussed it with C she agreed, so I decided to just push ahead and go for the earliest date I could. This meant seriously contemplating losing weight because one of the stipulations (more gatekeeping) was that my BMI had to be under 15 for the surgery to go ahead. At that point, it was up around about 19 so I needed to at lose at least a couple of stones.

Between the time I was referred and actually going to

Brighton I had several telephone conversations with the staff at the hospital in order to make sure things got arranged as quickly as possible. During one of these conversations, the nurse I was speaking to re-iterated what I had been told about losing weight and explained that excess weight could actually affect the aesthetic outcome of the surgery. She didn't say it quite like that though. She told me that I needed to lose weight because I wanted my 'lady garden' to look beautiful. I handled it perfectly and managed to hold in my laughter until the end of the conversation, nor did I say anything about how very wrong it was to describe a vulva in those incredibly gendered terms. My major regret, however, is that I didn't come up with the perfect reply until several hours later. I realised that what I should have said was that I actually already had a lady garden. I just needed a stump uprooting.

My job continued to get worse, and I finally decided that once my surgery was out of the way I was going to start looking for a new job. I had gone from thinking my line manager was okay (this is the same man who said that he liked me because 'I challenged him' remember. Apparently, that appreciation for challenge only goes so far) to loathing him. A couple more things finally cemented my dislike. Firstly, when he told me that I should have been released from the disciplinary process after the initial eight weeks. I don't know when he discovered this, but he didn't tell me until the six months was over. Secondly, telling me that my temporary band 4 salary - which had been given to me to help the new Team Leader find her feet - had ended and I had returned to my band 2 salary. Three days after it happened.

The bright side was that I had managed to get another

secondment, away from the team, which came with a bit of a salary bump, although this in itself was not to be without it's difficulties. Up until this point, the Trust had been using a rostering system for the staff called 'Smart'. The name was more of an aspiration that it never quite reached rather than a description of its true potential. It was no longer supported by the company that had designed it, so a new system needed to be brought in. My secondment was to set the system up and then train the managers. It wasn't a perfect result as I was only promoted to a band 3, which was still less than £20,000 a year for training people on significantly more than that. However, it got me away from my 'real' job and meant I was improving my skills. And, of course, by training all of these high-powered people I was becoming more visible to them which (assuming I did a good job) could only be a good thing.

I got the job in May but, as seems inevitable when it comes to recruitment in the NHS, I didn't actually start until July. There were problems right out of the gate. Not the least being that the software company recommended a minimum of eight people doing my job while the people in the Trust who set up the project (the head of the department, AKA my line manager's line manager, and the person above her) had decided that three would be enough. We were flat out from day one and quickly realised that it was going to be basically impossible to do the job as well as we should have been able. On top of that, as time went on, those two people in particular seemed to prefer to get in the way of the smooth running of the project rather than actually help. At one point, in a meeting well before we had reached the end of the project, they told the project manager who had a temporary contract that as his contract would be ending soon his views didn't really matter. In the same meeting, I was told that they didn't see the need for them to send out communications on our behalf to chivy managers into coming along for training as any email that came from the team should have been read as if it was coming from them. Which was helpful.

There is a reason why I am being so damning towards these people - firstly because I am pretty damn sure they'll never read it and secondly because neither one is with the Trust anymore. One left to go to another Trust essentially before they got pushed and the other was (reading between the VERY wide lines) allowed to resign rather than be sacked. The email announcing her departure was circulated twenty four hours before she actually left, coincidentally on the same day as the other person left to go to their new job. However, all that was to come. In the meantime, I was finally given a date to see Mr Thomas, the surgeon who would perform miracles on my genitals. It was to be on the 31st of July, two days after my birthday. I immediately started to worry. What was he going to say? Was he going to tell me to go away and come back when I had lost the required weight? Was he going to take one look at me and refuse to do anything because he could immediately see that I wasn't really trans? It was the usual over-thinking and utterly standard for pretty much everyone else in this situation. There are times when it becomes really quite dis-spiriting to learn that you are so incredibly average. Just once it would have been nice to have an anxiety that thousands of others had not.

In common with any other woman who differentiates from the norm, trans women have to put up with people who are described as 'chasers'. You can have 'fat chasers', 'black chasers', 'Asian chasers' and so on. They are, usually, straight white men with a fetish and only see those who 'fit' into their fetish as just being that thing - i.e. fat, black, Asian or trans. Some people think that a lot of the Gender Critical bunch are repressed trans chasers. Which makes an awful lot of sense. Especially when there is a rumour with quite a strong basis for believing that one of the main male gender critters became one after being rebuffed by a few trans women. While they aren't a recent thing, social media makes it far easier for them to find a person to fetishise I have been lucky enough to avoid them although there is a small part of me that wants to know what's wrong with me that these people don't want to fetishise me. Which is just weird. Don't get me wrong here, I am not kink-shaming or saying there's anything wrong with finding a fat woman or a trans woman (or a fat, trans woman) attractive. The problem lies when that is the be all and end all of someone's interest in a person. We are more than that single label and deserve to be treated as such. If someone foregrounds and sexualises a trans person's identity as a trans person over and above the rest of their identity then I think that is as problematic as someone who refuses to have a relationship with a trans person because they are trans. They are reducing us to one single aspect of who we are and let's face it, we're talking about genitals here.

To date I have - as far as I am aware - only had a single interaction with a chaser. At the time I wasn't even certain that is what it was. I got a friend request on Facebook from a man who was mutual friends with quite a few other trans women which made me think that he was going to be okay, so I accepted his request. I thought that maybe he was a closeted trans woman who was reaching out for help and support or something like that. However, the first time he sent me a private message he asked if I was married and where I lived. I gave generic answers and he continued on with similar questions which gave me a very weird vibe. When I asked him what I could do for him. His response was 'I'm naughty'. I should have immediately blocked him, but I just couldn't understand why these other women were friends with him. There had to be more to him than this. I asked him to explain what he meant and he said 'i don't know what you doing' (lack of punctuation and capitalisation in the original because I took a screenshot). This in itself led to a short exchange which I quite enjoyed:

> Ellen and the Chaser. A short play in one act.
>
> Him
>
> I don't know what you doing
>
> Ellen
>
> Not a lot.
>
> Him
>
> Really
>
> Ellen Yes
>
> -fin-

I think you can probably tell that I was not fully engaged with the conversation at this point.

He went on to say they he liked trans women 'our height' which was odd as I had not told him how tall he was. Maybe

I gave off an aura of 'nearly six feet tall'. After I told him that the conversation was making me uncomfortable, he said 'sorry' and followed up with the fact that he had been deaf since birth. He went silent after I told him that mentioning that sounded very much like a play for sympathy to keep me talking. I gave up at that point and blocked him. It wasn't a fun experience but as he didn't share pictures of his dick with me I think I probably came out of it relatively unscathed. Although if he had done, I'd have known what to do far earlier.

Much of the summer of 2018 was spent focusing on the government's consultation of the reform of Gender Recognition Act.

It wasn't just about filling out the consultation questionnaire form myself but getting the word out and trying to get others to do the same because if there was one thing that went without saying it was that the transphobe set were going to be completing it multiple times. By some bizarre coincidence, the media suddenly started to spout a lot more transphobic nonsense with articles and reports that deliberately and blatantly blurred the lines between the Gender Recognition Act 2004 and the Equality Act 2010. The former allowed someone to change their gender on their birth certificate. Other than that, it didn't really have a lot of effect on day-to-day life. If someone with a Gender Recognition Certificate were to be sent to jail, then it would mean that they would be sent to the Women's Estate rather than the Men's. Or at least, in theory that's what meant to happen. In practice it's still a bit of a lottery. There are a few other things it affects - pensions and life insurance and the like but, on the whole, it has very little effect other than to say that you are legally the gender you are (unless you are non-binary. In which case, you're screwed). The Equality Act 2010 is the one that has the biggest effect - it's the one that says that trans women are allowed to use women's toilets, changing rooms and the like (or rather, it doesn't prohibit us from entering them. There is a clause that says that trans people can be excluded from single sex spaces but that it needs to be a 'proportionate means of achieving a legitimate aim' and should only occur in 'exceptional circumstances'. So not wanting to pee in the cubicle next to someone with a willy is not included). Gender Critical types tried to muddy the waters as much as possible by claiming that if self-ID was allowed then any man would be able to go into single sex areas just by claiming that they were women even though it's never happened in any country where self-ID is already the law.

They dismiss this by saying that you can't apply arguments around what goes on in other countries to this one, as if British men were more rapey than those in other countries. Self-ID is something of a misnomer anyway. I already self-identify as a woman. My passport, my drivers' licence, my bank account, my medical records and just about everything else has a little 'F' on them denoting my gender and it only shows that because I told them to change the marker and they complied. I also use women's public toilets and have never felt the urge to ogle anyone else.

The day after my birthday I found myself on a train down to London and then on down to Brighton accompanied by my friend Karen from Rickmansworth (who assures me that she has never had any revelations about "what it was that had been going wrong all this time" in small cafés) who came along to support me and have a wander around the place. I had been to Brighton once before but this time it was a bit more important. The Nuffield Hospital is actually on the way out of town towards Hove and was every bit as nice as I expected it to be. I had a tour of the hospital followed by a short talk which included a presentation of Mr Thomas' 'work'. It was potentially the least sexual presentation of multiple vulvas (vulvae? Vulvapodes?) I've ever seen. But god damn, his work was good, and I would have been pleased to ....er... come across... examples of his work in a more intimate setting. It also made me really excited for how mine would ultimately look (not excited like 'that' you pervert).

The major part of the appointment was however to meet Mr Thomas and introduce him to my genitals. Ostensibly this was so he could see what he had to work with and how much hair removal I needed. His decision would dictate how long it would be before I would be ready for surgery and also how much pain I was going to be put through. Having laser and electrolysis on my face had been bad enough. The thought of having it on my genitals was enough to make me just curl up in a corner whimpering. In the end, I spoke to him for about three minutes while he explained a couple of things then I went behind a curtain, whipped off my skirt and knickers and lay down, legs akimbo. He came in wearing rubber gloves, gave my bits a yank to see what he was dealing with and said that I didn't need any hair removal. Or rather, he mumbled that I didn't need any. I didn't quite catch what he said and had to double check with him before I was certain.

All in all, for a journey that lasted two days and cost me a couple of hundred pounds, I was in and out of there in significantly less than hour. But it was worth it. It was going to happen and - all being well - within the next five or six months. I would have a vulva for Christmas!

The drawback was that I found out that I also needed to lose more weight than I thought as the hospital said my BMI needed to be under 28 rather than the 30 which I had originally been told which, meaning I had to lose an extra 10lbs. I was going to have to be even stricter and up the exercise if I was going to manage. There was one day when I thought I was doing better than I actually was after visiting my GP for my regular blood test to check my hormone levels. I had weighed myself before going so I wouldn't be surprised when I stepped on the nurse's scales, and it was lucky that I had because her scales told me that I was a stone and a half lighter than I thought I was. If that had been true, I would have smashed my BMI target and would be totally ready to go. Being the suspicious person that I am, I decided that I needed a third opinion. Disappointingly, my suspicions were correct, and I was exactly as fat as I thought I was which, although expected, was still dispiriting.

Waiting for the surgery was much harder than I had expected. The dysphoria got stronger and stronger, washing over me more often making me feel like my heart, head and soul were weighing me down and making it impossible to think straight. I knew that I was ugly and male, and no matter how much make up I put on, how many pretty dresses I wore or indeed whatever surgical interventions I had this would be my life. Understanding that I felt this way because I was stuck in another period of waiting for someone else to make a decision about my life didn't help either. Recognising the situation didn't mean that I had a solution. All I could do was hold on as best I could and hope that I would get some good news soon.

Ellen Mellor

It wasn't all entirely bleak and awful though. *Ghostkin* finally came out that September. I was so proud of it: My first ever non-self-published book and also my first ever book launch. Although, of course, it wasn't going to be plain sailing. I had been planning on holding the launch at the charity where I was writer in residence until I started to organise it, when she withdrew the offer, citing her health as the reason why she was pulling out. I wasn't going to argue, her health was not good, but it was frustrating that she waited until I was starting to prepare for it. Unfortunately, anywhere else suitable would have cost money. I didn't want to have it in a pub function room and couldn't have it in a bookshop because the book wasn't actually available to buy anywhere other than Amazon. In order to avoid calling it off, I decided to run a pre-sale with people buying it directly from me at full price while I got it from the printer at cost price. Any profits I made went towards organising the event. It went very well, and I sold plenty of books, both more than I needed in order to fund the book launch and more than I expected meaning I could hire a room in the Literary and Philosophical Society, a wonderful private library in a beautiful old building in the centre of Newcastle. About thirty people came along - admittedly I knew them all but that was rather to be expected. They were a very appreciative and generous audience, and I signed my name on lots of copies.

The one thing that cast a pall over the proceedings was my angsting about the possibility of my Own Personal Transphobe discovering what was happening and deciding to gate-crash, which wasn't entirely impossible as she did lots of events with the society. Then, on the day of the launch, just before I left to drive to the Lit & Phil, someone who had chosen to remain friends with her as well rang me, first to wish me luck and secondly to tell me that my OTP had actually decided not to come because she 'had a nasty cough'. My immediate response was to say 'good, because she was not welcome'. Right up until it started, I was nervous that she may have changed her mind and turned up anyway but lots of people promised that they would act as a bouncer if she did.

Rather than wait for the Nuffield to get in touch with me, I decided to take matters in my own hands and rang them as I had a fairly tight window for when I could have my surgery. Basically, it needed to be during the February half term to ensure that C could accompany me and, possibly more importantly, drive me home again. They strongly discouraged patients from taking a train or (god forbid) a bus because it would have been nightmarish and painful. They actually recommended flying except there were no direct flights from Newcastle to Brighton. Although I could have gone via Alicante. If I just left it to chance, then I probably wouldn't get the dates I needed so I thought it made sense to pre-empt the problem. As it turned out they were very amenable, promising to try to accommodate me and that they would let me know the date 'soon'. That was in October which meant that if it was going to happen then I only had eighteen more weeks to wait. I was suddenly very nervous and jumped every time my phone rang.

As well as being a bolshy trans, I was also reconnecting with my union. After the disaster that had been my introduction to union work in the Council, I had been very unsure of getting involved again, but seeing how much C got out of her union involvement inspired me to start again. I didn't dive straight in and become a rep again, instead getting more involved with the LGBT side of things, which included going to the regional LGBT Committee meetings.

It had taken losing my cis, straight, male privilege to finally see what I had had. During a quiet moment at work, I tried to explain this to my straight, white male colleagues and despite the fact that they were intelligent people they just couldn't get it - arguing that they themselves had not benefited from privilege because they themselves were not rich and powerful. Try as I might, I couldn't get them to understand that it wasn't about where they were but rather it was about how much easier it had been for them to get there.

And then one of them said that he couldn't understand how someone could be a transgender lesbian which, speaking as a transgender lesbian who had been working with this prick for six months, absolutely floored me. I didn't question him about it because I knew that he would have just bullshitted and gaslighted me, but the only way I can see why he would think that was because he didn't see trans women as women. He didn't say that liking women just meant that I was straight or ask why I had transitioned if I liked women but I could see those thoughts going round and round in his head. And he had absolutely no idea why this may have been an inappropriate comment to make. Because of his cis, straight, white male privilege. One of my other colleagues complained that by explaining the concept of privilege he felt attacked which made him feel like 'a piece of shit'. I told him that I was sorry that I made him feel like that and it wasn't intended but a large part of me felt that if he thought that this was being attacked then he should spend some time as a trans woman...

Tea, Comics and Gender

Anyway, this sort of interaction made me reflect more on my own privilege. I had come to understand more about the concept of intersectionality (the idea that people's advantages and disadvantages in life are based around the interaction of their various different 'labels' - for want of a better word) and was trying to apply it to myself and also how I saw other people and their various issues. So, while I may have lost the straight, cis, male part of my privilege, I still had the white, middle class, home owner in full employment aspects of it that meant that I was, on the whole, on the top of the pile when it came to trans women. I thought I had a pretty good handle on the trans aspects but those surrounding ethnicity were harder for me, not least because, as a white person I benefitted from the racism inherent in Western society. In the same way that it is not my job to educate cis people all the time about the various aspects of living as a trans person, I should not as a white, British person expect people from other backgrounds to educate me on their lives. So, when the union offered a chance to take a course offered by Show Racism the Red Card I leapt at the chance. Despite what I said about not expecting others to educate me, hearing from the Black people who came along, especially those who came to the country from elsewhere, was incredibly enlightening. Just to give one example, their description of the immigration process and what it takes to apply for British citizenship was astounding and appalling and I didn't have the faintest idea about what it involved or what it cost - it certainly put the cost of applying for a Gender Recognition Certificate into perspective.

However, as a trans person there were issues with the course. Guest speakers had been invited to come and talk to us which was, on the whole, excellent but there were a couple in particular who made me feel uncomfortable. The first was a woman who introduced us to the basics of mindfulness and assertiveness. She started by explaining techniques around taking quiet time and focusing on yourself which we then practiced. It was a very difficult three minutes. Focusing on myself so intently didn't relax me, instead I became uncomfortably aware of everything wrong with my body. Once the time was up, she asked how we had found it. It took a lot for me to disagree with everyone else saying it was positive, comforting and relaxing but I forced myself to speak up and explain what it did to me. She either didn't get it or chose to ignore me, presumably because it interfered with her carefully thought out lesson plan. As soon as we had told her how we felt she asked to do it again. I decided not to take part but just sitting there in silence made things worse.

Finally, to end the session and to prove how little she understood, she finished with a longer, more 'guided' meditation. She had us start by being aware of our feet and then slowly moving up. Even trying to do this a little freaked me out, especially as we got up towards the waist. I didn't last long and left the room in tears, not returning until the session was over and I had managed to regain some control. At the end, she congratulated me for being 'properly assertive' and knowing when I couldn't do something, without her showing any understanding of why I reacted the way I did and how she had forced me to be assertive. Instead, she firmly insisted that these sessions had always been very successful, and nobody had found it difficult or problematic before.

Afterwards, in discussions with others who understand

more about mindfulness than I do, I discovered that this sort of body scan meditation can be bad for people in many different situations - survivors of sexual abuse, people with disabilities and indeed trans people. There should have been trigger warnings and much more notice given to the participants in case they had issues with what they were being asked to do. It was also pointed out to me that the sessions had always been problem free in the past because in order to make a fuss people have to out themselves, discuss their trauma or in some other way 'other' themselves. It was very hard for me to say anything so I can see how other people with other issues may not have been able to do so. As I write this, I realise that telling me the sessions had been successful and unproblematic was a form of gaslighting, implying that the issue wasn't with the session but with me which is making me angry about it all over again.

The other issue I had was when a couple of Muslim people came to talk about their religion and the problem with Islamophobia.

While I have no issues with the Islamic faith beyond those I have with all organised religion and found the talk absolutely fascinating, the problem came when I asked how their faith dealt with the transgender people. One of the people told me that being trans was 'haram' - an act forbidden by Allah and therefore immoral. I then asked the woman if she would feel comfortable taking her hijab off in my presence. She couldn't answer it, saying only that she would have to speak to her imam which, to be honest, was all the answer I needed. I remained polite because they were guests, but I was more than a little annoyed. Since then, I have spoken to LGBT+ Muslim people who have a far more nuanced understanding of the subject and explained a little about the history of gender non-conforming people in Islamic history but to be told explicitly that this person thought I was immoral for being myself was upsetting.

Continuing with the current theme of being a loud, bolshy trans woman, I went to the Unison LGBT conference for the first time that winter. I had been to the NASUWT conference several times with C but only ever as a guest. This time, I was an actual delegate. There were two motions that I decided to talk about, the first in favour of a motion on transphobic feminism and the fight for trans rights, the second opposing an amendment on changing the name of the LGBT group to the LGBT+ group. Someone had put forward a motion saying that we shouldn't add the '+' because doing so would mean that we could be attacked for including paedophilia in our remit which, as you can imagine, went down a storm. I was complimented several times on my speeches and told that I didn't come across as a first time speaker but this was purely because I was used to standing up in front of audiences. It was, for example, nowhere near as terrifying as my book launch.

At the end of November, I rang the Brighton Nuffield - again - to find out what was happening to be told that they weren't booking any surgeries at the point as they needed to apply for money from NHS England. While this was concerning, I wasn't overly worried as the secretary said that it was just a formality and, while I wasn't at the top of the list, I would still be having my surgery in early 2019. This was followed the following night by a dream where I was standing in a queue that wasn't moving. Not that the two were connected in anyway whatsoever...

Tea, Comics and Gender

Medical shenanigans unconnected to my genitals were all the rage at the end of 2018. I had, for a while, had issues with being constipated which frankly I'm not going to go into because while I'm happy to talk about my bits and my mental health and all of that stuff, nobody (or at least very few people) wants to hear me talk about poo. Anyway, I had another appointment with my GP for a blood test to check my oestrogen levels as they were still fluctuating far too much and failing to settle down in a sensible range. I mentioned my lavatorial issues - because if anyone wants to hear about my poo then it's going to be my doctor - and she said she wanted to refer me to have a camera put up there for a look. Which was all well and good.

Checking my records on the online service a few days later for the blood test results, I was also presented with an entry saying 'Hospital fast track referral for suspected lower GI cancer' which sent me into a complete panic. This was the last thing I needed. If I had cancer, then not only would I have to deal with that it would also put the kibosh on my GRS for the foreseeable future. Upon ringing the surgery, the person who spoke to me told me that it was a standard procedure but did absolutely nothing to try to reassure me or apologise for the way I found out. I didn't get an awful lot of work done that afternoon, spending most of it researching and confiding in Facebook (although I did that in a private group page rather than on my own timeline as I didn't want to scare my family until I knew more). Discovering that the chances of it being cancer were actually quite slim helped a bit but not massively as even a slim chance of a specific cancer was higher than a slimmer chance of a non-specific cancer.

The letter of complaint which I wrote was far calmer and

more polite than I actually felt, explaining to them that while I was reasonably healthy mental stable being presented with that piece of information with no warning could still have been very dangerous.

Then I realised that when I went for the colonoscopy, I was going to have to be naked from the waist down in front of people who weren't necessarily going to be aware of my transness. I discussed my worries with the nurse in the hospital when I made my appointment, and she took me seriously and reassured me that it would all be okay but it was just extra stress on top of everything else that I could have really done without. My GP finally got in touch with me. She only worked the back end of the week and so was unaware of the issue until she came in. To her credit, she was very, very apologetic, saying that she didn't think it was cancer but had decided to refer me through that route because some of the cancer checkboxes were ticked when she was writing the referral. She also said that she didn't realise that was how it would show up online and if it had she would have rung me immediately rather than leaving it until she was back.

The colonoscopy went well, if uncomfortably, although the worst bit about the whole thing was the preparation I had to take the night before in order to clear my bowels. There were several points when trying to drink it made me feel as if I was actually going to empty the top part of my gastro-intestinal tract rather than the bottom. The doctor who performed the procedure informed me that I have a long, twisty bowel which made the procedure a little more difficult to do but I'm unsure as to whether it's a good thing in general or not. I mean, presumably the longer the bowel the more nutrients I can absorb?

Ultimately, the report came back that there were no issues and my bowel was completely fine, other than its length and twistiness.

I should have probably followed it up but by that time I had other issues to deal with.

The colonoscopy took place the week before Christmas. While recovering from it I rang Brighton again as I still hadn't heard from them and it was fast approaching the latest date at which I could stop using the hormone patches if I was going to have my surgery in February. They told me that they had run out of money - whether they were unsuccessful in getting the money for more procedures from NHS England, didn't get as much as they wanted or just hadn't bothered to apply for it is unclear - and so wouldn't be offering any more dates until the next financial year and I would probably be offered a date in May or June. Which was exactly when I couldn't have it as it was right when M's GCSE exams were taking place. C was also taking pupils on a week-long school trip in the middle of July so that essentially meant that I wouldn't be able to get a date until the beginning of August. While this was the date I had originally envisioned it sort of meant that my original plan had been the right one, except that plan had been abandoned long before due to the GIC telling me that if I said that I wanted to delay I could have lost my place on the waiting list and then subsequently the staff at Brighton telling me that they didn't think there would be any problems with having the surgery in February without mentioning the possibility of running out of money at all. So, while I know that a spoken promise is as strong as the paper it's written on, I had still trusted them and taken them at their word. And then, they hadn't bothered telling me that it wasn't happening and seemed happy to let me wait.

5
Annus Horribilis

I have never really explained why I called myself Ellen, always saying that I couldn't remember why I had chosen that name.

Well, that's not entirely true. After settling on the name, I decided to keep the reason behind it secret, mainly because I didn't think that it was anyone else's business.

However, I made a pact with myself that if I ever wrote a memoir, I'd reveal the truth.

So here it is:

When I was trying to decide on a name, I discovered that Ellen is an old English word that means "zeal, strength, power, vigour, valour, courage, fortitude, strife, contention" and I really liked that connotation. I sort of hoped that by taking that name those things would become part of me. Except for the last two, obviously.

Both the depression and dysphoria ramped up immediately after that which, considering it was Christmas and I had a fortnight off to do nothing but brood was exceptionally bad timing. I became hyper- aware of what was between my legs and every time I felt them I physically shuddered and felt nauseous. Dark thoughts floated around the edges of my consciousness. I knew that I would never act on them but at the same time knowing that they were there was very worrying. The knowledge that I was having surgery soon had been a dam holding back all the really bad shit but it proved to be gossamer thin and shattered entirely.

Ellen Mellor

Surgery wasn't a magical cure-all, nor would it make me look like the 'perfect' woman but as most of the dysphoria was centred on what was down there getting rid of it would have to help. It was almost like I didn't really need a vulva, even though I was really looking forward to having one. What I really needed was just to get rid of what I had then.

As a slight aside, I was reading my copy of the *Tales of Earthsea* by Ursula LeGuin. I'd read the original trilogy before but none of the subsequent ones as I'd been told that *Tehanu*, the fourth book, was not as good as the first three being a clumsy attempt to put a feminist veneer over the original trilogy and so had never bothered with it. And this will (it won't but it sounds good) teach me to never listen to the opinions of others when it comes to media. *Tehanu* was lyrically beautiful, intelligent and deeply feminist, utterly different in tone to the original trilogy but absolutely fitting. It continued Ged's story but, for the first time looked closely at the role of women (the original trilogy was nearly as much of a sausage fest as *Lord of the Rings*). Contrary to those who had said it wasn't as good, I felt that it far outstripped the quality of the original trilogy and became my favourite of the entire series. There was a passage in the book that, considering how I felt at that point - you see? It does link with what I'm talking about! - made me cry.

> *"You are beautiful," Tenar said in a different tone. "Listen to me, Therru. Come here. You have scars, ugly scars, because an ugly, evil thing was done to you. People see the scars. But they see you, too, and you aren't the scars. You aren't ugly. You aren't evil. You are Therru, and beautiful. You are Therru who can work, and walk, and run, and dance, beautifully, in a*

red dress."

Ursula Le Guin - Tehanu.

Christmas 2018 was terrible and I hated every moment of it. Knowing that I was also bringing C and M down made it worse. It was one thing to do it to myself but to inflict it on those I loved was awful. There is a selfie I took to show off the gorgeous jumper and scarf that my mother gave me and I just look dead inside. There is no hint of a smile, I tend not to when I take a selfie because it feels forced but in this one, I look like I've never done it. Ironically, other than that, I look pretty good. My hair was lovely (I had recently discovered the joy of the asymmetrical hair style and had gone full trans lesbian with it), my nails were perfect, my legs looked wonderful and I was reasonably slim. But my face didn't show any of it. Even when C described me as 'pretty' it drove me to tears although they weren't happy tears. I just couldn't accept her compliment, it felt like she was just saying it to try to cheer me up because nobody could ever think that the ugly man in the mirror was anything like 'pretty'.

Just to add to my unhappiness, my trans-sister, Amy, got a date for her surgery. It had been delayed for various reasons but now they were ready for her. So, while I was being made to wait, they seemed able to find the money for her. It wouldn't have been so

bad if the offer hadn't been made in the week when I had been hoping to have my surgery and exactly a year to the day since I had been in Edinburgh for my second opinion but it did and it was. Don't get me wrong, I do not for one moment begrudge her the surgery, I was very happy for her. It was just how badly the timing sucked. Feeling the way I did meant that I was unable to show her the love and support she deserved. She was absolutely over the moon about it while I was struggling to hold back tears. Knowing that I was letting her down because I couldn't handle the emotional work needed to show empathy and share the joy with her made me feel even worse. Her 'V-Day' was a moment for celebration and I was acting like the proverbial ghost at the feast, making it all about me and my pain. I tried to hide how I felt but I know that I really didn't do a good job of it.

Knowing that they were giving out dates inspired me to ring them up and try to get in first. And this time I was successful. Ish. They gave me a tentative date for the week commencing the 22nd July which was in itself a pretty auspicious time for me as it would mean that I could look at the installation of my new 'lady garden' as a birthday present. All I had to do was get through the next five months. Which was proving ever harder. One evening sleep proved particularly elusive because everything I did, however I lay, 'they' were there. I felt them more keenly than I had ever done before and it was nauseating. Getting out bed and doing other things to try and distract myself failed. Nothing would make them go away and I found myself contemplating self-harm.

The fact that this was the first time I had ever considered it makes me one of the 'lucky' ones. (There's that word again.) A survey of trans young people from 2014 (I know I'm not a trans young person but there's not a lot of research on the subject) discovered that 72 per cent had self-harmed at least once. I know people who have self-harmed and struggle to stop themselves from doing it again. One trans woman will have major issues having GRS, to the extent that it may not even be possible, because her penis is so scarred from damage she did to herself when she was younger. So for me to have taken this long to even contemplate it is nothing short of miraculous.

I was at the lowest point I had ever been and, really, not even the prospect of a surgery date which wasn't really any more definite the one in February did a lot to improve my temperament.

There were a series of other things that increased the dysphoria and self-hatred around this time as well. Four years to the day since I starting to transition, a man stopped his car as I walking down the street to scream at me that I was a 'fucking crossdressing slag' (which confuses me because 'slag' is such a deeply gendered term that even while he was calling me a man in a dress, he was also saying that he thought I was a promiscuous woman. Transphobes. They're fucking weird). The following day I saw a BBC report on Facebook from referring to a murdered with my Deadname - as in my old forename and the surname 'Mellor'. Normally, that wouldn't have worried me too much but because I was feeling so low, it was so unexpected and in connection with an ex- murderer (even though he had completed his sentence, reformed and wanted to make good), it really shook me up. Then, on another day when I was having trouble persuading myself to even go to work, Daily Telegraph reported on a potential review of the rules around allowing trans women patients on women's wards if they have not medically transitioned and were still 'legally' male as Nick Hancock, the then Health Secretary was 'uncomfortable' with the current arrangements. The 'Torygraph', headlined it as allowing "men to share women's wards if they identify as female" because of course they did. I couldn't help but wonder if they could make it harder for trans people who work in the NHS as well. Would I need a GRC as well as a DBS (an official certificate used to 'prove' that the applicant is suitable for various kind of work, especially those which involve children or vulnerable adults) in order to be allowed to work in the public sector? While nothing overt specifically happened around that idea, the Tory government continued to slowly erode LGBT+ rights in general and trans rights in particular. Just this week (as I write) there was a debate in Parliament about outlawing conversion therapy during which the Secretary of State for Equalities, Kemi Badenoch, failed to give a timeline for any action or even actually use the word 'ban'. There has been a consultation on the provision of 'single sex' toilets (a standard talking point for 'gender critical' types) designed to allow transphobes to rant about men in dresses coming into their spaces, especially as the term 'single sex' is a transphobic dog whistle used to say that only cis women (not that they use that term because cis is apparently a slur) should be allowed to use women's spaces.

Work was also getting harder. One of my colleagues had successfully applied for another job and left. I had also been interviewed for the position and was shocked when he got it because I was objectively the better candidate (in my own humble opinion but backed up by the number of people who told me that I was the best one out of the team). However, he was a young, cis, straight man while I was none of those things. That left two people (plus the project coordinator/ team leader) to do the bulk of the work which, if you remember, had come with a recommendation of employing a minimum of eight people to successfully do it. And then my other colleague got another job (which I hadn't applied for this time) and was out of there as well. Leaving one person who was already having a really rough time. And then the project manager told me that I was being paranoid because I had said that people wanted me dead because I am a trans woman. While people may not want me dead specifically, many people want all trans people to stop existing and absolutely would not be upset if some bigoted psychopath decided to take me out. This was the same cis man who had told me that by explaining the concept of privilege I had made him feel like a 'piece of shit' so I already had experience of him gaslighting me but this felt like it was taking it another level.

At the same time, the woman who had excitedly invited me to become a writer in residence for her charity told me that she thought I was the most selfish person she had ever met and never wanted to see or hear from me again.

This came about because of my inability to keep in touch with people and my tendency to be very open to those I trust when I do talk to them. Although I had not seen her for several months due to her essentially shuttering the charity due to her illness as well as starting a Theology degree, we still exchanged emails and updated each other about what was going on, promising we'd see each other when she was in a better place. As the depression and dysphoria started to get stronger I withdrew from everything. I posted on Facebook but that was the only writing I was capable of doing. She emailed just before Christmas telling me that someone she had once known quite well but, from what I could gather, hadn't talked to for a while had recently died after an overdose and how it had upset her. I had wanted to reply but had neither the energy nor the brain-power to say anything that didn't sound trite, on a par with the 'thoughts and prayers' of American politicians after yet another gun massacre. As time passed, it got harder and harder to say anything. I finally wrote back in early February, apologising for how long it had taken and explaining why. She quickly replied expressing her sympathy, telling me she understood and then going on to tell me about her brother's friend who had also died suddenly and how she was struggling with writing a letter of thanks to the pastor who had performed the funeral ceremony. Once again, I failed to reply having exhausted my ability to say anything the first time. Another month or so passed before I got another email from her in which she berated me for 'dumping' all my problems on her, when I had other friends who could support me, and, furthermore, how I had caused significant emotional distress by failing to show the appropriate amount of sympathy for what she had gone through with the death of these two people. She had been to see a counsellor at the university and had come away from that convinced that I was a selfish, toxic person who needed to be excised from her life. And therefore, I was never to try to contact her again. I was shocked and distraught by the level of vitriol she levelled at me especially as we had been entirely open and honest about what was happening in our lives, spending hours discussing the different issues we faced. The last thing I did to honour our friendship was to comply with her request. I didn't reply to her, I blocked her on social media and added her email address to my spam filter. If she wanted nothing to do with me then I would oblige. I may have forgotten the saying 'once bitten, twice shy' but I wasn't prepared for her to have a third chance. I have seen her once in the street since then and got away from her as quickly as I could, hoping that she didn't see me. That close encounter upset me but it was nothing compared to the time that my OPT got onto the Metro and sat right next to me, as far as I could tell without recognising who I was although I kept my face turned to the window for the entire journey to reduce the chances of her doing so.

All of that happened in the first three months of 2019. Is it any wonder that I had to take a day off work because of stress?

That day, I went back to my journal in order to put down the thoughts and feelings that I didn't think I could express elsewhere.

6th March 2019

It's been four years since I last wrote anything in here. Apparently I only feel like I need to write the really, really shit stuff rather than the absolutely wonderful stuff. But, I'm going to force myself to do that before I talk about the bad things.

So, despite everything that I'm going to talk about after this, I'm overjoyed with who I am now. All of this pain and angst and suffering I'm feeling now - it's only temporary. This time next year I will be so much better and in a much better, happier place. I love the changes that the hormones are making to my body. I adore my breasts and the fact that people do genuinely think that I am to any extent an attractive woman even if my dysphoria doesn't let me see it or believe it. Or at least not very often - I do occasionally catch glimpses of her and they are happening more often but they are still quite few and far between.

However, all that being said, I am not in a good place at the moment.

I have not slept properly for weeks, averaging about four hours a night for the last couple of weeks at least and not much better than that probably for the last couple of months.

My dysphoria is absolutely through the roof - specifically dysphoria focused on my genitals. I feel a deep sense of revulsion and nausea about them and can't bear to look at or touch them. I haven't had it as bad as it was a few weeks ago when I was contemplating self-harm but it is constant. I shudder whenever I become more aware of them and this can be every minute or so sometimes. Writing this has made me acutely aware of them and it's making me feel somewhat sickened.

All of this has of course happened because I didn't get my GRS when I was hoping for it in mid-February. I obviously had walls built up around my dysphoria that allowed me to cope with it but discovering that it wasn't happening just knocked them all down. It's similar to the increase in dysphoria I felt when I first started to transition - there's nothing there to filter it out any more so I'm just feeling it all.

Then, of course, there is my ongoing worry about what is going to become of me and C. I just can't see us lasting beyond the recovery period of my surgery. It's not that I'll be finished with her and won't need her anymore, it's that she won't feel the need to support me as much or as closely anymore. And I won't blame her at all. This last four years has been all about me - she must be utterly exhausted by it. She absolutely deserves a break from it and a chance to find the happiness she deserves and I have denied for - how long? I hope I have made her happy for most of our time together, I know she has certainly done it for me. I have to support her in whatever she decides, the same way that she has supported me.

I'm also worried about M. The upcoming GCSEs this year are

causing so much stress and worry and I have no idea how to offer the right sort of support and encouragement to get through them but I don't know if anything I do is going to make any difference or if I'm making things worse. I want M to do well obviously but at the same time not at the expense of his own mental health.

I'm worried about the massive fuck up that is Brexit - both what it means generally for the country and what it means for me in terms of continued access to HRT and ongoing treatment. I really wanted to have had my surgery before the country got to this point but that obviously hasn't happened. Treatment for trans people is one of the obvious targets for the ongoing cost-cutting and privatisation of the NHS and the hideous thing is, if it were to be cut, there would be so many people who would be fine with it and would think it was a good idea. Too many people seem to think that the slow eradication of trans people - first by refusing them a voice and then by the erosion of our rights, which we have seen really clearly this week with the announcement of a special wing being opened up for trans women prisoners and the Health Secretary's pronouncement of his 'discomfort' with trans women in female only wards and his desire to re-examine the legislation - is a reasonable price to pay, although I'm not sure what it is they think they are actually paying for.

All of this has come together in a perfect storm this week meaning that my mental health is absolutely fucked. I'm just utterly messed up right now. I am not contemplating suicide but what I am doing is listing all the reasons why it's not an option - the things I have to live for.

Before I get to that though, I realise that I've missed one of the reasons for my headfuckery - work. Work is just awful at the moment. The knowledge that R is leaving means that the pressure for training now sits squarely on my shoulders. P can say that he will try to get other people in to take some of the strain in the next stages but there is no guarantee that he will be able to get anyone - either that he'll be allowed to do so or anyone will apply. I'm pretty damn sure that I wouldn't under the current circumstances. P himself hasn't the done the project any good either by pretty much alienating everyone around him at every level with his shitty behaviour and immaturity. But also there has not been a single iota of support from those around us both in senior management and in the Trust as a whole. The whole thing just feels like a toxic mess that needs to be buried and forgotten about. When I'm training I can hear myself almost pleading with people to take this seriously and my voice filling with a fake bonhomie that I really just don't feel - frankly, when I get up in front of people to deliver training, I become the world's best actress.

So, those reasons for not killing myself.

The biggest one is that at some point within the next few months I *WILL* have a new vulva. And it *WILL* be what I need and want. Having the rest of my life to explore what it means and to properly discover myself as a woman has to be worth any amount of short term pain and discomfort and distress. I want the happiness and calmness that I can see in the faces of other women immediately after their surgery.

I want to see M grow up and become happy and strong. To fully discover and share in the joys that are to come.

I want to be here for C - to help her find her own happiness, whatever form that may take. If that means finding a man who can give her what she needs then I want to be by her side urging her to take that step.

I want to be at Amy and Rachel's re-marriage next year. I am truly looking forward to it.

I want to travel the world and meet all of my friends that I only know through Facebook and Twitter. I want to see Katrina again. I want to meet all of the Sloths from everywhere and hug them.

I have books I want to write and so many books I want to read.

I want to bask in and share the love of my friends and family for many years to come. This world is too full of amazing people to leave it just yet.

Tea, Comics and Gender

I want to be an even louder and even prouder trans woman. I want to take my activism to the next level and to fight against all the shit I talked about earlier. I want to leave the world better than it was when I found it and I can't do that if I'm not here.

I really, really want to piss of the transphobic idiots that would prefer that I didn't exist by staying around and getting in their faces as much as I can. By proclaiming my presence and staking out territory for all trans people to live in and thrive in.

The greatest thing is to love and be loved in return. And *THAT* is what I want.

That last line makes me cringe a bit - it's a (slight mis)quote from 'Nature Boy', originally by Nat King Cole, although the version I know is David Bowie's from *Moulin Rouge*. And, while it's entirely true, it just feels like I was trying too hard to be profound.

That first day off due to stress increased to two and then, after a visit to the doctor, a fortnight. I spent most of it focusing on myself - reading as much as I could, writing as much as I could - which wasn't a lot, doing a lot of cycling and drinking an awful lot of tea. It helped a bit although my insomnia didn't get any better with my dreams contributing to the stress when I did manage to sleep. One night, I dreamt that I was in a changing room. There was nothing particularly ominous about it but I remember clearly the anxiety I felt just by being there.

Later that month, I had intended to head up to Edinburgh to go to the Scottish Trans Pride event. Instead of doing that, I sat in A&E for several hours after tripping over in the street and cracking my chin off the ground. There was an awful lot of blood and I was quite dazed but the one good thing that came out of it was the number of people who rushed over to help me - one man who worked in the local Sainsbury's ran back into the shop to get the first aid kit and an off-duty nurse bandaged me up a bit and then drove me home. Despite the pain and the upset it was a moment that showed the depth of community spirit and caring that people have for others and I was not misgendered once the entire time. Ultimately, the injury wasn't too bad and I avoided any significant damage. In the end, the worst part was that I couldn't let the dressing get wet for seven days afterwards meaning I had a week of not shaving.

On that same day I also started a Patreon creator account, as it was originally intended to inspire me to write *Ghostkin 2* you could claim that it has failed entirely, I have, instead, been writing and sharing short stories to go into *All The Books of Earth,* starting slowly to begin with, managing only two in the first year but in late 2019/2020 I managed to get something out on a more or less monthly basis. One of these had been written in around 1990 and I had fond memories of it. The original version was an introduction for a character I had created for the original *Star Wars Roleplaying Game* but even back then I had the idea that I could do something more with it, giving it a re-write to change all the movie references to something original. I had a print out of the story, although once I unearthed it again, I discovered that while the story itself was reasonable, the writing was significantly less so, reading like something written by someone still deep in the 'million bad words' that writers with more experience and success than I (Ray Bradbury and Neil Gaiman, for example) said needed to be written to learn how to create a story. It felt like there was something that could be saved though, so I went to work, creating something that seems to work. Although, whether I come back to it in another thirty years and have the same feelings about this version than I did about the original, only time will tell. The same can not be said for the other story that I had from around the same time, a 'humorous' fantasy that fell entirely flat at every turn, reading like someone who had read a lot of Terry Pratchett and Douglas Adams but didn't have the skill needed to see how difficult it was to write the sort of prose that they had done. The jokes were clumsy (although I do quite like the messenger named 'Facks Mackin') and what little story there was acted only as a framework for those jokes. Reading it was painful and as far as I could see there was nothing worth saving, so it has been consigned back to oblivion. That year, for Transgender Day of Visibility, I wrote a poem to be published as part of an initiative by the Northern Unison LGBT+ group to show that trans people were more than just trans. Ultimately, only three of us wrote something but it still felt good to be visible and to stretch my creative abilities.

#MoreToMeThanTrans Who am I?

I'm Ellen.

And I contain Multitudes.

I'm a wife

And a parent.

I'm a daughter

And a sister.

Ellen Mellor

I'm a reader

And a writer

(Three novels and a book of short stories – get them from your local bookshop!).

I'm a comic book collector

And a gamer.

I'm a massive geek.

I'm a tea drinker

And a tee-totaller.

I'm a non-smoker

With a GSOH.

I'm an administrator

And a trainer.

I'm a trade unionist

And an activist.

I'm a socialist

And a feminist.

I'm English

And British

And European.

I am all this and more.

Who am I?

I'm Ellen.

I'm also a trans woman.

Other than that though, I hid rather than proclaimed my identity. The depression and dysphoria that had lifted a little in the fortnight I had been off immediately crashed down on me again once I returned to work. I managed a week and a half before going off sick again. A few days later, while still off, I rang Brighton again pestering them for a date. The secretary told me that she was going through June's list at that moment but would sort me out. Having said that, though, she couldn't immediately lay her hands on my notes and so was going to have to look for them and ring me back. Another delay.

As I waited my heart was beating so hard it felt like my rib cage was barely containing it. I was terrified in case she didn't ring back or she did but only to tell me that she couldn't give me a date. Although it was only five minutes it felt so much longer in the same way that the last week of term feels like it lasts a month. But, she did ring and we agreed a date. I was going to have surgery on the 23rd July 2019. As soon as I hung up, I felt a huge weight lifted off my shoulders. I could finally see the end of the road along which I had been traipsing for the previous four years. The following day, I started a countdown on my Facebook page with the first one being:

Ellen Mellor

15 weeks 3 days
6 Apr 2019, 11:38

Although I was off work, I did go in for a meeting with the Occupational Health team to see what sort of support I could be given to keep me going until July. It turned out that they couldn't offer me much of anything really. There was an offer for counselling which I accepted although I wouldn't be seen before going to Brighton. On top of the depression and dysphoria, I was also starting to get increasingly angry at everything I had been put through, becoming an 'angry trans woman' who just wanted to tell cis people exactly where to go and what they could do with themselves once they got there. I knew that very little of what I was suffering from was the fault of those around me so I had to fight to hold it in and try my hardest to be 'sweet, genteel and girly' Ellen rather than 'bitch from Hell' Ellen but it was just so fucking exhausting. I just wanted to scream.

With ninety-nine days to go, I made a decision. It came to me while I was reading Mia Violet's excellent memoir *Yes, You Are Trans Enough*. Having spent the last four months letting my life be ruled by disappointment and letting it totally screw up my head and messing up my life, focusing on that and the dysphoria that had broken through because of it, I was absolutely, completely pig fucking sick of the whole fucking thing. My life was actually quite wonderful: After years of not knowing who I was, I had broken through and found myself. And I loved her. I saw the positive aspects of who I am and acknowledged them. I accepted that while my job left a lot to be desired there were aspects of it that I did enjoy and I could see that I now had direction and ambition. On top of that, I actually had a job and when one of the biggest issues facing trans people is finding employment that was absolutely not something to be sniffed at.

While I had been off I had been exercising as a form of therapy and self-care, cycling further and further until I was regularly managing twenty mile rides. I was healthier than I had ever been and well on the way to hitting the target weight needed for my surgery. I was finally starting to see the real me in the mirror and in selfies. I may not have been the cutest girl I knew but for a 47 year old trans woman, I thought I looked pretty hot.

The dysphoria hadn't gone away. Thinking about what I had in my panties still made me shudder but at that point it was only for another 99 days and I realised that what was down there did not define me. It was barely a part of me by that point but I had still been letting it dictate my life to me. I had hoped and thought that sort of behaviour and thinking would have been over once I started on the 'girl cooties' but apparently not.

I recognised that I was surrounded by people who loved me and who I loved in return (the greatest thing... and all that). All in all, I was probably one of the luckiest trans women that I knew and I was going to try to celebrate that and share my joy and happiness rather than spread depression and misery. So posted something on Facebook explaining all of that, saying that those around me made 'my life worth living. And dammit, I'm going to live the goddam fuck out of it". The following day, despite having barely more than four hours sleep, I still felt good. It seemed like there was something in the power of positive thinking. At work everything and everyone seemed surrounded with a warm, 'Ready Brek' glow. Almost overnight, I had become one of those annoyingly cheerful people . On the way home I listened to the soundtrack from *West Side Story* came on and had to fight the urge to sing and dance.

The next morning I looked in the mirror and said 'good morning beautiful' to the woman looking back. She smiled.

One of the definite positive aspects of feeling positive was that when Amy's 'V-Day' arrived, I was able to feel genuinely pleased for her with no issues with her having what I so desperately needed. It just meant that my sister was going to be happy with her body and she would be able to share her happiness and her experiences with me in the run up to my own day.

Despite the positive outlook, my sleep patterns weren't really improving. In desperation, I got myself a bag filled with hops and lavender and a packet of 'sleep crystals' - amethysts, rose quartz and the like whose 'vibrations' were meant to help you sleep. This was, however, one of the occasions when you discover the drawback to having a smart, funny kid. M's comment on seeing the crystals was to say "so, you don't believe in science anymore?" But the truth is I was just desperate. I did actually sleep a little better that night although I put that down more to the 21 hour long day I had just endured rather than crystal energy. Whether it's my scepticism that prevented the crystals from working or merely science could, I guess, be open to debate (but really, it's not) but, which ever it was, they didn't work.

My sleep pattern continued to deteriorate and I was taking more and more time off. I went to the doctor with the intention of getting either sleeping pills or a large comedy mallet with which to hit myself over the head although failed to get either which was probably a good thing. What I did get was some advice around changing my sleep routine and a recommendation for an app called 'Pzizz' which did initially seem to work. The nap/relaxation session with which I started felt really good and when I woke up at 2am that night, it helped me get back to sleep again. It didn't stick though and, less than a week later I was back in the same place I had been before. The problem was the same as it was with all the other sleep apps I had tried and with the mindfulness session from the Show Racism the Red Card course. They focus on breathing, and being 'in the moment' and aware of yourself in a positive and relaxing manner. Which is all well and good when focusing on yourself doesn't send you into a shuddering mass of dysphoria.

Eventually I went back to see the doctor and was prescribed medication. To be honest, they didn't help very much either although they were probably a little more effective than the pretty rocks. The rocks did win out in the end though as while neither one helped me sleep, they didn't leave me hungover. After the positivity I had been feeling from 'changing my mindset' and having a firm date for surgery, I could feel the tide of depression rising once again. It was not a good feeling.

After the Labour Party's massive defeat in the 2019 General Election, Jeremy Corbyn was ousted as leader and replaced with Sir Keir 'Keith' Starmer. I wasn't hugely overjoyed by this as it felt like a swing back to the right and away from the Socialist principles which had persuaded me

Ellen Mellor

to join in the first place. Nor did Starmer seem to be much of a trans ally either. He was the only candidate in the Leadership election to refuse to sign the 'trans pledge' created by the Labour Campaign for Trans Rights (although he did sign a different, watered-down version of it). I was mollified by Angela Rayner becoming Deputy Leader as when I had met her at the previous year's Durham Miner's Gala she had marched with the NASUWT telling me to my face that "trans women are my sisters". I thought that even if Starmer wasn't completely on the ball, Angela would be on our side. But then, everything went very quiet. There were multiple transphobic incidents, including from some quite prominent Labour MPs, that went unaddressed, nor did the Party speak out when the government leaked their proposals for some harsh anti- trans legislation, including 'protections to safeguard female-only spaces' and abandoning GRA Reform. Despite the massive outcry from the general public against these proposals which ultimately led to the worst ones being dropped, it took a week for anyone from the Party to make a statement. They said it was "a nuanced debate, a very important debate, and what Keir wants to do is work closely with all sides of this debate in scrutinising the government proposals and ensuring that we remain committed to trans rights." This was the point at which I knew that the Labour Party was not a safe or welcoming place for me. Nor has anything that has happened since convinced me that I was wrong. When I officially resigned, there were two things that helped me accept that I was making the right decision and they both came from the Secretary of the local Constituency Party.

I emailed him to tell him that I was thinking of resigning and he rang me to talk about it. Rather than discussing the issues I had and why I felt the need to resign, he instead spent twenty minutes telling me how and why I could be useful to him in order to combat the right-wing elements of the party. Hie response to my officially resignation was the word 'fine' although, to be honest, maybe including an assessment that his allyship was of the "'tell don't show' variety" didn't go down particularly well. And then, the following week, he chose to email after "Starmer's lot" (to use his description) won a vote at a local constituency meeting that I would have apparently swung the other way had I chosen to attend, ending by saying "Thanks a lot for your effort. Perhaps in the future you might make more of a contribution. Who knows?" I was not best pleased by this email and told him so in no uncertain terms, instructing him not to reply to me and to delete my contact details. I considered making a formal complaint to the Party about his behaviour but, in the end, couldn't be bothered. They all deserved each other.

    Although I was back at work and trying my hardest to cope, it just kept getting harder. A restructure had been talked about for a while although little information was circulated other than the team I was then working in was to be amalgamated with the team from which I was seconded. My old line manager looked very much as if he was trying to get the top job when it was finally announced - there were at that time two band 7 posts, one of which was his and one of which was the line manager of the old e-rostering system who should have been put in charge of the new system once the project was complete. The old line manager had already started to act as if he was top dog by trying to give me extra work although the project manager put a stop to it. He may have been a prick but he was mostly a prick on my side.

However, he was taking a much needed holiday and had been told that upon his return he would have to go and work at the other site meaning that I would be the only person on the main site with real expertise when about a third of the managers still needed training, more infrastructure needed building as well as day-to-day duties like staffing the phone lines and answering e-mails. The two women working on the old system assisted as the new system took over more and more of the tasks as well as the women who worked with Bank staff, although that was more than a full-time job so they weren't always available.

Essentially though, I was doing the work of four people with nobody to protect me from other demands. The team leader of the old system did all she could but she had a lot of worries and concerns of her own, not least of which was the fact that she was more than likely to be demoted (while undoubtedly still having to do exactly the same job) once the restructure finally came about.

As the 'token out Trans person' and as part of the Trusts 'token minorities' group, I sometimes found myself being photographed doing 'something queer' at work - i.e. Existing. Usually I was okay with it but with the dysphoria spiking it got harder to see the results. Looking at them, with me more often than not standing next to AFAB people I couldn't see anything other than a ridiculous hulk towering over them, looking like an idiotic man in a short skirt. I started to avoid drinking because doing so meant that my bladder filled meaning that I needed to pee meaning that I would have to look at and touch my genitals. Considering that drinking tea is one of the core attributes that defines my sense of self, it shows how much the dysphoria was getting to me and I still had over two months to go. I was really starting to despair and the positive attitude that I had attempted to cultivate had been totally lost.

Early in the morning of the nineteenth of May I had a major panic attack. There had been smaller ones in the past which I had managed to control quite quickly but this one wasn't going away. Both my head and my heart were pounding, I couldn't catch my breath and I felt as if every single muscle in my body was as taut as could be and twitching uncontrollably. Hideous thoughts kept circling in my head. My weight and my mental health would disqualify me from surgery. If I took any more time off, the entire project would come crashing down and everyone would blame me. I posted on Facebook but even that was terrifying because I was scared that doing so would be the catalyst that would set everything off and everyone would end up hating me. Intellectually I could see that I was catastrophising like mad but I couldn't stop. It took most of the week to recover and resulted in being signed off with stress for another fortnight, coinciding, ironically, with my last ever testosterone blocker implant injection. These implants (which, as a counterpart to the HRT being my 'girl cooties' I came to describe as my 'cock blockers') lasted for around about twelve weeks before they needed to be replaced although the ideal to ensure that there was no unpleasantness associated with an increase in T as the blocker grew weaker was to have a new shot every ten or eleven weeks. This one came sixty four days before I would no longer have anything in my body that would generate testosterone (well, I would still have a tiny amount from the adrenal glands but really nothing to write home about). After that, I would have far lower levels of the hated hormone than the average cis woman and I couldn't wait.

Towards the end of the fortnight away from work I realised that there was no way that I could go back. Nothing had been put in place to protect or support me so I would be returning to the same issues that had driven me away in the first place, that I would manage for a week or so at most before losing it again. If I remained off then I would at least have one fewer instances of sickness. I was also worried about money, as if I remained off up until I had recovered from surgery I could be in serious financial difficulties by the time I went back as I would have used up the four months sickness on full salary I was allowed before it got halved. If that happened I would once again have to rely on C's salary and generosity even more than I already was. Of course, worrying about money just made everything that much more stressful. However, it couldn't be helped and at the end of May my sick note was extended for another fortnight.

Six weeks from the 'due date', I stripped off the patches on my skin and didn't replace them. For the next two months (six weeks before and three weeks after) I would be hormone free which meant experiencing the joys that menopause has to offer.

For the first time since I had been signed off with stress I had a meeting with the project manager and the head of the department to try and find ways that I could be supported to help me back to work. I didn't go into the meeting with much hope although I wrote a document discussing my issues and offering some suggestions so it didn't look like I didn't care. I absolutely did care, I felt a responsibility to the project as I had been there at the very beginning and desperately wanted to see it through to the end.

Immediately afterwards, I felt relatively positive although nothing definite had actually been put in place. That feeling quickly died away as I thought about what had actually happened in the meeting. The department head had dominated the proceedings with her own agenda consisting of focusing on one of the points I had made - that of the uncertainty surrounding the restructure. It was going to be worse than I thought. I had hoped that being the only person in the entire Trust who had been with the project from day one that my secondment would be made permanent. I thought it sounded reasonable me and everyone to whom I had spoken about it had pretty much assumed that it was a done deal. However, the old saying 'to assume makes an ass of u and me' proved entirely true when she told me that I would be going back to my old position and salary much sooner than I had anticipated. There would be a band 3 post and also a band 5 post but if I was interested in either one then I would have to apply for them. I didn't know if I had the energy to do that or even if I would be able to do so because depending on when they were advertised and how well my recovery was going I could be flat on my back in absolute agony. Despite feeling that I needed to go back to make sure that everything was in the best place possible before I went off for my surgery there was another part of me that just said 'fuck it. I'm taking the next six weeks off. Let them work it out for themselves'.

The following week I crashed headlong into a deep and serious depression. Thoughts about how everything would be easier for everyone else if I wasn't here circled around and around in my head and wouldn't go away no matter how much I tried to tell myself that it was just a side effect of coming off the hormones. I pushed myself into talking to C about it in the hopes that verbalising those thoughts would dilute their strength but it didn't work. She said that I needed to talk to someone but I was terrified that admitting that I was potentially suicidal might have prevented me from having surgery and if that happened then all bets were off. I tried to hold on to the thought that I would get through it and soon I would be on the other side but at that moment I found it very hard to see how I was going to be able to get there.

On the plus side, I seemed to be getting stronger in my anti- transphobic stance. Until then I had tolerated having friends who were also friends with transphobes - including those who remained in contact with my OPT - but in an attempt to make the world safer for myself, I decided that it was time they made a decision - me or them. To be honest, I didn't particularly care which way they went but I was sick of allowing people to sit on the fence when it comes to this particular form of bigotry. If someone was saying the sort of stuff that transphobes say about people of colour, Jewish people, gay people or cis women and demanding their rights be removed then I'm damn sure that those people who were in my circle of friends would stop being friends with that person. I wanted to know what it was about being trans that made it okay to remain friends with someone who thought I was mentally ill and a potential (if not an actual) rapist?

To follow this up I had a dream the following night where a bully discovered my Deadname (not hard if you search for approximately thirty seconds) and was using it. I warned him that if he used it again I would kick the shit out of him but he didn't believe me and I woke myself up punching the bedside table. It's funny now looking back but at the time I found it upsetting. The bully in that dream was someone I used to know at school who would do exactly what I had him doing but I knew that the truth was that I was deadnaming myself.

At the same time, M finished school and exams and all the palaver that went along with it. Next up was Prom. M didn't exactly go with the standard tuxedo, choosing instead a 'steampunk pirate' outfit - a gorgeous long brocade coat over a waistcoat (with a pocket watch on a chain), black silk shirt, black tie and black jeans tucked into brand new green DMs. It was a gorgeous look and I had never been more proud of my kid than I was then, choosing to rock a unique style that guaranteed admiration.

I decided that I would go back to work on the first of July for the final three weeks in order to make sure that I properly handed over to whoever was going to take charge for the time I was off. Despite my determination, I was fairly certain that it was probably the wrong decision. The meeting had failed to generate any change and indeed the follow-up email which had been sent to my work email - after having been told to avoid looking at it - was three lines long and without substance. I was going to try to take it as easy as could which would include taking at least one day of holiday each week but even then I was far from convinced that I was going to manage.

My resolve lasted exactly one and a half days. The night after my first day back I had an anxiety dream wherein I caught a cold which meant that I couldn't have surgery and I ended up catastrophising about everything that could go wrong over the next three weeks. And then I got to work. The morning went okay, my colleagues were pleased to see me back and did everything they could to help me but then, just before lunch I had another meeting with the head of the department. I had resolved not to go into meetings with her without union representation but she caught me unawares and implied very strongly that it was just a quick 'catch up' chat. Having seen her the day before when she hadn't said anything to even hint that there may have been anything amiss I was totally unprepared for what she was about to tell me. From her point of view I'm sure everything was fine and dandy and she was just doing me the courtesy of taking time out of her busy schedule to get me up to speed on everything that had happened despite quite a lot having actually happened.

To begin with, the restructure had finally taken place meaning that I had returned to my previous post and salary. On the first of July, the day I had returned from my time off due to stress, which had been exacerbated in part by worries about money. Perhaps more importantly, it was the day before this meeting took place. Her reason for doing this was because in her opinion the project was complete and so the position to which I had been seconded was no longer needed. Despite this bold assertion - I had already arranged several training sessions in the upcoming weeks - she then asked me to run some 'train the trainer' sessions and was actually surprised when I refused. Her exact words (and I can still hear them echoing in the exact tone of confused condescension that she used) were that I should 'help her understand why that would be' and didn't seem to understand how insulting she was being when I told her my reason that I wouldn't do it was because it was above my pay grade and if she wanted me to continue with any sort of training then she should continue to pay me to do so. She went away to find out if it was possible to keep paying me at a band 3 rate for the rest of the time before surgery. Leaving the meeting, I was stunned, close to tears and even closer to just resigning. Even more shockingly, they had not had the courtesy to inform either the project manager or the team leader of the team to which I was returning. I immediately went to speak to my union and then left, unsure if I would be returning the following day. Eventually, after a lot of very deep thought, I decided that it was too much of a risk to my mental health. It was a decision that had been made a lot easier when the head of the department failed to get back to me either to tell me what was happening about my salary or with the official letter notifying me of the reversion to my old job, both of which had been promised to me by the end of the day, showing once again that what she said was nothing but hot air.

As I was going to be lying on back at the far end of the country for my actual birthday, I had decided to have an early birthday/pre- surgery party. On several occasions I had come very close to cancelling it but my stubborn streak won out and so the 'At Last The Balls Are Over' party happened. Contrary to any worries I may have had about feeling overwhelmed by having so many people around, I instead felt enclosed in a tight embrace of love and support. So many people came along that there were people to who I barely got to say more than welcome and goodbye and received many beautiful presents including, of course, lots of chocolate. Initially I decided to leave them until after I coming back from Brighton when I wouldn't have to worry about my weight but my resolve lasted about forty five minutes. They were so good, made all the better by the hint of 'forbidden fruits' they had.

Ellen Mellor

The last few weeks before my surgery were actually reasonably good. M was offered a place at Durham Sixth Form College and I received my author copy of *Maiden, Mother, Crone: Fantastical Trans Femmes*. I also got back to cycling and writing - starting work on a story called 'Marooned Off Ceres' based on a picture by one of my best internet friends, Piper Strange. This wasn't the only collaboration we had going as Piper was also illustrating my story 'The Princess and the Elephant' with the intention of creating a trans inclusive children's book. We weren't sure whether we were going to try and get a publisher interested or run a Kickstarter for it. One thing we both agreed on though was that we both wanted a plushie of Edgar the Elephant. Piper had drawn a picture of Edgar as a warm up exercise and I fell in love with it. They had managed to exactly capture everything I had imagined Edgar would be and seeing it made me so excited for the finished product.

I had one last huge bout anxiety a few days before the surgery. I was still worried about everything up to and including the possibility that they were going to change their minds once I got there, the possibility that they could screw up my surgery, and that I would regret the whole thing after I woke up. I knew that two out of the three were not going to happen and the third one (that something could go wrong) was a possibility but I was in the hands of one of the best surgeons in the country which minimised the possibilities.

And then I was on a train to London, staying overnight with my mother in law, introducing her to Dylan who had come down from Edinburgh to be with me for the weekend and to accompany me to Brighton Trans Pride, and Karen who joined us for dinner.

One of my many concerns was that going to Pride might have been just one too many things to deal with but, once again, I proved how little I actually know myself by finding it exhilarating and empowering. If not a little exhausting. I had never been in such a huge crowd of trans people before. There were hundreds of us proudly walking through the town and along the sea front, people cheering and waving as we passed by and everyone hugging everyone else whether you knew them or not. The day was beautiful - warm and sunny and without a cloud in the sky.

I returned to London to stay with my Mother in Law on the Sunday night as it was cheaper to get a train there and back rather than spend another day in a hotel, especially as Dylan was going on to Northern Ireland to see their partner so I would have been paying for the whole thing myself. On my way back to Brighton, I listened to my iPod and purely by chance, I Want That Man by Blondie came up. The lyrics 'Here comes the twenty first century/it's gonna be much better for a girl like me' was exactly what I needed to hear and it sent me to the hospital buoyed up and feeling like I was ready for anything the world could throw at me. Until I discovered that the hospital only had PG Tips. However, despite any ideas that you may have formed from reading this book, I am not daft. I had brought a box of Yorkshire Tea with me.

As midnight approached, I had my final cup of tea, settled down in bed with nothing but a cuddly Chewbacca to keep me company and tried to sleep. The next day was going to start bright and early as I was first on the list.

6
Nevertheless, She Regenerated

I have never really explained why I called myself Ellen, always saying that I couldn't remember why I had chosen that name.

Well, that's not entirely true. After settling on the name, I decided to keep the reason behind it secret, mainly because I didn't think that it was anyone else's business.

However, I made a pact with myself that if I ever wrote a memoir, I'd reveal the truth.

So here it is:

Growing up, I was obsessed with the books of James Herriott. I read my parents' book club edition of All Creatures Great and Small over and over again. At one point, I wanted to be a vet and wrote stories at school which were essentially plagiarised versions of the Herriott stories. But, to disguise them, I wrote about a girl who was learning to be a vet, naming her after James's wife. Except when I was first writing the stories I forgot her name and called her Ellen rather than Helen.

I had set my alarm to play This Is the Day by The The on the off- chance that I managed to sleep. It had always been one of my favourite songs and it's sentiment was absolutely spot on for the day. The lyrics of the chorus 'This is the day your life will surely change/This is the day when things fall into place' hit an obvious chord.

The first thing I did that morning was to put a post on Facebook saying '0 days'. I was to be first in about which I was glad because it didn't allow the fear and the trepidation to build up.

Anaesthetics tend to hit me pretty hard and fast and this one was no exception. There was the usual malarkey about counting backwards from ten but I doubt I even got past nine before I was totally under. I was out for around three hours and woke with a beautiful angelic nurse looking down at me, a dull throb down between my legs and a feeling of intense euphoria. There was a massive smile on my face as I realised that I was finally rid of the thing which had plagued me for so long. There were no questions of whether or not I had done the right thing, it was absolutely, unequivocally the correct choice. So, of course, the first thing I did upon waking up was to flirt with the nurse. But, to be fair, she was very pretty with beautiful, sparkling blue eyes, so I told her. Admittedly, there was still a pretty hefty dose of anaesthetic and pain killer in my system but at the same time, I'm sure she was a very attractive young woman.

During the surgery, my stomach cavity had been filled with gas in order to inflate it and give Mr Thomas enough room to work with. Unfortunately, there was only one way that air could escape so I spent the next couple of days, lying completely flat on my back, emitting some really quite impressive farts. I finally got to eat something the day after the surgery although, 'eat' is perhaps too strong a word as I was given three beakers of liquid that looked like a series of urine samples from people who are increasingly dehydrated - a consommé of some description, a cup of apple juice and (at long last) a cup of tea. The consommé - being the first thing in my mouth for two days that wasn't water - tasted great although not as good as the tea nor as good as the white toast with butter that I had the following day.

Tea, Comics and Gender

I finally got to see my crotch on the second day post-surgery. It was completely wrapped in dressings that looked like a weird mix between a nappy and some kind of fetish wear but even then it looked right without any hint of a bulge although it was weirdly small.

That evening, I got a hint that things were going to work out quite well for me, although that's not how it felt at the time. Ever since I had woken up I'd been absolutely, unutterably, euphorically happy, perhaps even verging on being manic which is difficult when you're tied down to the bed by a tube full of your own pee. However, nothing could touch my joy - not even the government announcing the first of many delays to the reform of the Gender Recognition Act. But, that evening it all came crashing down, induced by nothing more than a little tingle.

I was lying in bed trying to sleep when I felt a sensation in my clitoris. Because it is formed from part of what was the head of my penis and my brain had not had time to rewire itself, it just felt like I was starting to get an erection. All it took was for that to kick off the dysphoria and send me spiralling into despair, crying and howling like a lost baby, convinced that this was how it was always going to be. Without the reassuring presence of one of the nurses holding me and calming me, I'm sure I would have spent the whole night in hysterics. I had allowed myself to fly too high in my joy, totally avoiding anything which could have kept my feet on the ground. In a way, it was probably a good thing that I crashed so quickly as it meant that I was able to achieve some kind of stability more quickly. If it had been left to go on longer the subsequent re-setting of the equilibrium would have been far rougher and harder to get past.

Ellen Mellor

The positivity had returned again by the following morning. I wasn't as high as I had been but I still felt good and, to make the day better, I was allowed a bowl of Rice Crispies and a shave. While I hate having to shave, not shaving is even worse so having been unable to do so since just before the surgery had been pretty unpleasant. The one positive aspect that came from allowing the stubble to grow for a few days was that it meant I could get a really close, smooth result.

The day continued improving when I was allowed out of bed and into my chair for half an hour. I also managed to impress myself by coming close to bursting a catheter bag. I had been left alone for most of the afternoon as I didn't really need any assistance and so the nurses could get on with looking after those who did. At one point I thought to myself that the bag hadn't been emptied in a while and checked over the side of the bed. It was literally straining at the seams with two litres of pee, all of which I had produced in a single afternoon. The nurse responding to my call was also quite impressed, he'd never seen one get so full so quickly. After that, we all made a point of checking on it a little more regularly.

Finally, after four days of it being covered by padding and bandages, I finally saw my new bits. It resulted in bad poetry:

I am totally overwhelmed.

My mind is blown.

I feel amazing.

Tea, Comics and Gender

I cried when I saw it and touched it.

It's perfect and beautiful.

Scarred and swollen and bruised and smelly

But perfect and beautiful.

It feels so right.

More so than that other thing ever did.

Even before the dysphoria kicked.

When something creates emotions strong enough to make one write poetry that bad and yet still feel comfortable quoting it eighteen months later then it shows how powerful a reaction it was. Obviously, I'm being facetious here. But only a little bit. Up until that point, because my vulva had been covered by a huge dressing it felt quite abstract and somehow still unreal. But, after the dressing was removed and I saw what I had been given... well, the abstraction had been removed and it was extremely real and concrete. I did write more on the day other than that though:

So, the nurse came in, stripped the dressing off and pulled the packing out like a magic trick with the flags of all nations.

Then she washed me, lubed up and put first a finger then the small dilator inside me. After 10 minutes, it came out and it was my go. Lube on the finger and in. And just... Wow... I had to leave it there for a minute and just come to terms with exactly how right that was. It wasn't sexual in the slightest but it was just right.

Then the small dilator, followed by the large one.

Then douche and clean up, tea, biscuits, lunch then shower.

I said there that it wasn't sexual and it wasn't. I got a little tiny tingle with the larger dilator but my nerves down there are still in shock.

But what I did feel was this sense that at last, this really was right. I could look at her, touch her and wash her all without wanting to die. The photo I took is the very first picture of my genitals that hasn't made me want to throw up and delete it immediately.

Putting my finger inside. Feeling that space between my legs (my ladycave). I'm actually finding it really difficult to put into words. I cried both when I first saw her and when I first touched her. She is bruised and swollen and she was very smelly but she was beautiful and perfect. I couldn't stop looking at her.

It really feels like every single day has just been leading here. My future is completely open to me now.

I mean, on the grand scale of things, this is quite minor. What I had last week and what I have now makes absolutely not a jot of difference to who I am. I'm sorry to say that the vast majority of you will never get to see her.

But being able to look at myself in a mirror and not shiver with disgust. To have that dysphoria around my genitals completely dissipated - so far anyway.

I feel lighter and more free and more me than I have ever done at any point in the past.

It's like when you have your first baby and all the parents you know tell you that everything is going to change. Obviously you know that. It's obvious. You are going to be connected to this helpless being for the rest of your life. They will bring you the deepest pain you will ever feel as well as the most euphoric joy. But, it's not until you first look at them, lying staring up at you with the most beautiful eyes in their pissed off, old man scrunch of a face that you know. Everything has changed.

Seeing my bruised, swollen, smelly, scarred, stubbly little cunt that first time.

Touching her.

Tea, Comics and Gender

Every.

Thing.

Has.

Changed.

The following day was my birthday - 'my third first birthday', after my real first birthday, my first birthday living as Ellen and now my first birthday with the correct body parts. It was also the first time I actually got to go outside. The hospital is located in a beautiful area on the outskirts of Brighton. The south side looks across a mile or so of fields towards the English Channel and is utterly idyllic. My room was on the north side of the building and so just looked over the car park. There were advantages to this, however. That week was the warmest one of the year with temperatures remaining consistently above twenty degrees Celsius so those on the south side roasted in their beds. I was still very warm but I was at least in the shade which, considering I was unable to move much beyond my bed for the first few days meant that I couldn't see anything other than a bunch of trees anyway.

Getting up, dressed and going outside on my birthday was really quite special, literally and metaphorically. It was the first step into a whole new world, one where I would not have to worry about my genitals betraying me or making me feel horrible. So, of course the first thing I did was to take a photograph of the cake and hot chocolate that I had bought myself from the Costa in the reception area.

The following morning, I was discharged. Mr Thomas was delighted with how well I had come through the surgery and the results of it. The entire week had been relatively enjoyable for values of 'enjoy' that include major surgery and being tied to your bed with a tube full of your own pee. But, the pain had been minimal and my happiness, while not reaching the giddy ecstasy of the first couple of days, had not dissipated noticeably in the days since. I hadn't been looking forwards to the journey home - even on the best of days an eight hour drive is very few people's idea of a good time. I was pretty sure that it was going to be gruelling and I wasn't wrong. While I was taking paracetamol for pain relief, that's all I had. The tiredness, discomfort and pain from being scrunched up in the back of the car quickly overtook any comfort that the drugs supplied. We stopped quite regularly - the first time I used a public loo I was convinced that the universe was going to play its 'Cosmic Irony' card and it would be my first time being challenged. I wasn't but having to worry about it added to how awful I was feeling.

The journey was worth it though because my bed felt so good when I got into it.

The following day, the thirty first of July, was the one-year anniversary of my first visit to Brighton with Karen to see Mr Thomas.

It had been a very long, very difficult year and there were points when I felt like I was never going to make it but waking up in my own bed that morning, opening the cards and gifts that I had received and feeling that all was right with the world put the whole thing into perspective. It had been hellish, but it made the rewards all the sweeter.

After returning home, I had several weeks of essentially doing nothing to look forward to before I would be going back to work. The only task I had to focus on was dilation. I mentioned using the dilators in the quote earlier on without actually explaining what they are or what I did with them, although the name is probably something of a giveaway. Essentially, they are a pair of dildos, one quite slim and one fatter, that I have to use in order to ensure that my vulva remains open. It's certainly not sexy nor is it particularly comfortable but unless I have regular penetrative sex, it's something I need to do - ten minutes using the smaller one and then another ten minutes with the larger one. Immediately after surgery, it was three times a day, dropping to twice a day after a few weeks, then once and finally weekly which is, in theory, where I am now. It doesn't always work that way though as there are times when I just don't seem to manage to find the time which is, admittedly, more due to laziness rather than actual lack of time. Back at the beginning, when I was doing it three times a day, my entire life was built around those sessions - I had to wake up early enough to do my morning session in order to make sure there was enough time between that and the lunch time session and that one and the evening session. Twenty minutes doesn't sound like an awful lot but the preparation and the cleaning up and showering afterwards meant that, especially early on, each session could take up an hour or more. Fortunately, I didn't really have much desire to go anywhere. While I wasn't in much pain, I got very tired, very quickly. Even lying on the bed literally doing nothing other than holding something inside yourself for twenty minutes was exhausting. One of the things I discovered was that, unless you are quite careful, lube has a tendency to go everywhere and when there is an interested cat who is demanding attention immediately after you have liberally applied the stuff to both your bits and your dilator it can get bit awkward.

When I first started dilating, I was uncertain of my ability to keep the lubed up, smooth silicone dilators inside without holding them. After about a week, the awkward position of my arm resulted in getting a trapped nerve in my right shoulder meaning that, not only could I not hold the dilators in place, I could barely do anything else which, considering I am right-handed and about as ambidextrous as Captain Hook, caused something of an issue.

While my recovery was mostly plain-sailing, to the extent that I'm pretty sure that I had the easiest recovery of anyone I knew, there were a few issues, although really nothing to compare to some of my friends who found that they had severe complications - one continuing to bleed for months afterwards and another who has still not properly recovered three or four years later. Compared to the things they suffered my own very minor issues are barely worth mentioning. But I'm going to because it's my autobiography.

There are really only two very minor complications and one that could potentially be a little less so. Firstly, during the surgery itself, I think that a nerve must have been nicked in my groin leaving me with a patch in my right thigh that occasionally goes numb. The second one is that I find it far harder to hold my pee. As mentioned earlier, I appear to have an ability to generate a huge amount of urine in quite a short period of time meaning that I often find myself going from vaguely needing a pee to having to go right-the-fuck-now in the space of about thirty seconds and, if I leave it too long, I wet myself. Fortunately, it has not (yet) happened in a situation where I wasn't immediately able to strip off, wash and change but it does mean that I have to plan if I'm going on a long car journey and make sure that I pee at every possible juncture.

The last complication is more serious. Because my vagina is artificial and not actually connected to anything, it is not self- cleaning, therefore, to make sure it remains clean and I don't get a UTI, I need to douche which I do after I have dilated. However, one of the things I have discovered, almost from the beginning, is that the warm water from the douche comes out of my bottom. Slightly more embarrassing is that I found myself farting uncontrollably through my vagina. Because of the lack of post-surgical care information, I spent months trying to convince myself that either this wasn't what was happening or it was meant to happen like this but, eventually, I had to accept the truth that there may well be an issue and I might have a rectovaginal fistula (a small hole between my vagina and my rectum) which research suggests occurs in about 1% of post-GRS trans women. When I saw my GP about it, she tried and failed to insert a speculum inside my vulva so had to refer me to a gynaecologist. To be honest, I thought that she was making a fuss and was just being a bit rubbish and squeamish about a trans neo- vagina. However, once I saw the gynae and she also failed, telling me that they were going to have to perform an investigation under a general anaesthetic, I forgave her. Apparently, even with regular dilation, I have a very small vulval opening. There was another long wait, when all non-essential surgery was cancelled because of Covid-19 but I eventually had the procedure when my fears were confirmed. I do indeed have a fistula but it's so small - around a millimetre in diameter - that the gynae wasn't certain that I even had one at first. She had to put water in my vagina and then blow air up my arse causing bubbles to come through as if she was searching for a puncture on a bicycle tire. It's also in a very awkward position, right at the top of my vagina, that she isn't certain if the repair can be carried out by going up through the vagina so they may have to go in from above. At the time of writing, I have an appointment next week for a CT scan and then a decision will be made about how they are going to repair it.

Eight weeks after my surgery I had an appointment for a post- surgical check up. There is a certain irony in being told to rest as much as possible and only do what your body says that it is capable of doing while, at the same time, having to spend three days on a return trip to Brighton for an appointment that would last no longer than five or ten minutes. There were some definite plus points to my return though. Spending more time with Karen and having lunch with people that I had only known virtually up until that point. But, I was completely correct, my appointment was roughly ten minutes long, during which Mr Thomas mansplained my new genitals to me, handing me a mirror and pointing out my new anatomy with a pointer thingy, saying 'this is your clitoris' and 'this is your urethra' and so on. While he was doing so, I was thinking three things. Firstly, that if I had gone through all of this and not researched my new anatomy then there would have been something seriously wrong with me. Secondly, that there were people who probably needed this stuff explaining to them. Thirdly, I wouldn't say anything because after all, this man actually gave me the damn thing so complaining would be a bit rude. And it was kind of funny. As well as the mansplaining, Mr Thomas did also actually have a proper look and pronounced himself very happy with the results.

Tea, Comics and Gender

{PLEASE NOTE: THIS NEXT SECTION HAS DISCUSSIONS OF SEXUAL ACTIVITY. YOU MAY WANT TO SKIP THIS PAGE. I'LL PUT ANOTHER COMMENT AT THE END.}

After the appointment, Karen and I wandered around the touristy bits of Brighton. It was a glorious, sunny day and I felt good about everything. Except for the shop which had absolutely gorgeous clothes that suited me perfectly but didn't have anything larger than a size 14. I found something that fit me perfectly in a different shop though. One of the things I had promised myself was a vibrator of my very own and after my appointment I thought I deserved a treat. I found 'She Said', a sex shop which billed itself as friendly, feminist and inclusive. Being in Brighton it had to be pretty LGBT+ positive at the very least so Karen and I thought we'd check it out. I'd been in sex shops before but this was definitely one of the better ones and didn't wrap itself up as a lingerie shop which just happened to sell sex toys like Ann Summers. I worked up the courage to ask the woman who worked there for some advice. I was a little intimidated by the options from 'lipstick' and bullet vibrators, to rabbits, to devices that look like they'd been amputated from a Terminator robot, moving in every direction and lighting up. In the end, I got myself a little bullet vibe that claimed to be the first environmentally friendly, biodegradable vibrator. It would be a few days before I got a chance to play but just owning it felt good.

When I did try it, it was so very different from anything I had ever experienced before that I didn't really have the words to describe it apart from the knowledge that being penetrated sexually felt so very right, not that I wanted a penis inside me but just the fact that my body was now capable of that sort of... I don't know if 'acceptance' is the right word but it seemed to fit (as did the vibrator). Having a vulva and being penetrated feels like I am allowing the world into me in a way that having a penis doesn't and can't. Accepting and enclosing and protecting something and having it internalised rather than the external, liminal (in the sense of the penis being a part of the body that is in many ways disconnected from the rest of it - it reacts without any conscious control, it often seems like it is making the decisions for the body rather than the other way around, it is this 'extra' part that is just there) experience of having a penis that is all about penetrating and filling up a 'void'.

I didn't orgasm that first time. I needed to experiment and allow my body to recover further before that was going to happen, but at the same time, the sensations from penetrating myself and also running it over my clitoris were powerful and very, very nice. There was, however, one thing that worried me a little. My fantasies were gone. Pre-transition, I had some really quite vivid fantasies about having a vulva and being accepted as a woman. Post-surgery, being the proud owner of a vulva and being accepted as a woman meant that I discovered that the reality was really somewhat different to the fantasy. I mean, this wasn't exactly a shock but it meant that I couldn't really bask in it any more either. So, as I lay there, enjoying the sensations, I found it hard to focus. At that point, it wasn't much of an issue as it was more about exploration, discovering new sensations and how they differed from how it used to feel but it also felt a little like I'd lost something. I enjoyed those fantasies, they were fun and, yes, a bit silly but they were mine and they helped. As a writer, I'm not great at writing sex scenes - in the past I'd written two, neither of which were particularly explicit - and that was at least partly because I wasn't ever very comfortable with sex. It's one of the reasons why I write science fiction. It's very hard to get it on in a spacesuit...

{OKAY, THE SEX STUFF IS FINISHED FOR THE MOMENT.}

While all this was going on, something else also came to a head. In the middle of August, C and I had a visit from our friend Quentin. We had met him years before in a tiny village in the middle of the Massif Central region of France on a volunteer work placement holiday renovating an old hospital for sick children to turn it into a youth hostel. Quentin lived in Sunderland and worked as an Educational Psychologist. We quickly discovered that Quentin and my Uncle Nigel, who is also an Ed. Psych., knew each other and had worked together in the past. Returning home, we continued to see each other regularly until he and his wife, Marion, moved to New Zealand. Quentin comes back every year or so to visit friends and family and work with the Quakers but unfortunately, we have never yet able to save enough money to visit.

One of the things that C and I had often discussed was building an extension on the side of the house. There is an outhouse there at the moment with no insulation or heating and a tendency to get damp. For several years we had vaguely discussed knocking it down, along with the rather horrible porch and replacing it with a sort of L-shaped addition creating a spare bedroom/office. For some reason, I mentioned this to Quentin while he was visiting. Usually, C would have gone along with it and said that it was definitely something we would look into when we had the money but, this time, she was very reticent and said that she wasn't sure and it depended. I knew what she was really was saying. She wasn't sure because she didn't think that she would need the extra room any more once I had moved out. While she was still being caring and kind and affectionate, I had a sense that she was unhappy and uncomfortable with our relationship - not due to transphobia or homophobia, but because she is straight. She had never been able to refer to me as her wife - it just didn't feel right to her. After all, she hadn't married a wife. I had asked her for so much and she had given it all without hesitation. It really felt like it was time to allow her to find her own way and her own happiness without having to worry about me as much.

A few days later, I forced myself to bring it up, but there was no way I was going to be able to just come out and baldly ask the question. So, instead, I wrote a letter. It was the hardest thing I had ever written and I felt awful, as if I was saying that now I had my surgery, I didn't need her anymore and I was moving on. The few hours I waited between giving it to her and her reading it were awful. I had to hide how upset I was from M because that was a whole different conversation that I was really not ready for. There was also the fact that this made finding a new, better paid job even more imperative along with the knowledge that I was going to be living by myself, something I had never done before. There was never any doubt about which one of us would become M's primary caregiver and would remain in the family home. C had always had the higher income whereas I was going to struggle to even support myself.

C's response was to agree that we were done, that she had been intending to say something but couldn't. With that, my thirty year relationship with the woman who had been the love of my life was over.

It didn't end straight away with me immediately moving out. In fact we continued to share a bed for a few more months while I looked for somewhere new and If anything, we became closer than we had been in long time, although our relationship took on a different tone with us becoming more like sisters than anything else. There was still a lot to do before I could get to the point where I would be able to move. Not the least of which was finding a place that I could actually afford and wasn't horrendous. I knew that I needed to buy rather than rent because the way the private rental situation is in this country it made no sense. I would have ended up spending at least as much money each month on rent as I would on mortgage payments as well as having to find the initial deposit and still wouldn't actually have a place of my own which, considering there were things I wanted to do that meant I needed the freedom and stability that owning my own place would afford me. I was finally going to be able to get all of my books out of the loft and onto bookshelves and, if I was going to do that then I wanted to know that I was going to be staying wherever I ended up for a while. My original plan had been to buy a two or three bedroom house but quickly discovered that even the cheapest two bedroom house was well outside my budget. This was devastating, I knew that I was badly paid and things would be difficult without being able to rely on C's salary, but to fail at the first hurdle drove my hopes deep into the ground. I knew that I would never be homeless but it also felt like I was going to end up living in a hovel.

On top of all this, I was preparing to return to work. During my time off, I had a major revelation, although to be honest, the only surprising thing about it was that it took me so long to realise. My immediate line managers had been a lot less supportive of my transition than they could or should have been. Since my surgery - in fact, since I had gone off sick for the final time at the beginning of July, I had had no contact at all from anyone at work with the exception of my union association secretary who had arranged for a gorgeous bunch of flowers to be delivered and a couple of messages from work friends on Facebook. Officially, as far as anyone in management knew, I could have died on the operating table. It later turned out that there had been a card for me but the woman who had volunteered to give it to me failed to pass it on but, even so, there were some names on it which were very obviously missing.

Recently, the Trust had taken on a new Chief Executive and, from what I knew of her and her background, I was hopeful that the Trust could change. Under the previous CEO, there had been an atmosphere of cronyism and deceptive practices. Morale had been low and there was a general feeling of mistrust pervaded the place. Suffice it to say that when he left suddenly very few people were hugely surprised or upset. The new Chief Exec came from a different Trust, one that had a very different attitude to working with staff and also with LGBTQ+ staff, to the extent that it was actually in the upper echelons of the Stonewall

Tea, Comics and Gender

Top 100 LGBTQ+ positive businesses.

It was with a mixture of anxiety about returning to my old job under my old managers and hope about the future of the Trust under the new Chief Exec that I wrote her a long letter detailing my issues, explaining that I was actively looking for work elsewhere. I was very pleasantly surprised when she got back to me almost immediately, inviting me in to discuss my letter before I returned to work.

The meeting went well and, she was supportive and understanding but, ultimately, there didn't seem to be a whole heck of a lot she could do right then and there. She said she was aware of what was going on and if I held on, changes would be happening. We also agreed that, if I stuck around, I would act as a mentor to her on trans issues while she would help me with management type stuff, which was absolutely excellent.

But then I had to actually go back to work. I had arranged for a phased return to work with my Team Leader, who had told me that I would be sitting next to her and how much she was looking forward to me coming back so I felt a little better about things, even if still incredibly anxious. I knew she would have my back and I wouldn't be right in the middle of everything straight away but I also knew there were still going to be issues. Many, many issues.

My first day back as not great. It started off badly with both C and M being in foul moods due to running late meaning they pretty much ignored me on the way out of the house leaving me in tears and with no desire to get ready and go to work. The day itself wasn't as awful as it could have been but it felt like I'd never been away and nothing had changed. Team morale was at rock bottom and there was far too much work to do. I had a meeting with my Team Leader in which I was extremely blunt, explaining how hurt I was that nobody had been in contact and if things had not improved by Christmas then I was out of there. I don't think that she had realised that nobody had been in touch with me and immediately apologised for not doing so herself.

After that, things got worse. I had to set boundaries for myself and ensure that I worked at the level to which I was being paid. I was fairly well known as the person who knew the rostering system best so they would often come to me for help and advice and I had to turn them down. I hated doing it but I felt that I needed to for my own stress and personal integrity. Once again, my sleep pattern almost immediately fell apart, I had neither the time nor the inclination to wear makeup and my stomach started trying to eat itself - churning constantly and causing me to burp and fart. I was using a meditation app and it really wasn't working. I couldn't focus and do the 'not thinking' and 'gently drawing yourself back to your body' thing. At one point, narrator kept saying 'It's like this' and every single time she did it, I found myself replying 'And that's the way it is!', meaning that rather than having a quiet, calm and relaxing break from everything I was instead having a full-on rap battle in my head. By the end of my second week back, I was on the verge of going off sick again. I was at the end of my tether, couldn't concentrate and felt like either crying or throwing up all the time but I knew that I couldn't actually do it because I had used all of my full time sick pay. Physically, I was fine, with only the odd twinge. Mentally though, I was a mess with the list of things that were causing me stress and anxiety - work life, home life, money, relationships, the bloody country - getting longer and longer with no way to influence or change any of them.

In the meantime, I found a flat and secured a mortgage which was good but became another thing to add to the 'anxiety list'. It was a lovely two bedroomed flat in a small block literally over the road from the school that both M and I attended. It had a gorgeous view from the front room and the whole flat was surprisingly spacious. There was a little cubby hole created when previous owners had blocked out a part of the front room that would make a perfect office space. Apart from pretty hideous wallpaper on one wall (although I seem to be in something of a minority in holding that opinion), it needed nothing doing to it and it was right in my price range. Essentially, it was as perfect a place as I was going to find so when my offer was accepted, I was relieved and happy. I could start making plans, after all, there was no chain at either end so it should all be quite smooth and fast to get everything finalised.

Of course, moving house is never that simple and it ended up taking months to complete, mostly because the other person's solicitors were utterly useless. And all of that added to my stress. Less than a month after being back at work and even before I was back to full time, I was back to the same place I had been at the beginning of the year. Actually, I may have been in a worse place than because I didn't have any dysphoria. Instead, my brain was telling me that I was a worthless piece of shit who was failing in her commitments to her friends, at work, at home and in every other relationship. I had no idea what to do and just felt stuck. The only thing I was certain of was that I wasn't going to hurt myself or attempt suicide, no matter how tempting it may have seemed at the time. But, other than that single point, I didn't know what I was going to do. This happened partly because I had been prescribed a stronger antidepressant medication that meant that I had to wean myself off the old ones before starting on the new ones. But, even knowing that didn't help. Depression doesn't take into account anything like reason or intellect. I may have known why I was feeling the way I was but it didn't help fight it.

One of the ways that I tried to combat all of this was to throw myself into more things that could take myself out of myself. I tried to become even more of an activist at work - one of the first things that the new Chief Exec had done was to implement new, individual staff groups for various minorities - LGBT+, BAME and Disabled staff - and I joined the LGBT+ group in the hopes that it would be more useful and less of a box-ticking exercise than the previous, all-encompassing group had been. I became more involved in union activities, attending my second LGBT+ conference and my first Women's Conference where I forward amendments on a couple of motions to 'queer them up' by making sure that a motion about menopause referred to trans masculine people and another about women supporting women explicitly included trans feminine people.

Be:Trans Support, the local support group which had nearly died the previous year and was only saved by the efforts of Gemma and Kate, two lovely trans woman who took it over and reinvigorated it. As part of that, they created a new executive committee and I was elected secretary. Up until then, I had not been especially active and had allowed others to do most of the work. I made a vow to myself to change that and actually try to do the job for which I had volunteered.

Eventually, as these things do, all the paperwork and

legal tomfoolery was completed and at the end of January 2020 I left the home I had shared with C and M and became a single woman. I was utterly terrified. The closest I had ever been to living alone was the few months I spent sharing a house during the first term of my English degree in Middlesbrough. Once C and I had finished our degrees we immediately moved in together and had not been apart for more than a few days since then. I was going to have to finally find out who I actually was without having anyone else around to help me filter myself.

Unsurprisingly, work had failed to improve and I desperately needed out of there. Since returning I had been on back on the first step of the absence process both because of the time I had spent off in the first half of the previous year along with my recovery from surgery as there was no formal process of allowing time off to heal other than to treat it as sickness, although I recently discovered that the recovery time should not have been a factor - another case of my Line Manager either not knowing or not caring about how to look after his team. I had managed to only take a couple of days of sickness since my return but even so that meant that my Line Manager 'had' to move me onto the second step. If I had any more absence in the following eight weeks I would be moved on to the third step which meant appearing before a panel and could have resulted in my dismissal. This happened at the very beginning of February and I had two days of annual leave left to me before the beginning of April. I also owed twelve hours of flexi-time. I had no space to take a breather and get away from work and desperately felt like I was being victimised for my poor mental health. Ironically, this all happened during 'Time to Talk' week when we were meant to focus on and talk about mental health in order to help destigmatise it all. I needed a new job but knew that there was no way I was going to be able to focus enough to find one. I had had an interview the previous week but there was no way they would have employed me because I had in such a state that I could barely answer even the simplest of questions.

It wasn't all doom and gloom. I received my first ever real, proper royalty cheque. Admittedly, it was only for twenty five dollars but it was a massive boost to my battered ego. The speeches I made to the Unison Women's Conference and were very well received and appreciated and made me feel like I had a reason for being. And I got a cat.

Missy is a beautiful, tiny tortoiseshell aged around about nine or ten years and she came to me in a very roundabout way. She originally belonged to the mother of one of my mum's friends who became ill and had to go into hospital. Her daughter was unable to look after Missy and so my mum volunteered to take her in, alongside the two cats she already owned. While she liked her, my mum didn't really 'click' with Missy at least partly because she already had two cats that she had actually chosen to have. Missy also had a tendency to bite. Not a lot and not painfully, most of the time, but if she was annoyed it would be her first instinct. The old woman had been insistent that she would have her cat back once she was better and out of hospital but, unfortunately, it was not to be and she passed away that Christmas. My mum, knowing I wanted a cat and also that she didn't really want Missy to stay with her, offered her to me. I accepted eagerly because I had rather fallen in love with her. She came to live with me the day after I returned home from the Women's Conference. I took one of my two days leave in order to help her settle in. I actually asked for six months Caternity Leave and very nearly added a line saying that I knew that I had just had several months off to look after a new pussy but needed to do it again but my professionalism overrode my need for a cheap joke.

In early 2020, the rostering team were re-organised again and moved back to where they were again. Once again, I got a secondment to join them, meaning that firstly, I was away from the toxic atmosphere of my old team, I got a pay rise back up to a band 3 and I actually started to enjoy my job, which surprised me more than anything else. I had never in the previous three decades of working had a job that I actually enjoyed. But this one was fun. Communication was open and easy and the team were appreciated for what we did and how we did it.

Entirely unconnected with my increasing happiness and decreasing anxiety, the world was slowly becoming aware of a new virus that had started in China and spread with increased rapidity around the world. When I first heard about this new strain of Coronavirus, I dismissed it, assuming that it would, ultimately, be as worrying as the H5N1 bird flu scare had been. It would be a major news story for a couple of months and then would be forgotten. This was not the case. As Covid-19 took hold and cases skyrocketed the Trust had to quickly work out a pandemic strategy. My job was identified as of high importance, indeed I was described as one of the few people able to run the 'second most important system in the Trust'. During the first UK-wide lockdown I went in to the office every day with no option of working from home, worked hours of overtime to ensure that front-line staff were in the right place at the right time. While it remained at one remove, I was very aware that I worked in a place where people were being treated for and, in some cases, dying from, Covid-19. I didn't have a lot of close, regular contact with doctors and nurses but I saw them and spoke to them on a fairly regular basis meaning that when I was at work I felt unable to see anyone else because of the possibility that I may have been a carrier. I essentially had to say goodbye to C and M for an unknown period of time. With C working in a school and M at college, it was just too risky for me to see them. One of my biggest fears when C and I separated was that we would grow apart and stop seeing each other. I hadn't expected it to be this sudden and this vicious. In the few weeks since I had moved into my own place I had seen them once or twice a week which had been hard enough, leaving me in tears more often than not, but the knowledge that I didn't know when I would see them again devastated me.

There were Zoom got-togethers but I quickly came to hate them. The first one made me feel lonelier and sadder than I already was as I saw my friends there next to someone else and it emphasised how alone I was. It all felt so unfair. After all the time and energy I spent remaking myself into the person I should have always been, things should have been improving and I should have been getting happier as life got easier. Instead, though, the exact opposite happened. A friend had confidently predicted on New Year's Day that 2020 was going to be 'the year of Ellen'. It was a prediction that did not age at well.

And then I found a girlfriend.

The lockdown meant that the Be support sessions had to be cancelled. They were quickly moved to Zoom to try and keep something going and I volunteered to run the first one. For the first half hour or so the only other person in the call was a trans woman called Stargirl who had only recently started transition and had never been to any of the 'in person' support sessions. I found it hard to believe that she was so early in her transition. Despite only having been self-medicating with low doses of oestrogen for a few months I thought she looked really rather beautiful and very feminine. I had a strong mix of attraction and jealousy because, if she looked this good with so little oestrogen inside her, she was going to be absolutely astounding when it really hit her system. During that first half hour, we really clicked, finding ourselves in agreement about so many things. She was almost as much of a geek as I was, in some ways more so (especially in her love of bad movies). After that first meeting we called each other whenever we could. Even from that first time seeing her I knew that I wanted to get to know this woman,

I remember remarking to Amy afterwards how very cute this new girl was.

After a few weeks of talking we agreed that, even though we had not yet been in the same physical space, we were girlfriends and 'lockdown dating'. Once we agreed that was what we were doing things started to get more intense. Our video calls became far more explicit and I did things that I would never have even considered doing before but it just felt good and right. She was my girlfriend and I was hers. She made me feel like an attractive, sexy woman which I had never believed happen. How we spoke to each other and how we made each other feel was a potent, dangerous cocktail that made us both drunk with gender euphoria. Eventually, despite trying to hold back we had to break the rules and meet.

That first night, as I drove to her house I was terrified. We both were. I was desperately unsure if I was doing the right thing - it was less than three months since C and I had separated and I was really not sure if I was ready to date. Stargirl, for her part, was extremely nervous about being a 'baby trans', not knowing enough and not being far enough advanced in her transition to be woman enough for me. She was convinced that I was going to take one look at her in the flesh and be unable to see her as anything other than a bloke in a dress.

When I saw her in the flesh, I definitely did not see her as a bloke in a dress.

{THIS IS ANOTHER BIT WHERE I TALK ABOUT SEX AND IT'S PROBABLY MORE EXPLICIT THAN THE LAST BIT SO IF YOU SKIPPED THAT ONE, I'D REALLY RECOMMEND SKIPPING THIS ONE AS WELL}

Considering the sexual tension that had built up over the previous weeks and the nerves that we felt at meeting properly for the first time, it's hardly surprising that we immediately fell into bed. In fact, we nearly didn't reach the bed. We nearly didn't get out of the kitchen. As soon as we saw one another we were unable to stop ourselves and we were very quickly kissing, caressing and helping one another strip down to our underwear.

That evening was mind-blowing. I don't know what it was - the release of tension, the joy in being a woman with another beautiful woman or if Stargirl is just that good but I discovered exactly how loud I could scream when I orgasmed. She touched me in exactly the right places, knowing when to push and when to hold back, when to be gentle and when to be rough. That evening she gifted me with the strongest orgasm I had ever had, leaving me stunned and unable to talk afterwards. All I could do was hold on to her and try to catch my breath.

While I knew there would be fundamental differences between having sex with a penis and with a vagina and had slowly started to explore those differences, including finding out what I needed to bring myself an orgasm, it wasn't until that night with Stargirl that it truly hit home how very, very different it was. With a penis, the orgasm is very focused on that single area and the need to ejaculate. Once it's done then both the ability and the desire disappear quite rapidly. It was good and most of the time I enjoyed it but it always felt like something was missing, especially as it got more and more difficult to gain and maintain an erection, never mind reach orgasm. With a vagina, my orgasm started down in my vagina and clitoris and rippled out, affecting every single part of my body. I had never cum in my fingers before. When I listened to meditation and relaxation sessions, there was often an instruction to 'breathe out through your legs' or some other body part that was unconnected to the lungs and I never knew what it meant. That evening, feeling the orgasm throughout my entire body, I sort of understood.

I had always pretty much assumed that I would end up dating a trans woman at some point at least partly because it was easier. There would be no need to worry about or have to explain the dysphoria and we wouldn't have to educate one another about what it means to be trans. (Not that I was in any way against dating a cis woman. I'm sure that a bi or lesbian cis woman would have at least some empathy and understanding of what I had gone through.) However, this meant that I had to face the possibility that I might end up dating and being in a sexual situation with a woman who still had a penis (and may not want or be able to have bottom surgery). I had absolutely no interest in penises either before or after surgery and didn't want heterosexual penis-in-vagina sex. Knowing that I might end up in a sexual situation with a woman with a penis worried me. If I rejected her because I was unable to get over my distaste for them, it would be horrible for both of us, potentially causing a massive attack of dysphoria for her that could cause more harm than good and revealing a deep-seated streak of internalised transphobia in me meaning that I was unable to see a woman with a penis as anything other than a man.

It turned out that I needn't have worried. Whatever Stargirl had in her panties didn't phase me in the slightest, I was desperate to return the favour and give her as good an orgasm as she had given me. Unfortunately, Stargirl's dysphoria meant her panties stayed firmly on. I did everything else I could think of to bring her pleasure but always obeyed her refusal to allow me to strip her entirely naked. While I wasn't directly confronted with the object of my worry, I am certain that, had she allowed me, I would have quite happily done anything and everything to her that she wanted me to. As far as I was concerned she had the body of a very beautiful woman.

{SEX TALK OVER. YOU CAN READ TO THE END NOW. NO MORE SEX FOR ELLEN.}

Tea, Comics and Gender

It didn't last. It couldn't last. While the time we had together was enjoyable and affirming, nothing ever quite reached the heights of that first night. I loved spending time with Stargirl and she certainly seemed to enjoy being with me but I don't think either one of us was ever entirely comfortable. Stargirl had too many issues with being so early on in her transition and trauma from previous abusive relationships. She constantly worried that I was suddenly going to 'see sense' and dump her for someone further along in her transition. For my part, it was just too soon after my separation and I held on to a lot of guilt about finding someone else so soon. I still didn't really know who I was as a person, supporting myself and having nobody to answer to, which sometimes made me frustrated at her insecurity and need for reassurance. I don't think I was looking for a way out but, at the same time, I had a very strong feeling that it wasn't going to last. The few times I actually spent time with her often ended with me feeling upset and guilty because I knew that I was potentially exposing everyone around me to Covid-19. Neither of us took the sort of precautions we should have done and, I was very aware that I could be endangering her life and the lives of her children from my end and, if she gave it to me, I could also endanger the lives of others, including patients. The end, when it did come, was sudden and unexpected.

Most mornings, one or the other of us would text to say good morning and say something cute to get the other one off to a good start. That particular morning, Stargirl texted me and then followed it up with another message asking if I wanted to hear something funny. This sort of question gets to me a bit. I'm hardly likely to say no and, if I don't have time to respond then I'll say so but that shouldn't stop the message being sent in the first place. We had said that we would be honest with each other and so I told her that I found 'do you want to hear something' questions annoying and I'd rather she just told me. Unfortunately, this had been the sort of thing that her ex would say to control her and triggered her anxiety. I think I would have been okay and just apologised for upsetting her if she hadn't then gone on to say that if I didn't like her then I should just dump her. On top of the irritation that I felt at her suggesting that I was trying to control and change her, that just really annoyed me and the whole thing spiralled from there. I felt that if every time any little thing went wrong she was going to jump to the conclusion that I wanted to dump her then it could very easily become a self-fulfilling prophecy.

After messaging back and forth all morning we finally spoke at lunchtime. It did not go well with her finally suggesting that because I was the secretary of the only proper trans support group in the area, it made it so much harder for to access support. Feeling like she was blaming me, I responded very badly, told her to fuck off and hung up.

I'm not proud of how it went ended and I am very sorry that I hurt her. There was too much guilt and confusion and sadness at my end for this to have ever worked even without Stargirl's baggage. In the end, we weren't good for each other. I may not have been consciously looking to replicate my relationship with C but, looking back, I can see that it was definitely in the mix and, at the same time, Stargirl was looking for affirmation at a level that I was not going to be able to achieve. I am happy to say that after a while we were able to talk again and have managed to remain friends. There is a part of me that misses what we had but there is a far larger part that is grateful to her for showing me that I am an attractive, desirable woman. On the days when I find it hard to see, I can remember that there was an extremely cute girl that really fancied me and thought I was sexy.

Despite being single again, life continued. Although, having said that, it was really just work that continued. Everything else was pretty much on hold, although that did mean that I was able to learn to live by myself, surprising myself by discovering that I actually quite liked it. I was perfectly capable of entertaining myself and being able to really nerd out by organising my books was an absolute joy. I was also able to really start discovering my abilities as a writer. I had never been especially disciplined when it came to writing, often taking weeks or months long breaks between sessions. This was partly down to laziness and partly to not having a place to write without distractions. The little office space in my new flat meant that I had somewhere to work separate from the rest of my life and, being by myself meant that I didn't have to try to concentrate while other people were around, watching television or just existing. I was finally able to write the way I had always wanted and found myself getting better and better at it. I wrote more short stories and started to plan a second short story collection, intending to have enough stories ready by the end of the year to put it together. I also started working on a roleplaying game based on Ghostkin, had an idea for a television series and started to work on more ideas for Ghostkin 2, although without actually committing anything to paper. And then I derailed myself by writing this memoir. However, after writing more than 100,000 words in less than a year, I finally felt that I could actually call myself a writer.

Ellen Mellor

Somehow, Amy had persuaded me that running was a thing I wanted to do. I'm still not sure how she managed it as not running was very much part of my brand. And yet, I found myself downloading a Couch to 5K app and trying to keep to some kind of schedule. On three separate occasions I managed for a few weeks before something interrupted the flow, I lost the impetus and had to start again. So far, I haven't managed to complete the basic running sequence once. However, that didn't stop me from taking part in the 'virtual' Newcastle Frontrunners LGBT 5K. Rather than everyone running the same course, we were encouraged to run our five kilometres in different places. For some reason that I have not yet fathomed out, Amy, C and I decided to run around Northumberlandia.

Northumberlandia - 'the Lady of the North' is an enormous land sculpture of a reclining woman, built on land reclaimed from the adjacent surface coal mine. I had first visited her on the day she opened, becoming one of the first members of the public to stand on her boobs. While she is an absolutely beautiful artifact, the truth of the matter is that she is very much not flat which made running around and over her really bloody difficult. Nevertheless, this is what we chose to do. To be honest, I did not especially enjoy it. While the other two, who are far more experienced runners than I am, managed to keep going and run the entire course, I was reduced to walking about half of it. However, I kept going and finally got to the end. Amy, who has a sadist streak about which I had been unaware beforehand, had chosen to end the run on top of Northumberlandia's head. It's a beautiful spot where you are able to look out over a huge swathe of Northumberland but it's also the highest point of the whole sculpture and, bloody hell, it was hard to even walk up there.

Standing on top of Northumberlandia's head, hugging Amy and C, holding a trans flag and looking out across the countryside to the North Sea in the distance was a moment of total peace and tranquillity. I had never voluntarily done anything like this before. Another mountain climbed, (semi) literally and metaphorically. I was a strong woman, standing with other strong women. My life was my own, I was who I needed to be and it was great.

Afterword

I have never really explained why I called myself Ellen, always saying that I couldn't remember why I had chosen that name.

Well, that's not entirely true. After settling on the name, I decided to keep the reason behind it secret, mainly because I didn't think that it was anyone else's business.

However, I made a pact with myself that if I ever wrote a memoir, I'd reveal the truth.

So here it is:

When I was very young I had an imaginary friend called Ellen Emohpea who had the most amazing adventures with her cat Smokey (who was also my cat but snuck off to have adventures with Ellen). In a lot of ways she was the little girl I wanted to be. She looked like Anne from The Famous Five but acted like George.

It took me years to realise the alphabetical error in her name.

Choosing to stop where I did at the end of July 2020 was a completely arbitrary decision although partly motivated by the worry that I was going to end up writing "She sat down at her computer, opened up Scrivener and started to type 'She sat down at her computer...'" and that would just have become too meta for words. Obviously though, my story hasn't ended and hopefully won't for a great many years to come. I could have talked about how my job improved when I got a permanent band 5 position working in the e- rostering team, meaning that in 2020 I managed to get a £7000 pay rise and am now earning the most I have ever earned. I could have gone more into the process of writing this book although, once again, potentially far too bloody meta and desperately pretentious. I could have gone on for thousands of more words but ultimately, ending with me standing on top of Northumberlandia just worked. It was a positive, powerful image that would make a great final shot in the film of the book

In Sarah McBride's memoir, *Tomorrow Will Be Different*, she tells a story about meeting a 7 year old trans girl called Lulu. Lulu asked Sarah what her favourite part of being transgender was. When I read that it made me stop and think. It's a question that is so very rarely asked or answered. Sarah replied to Lulu and I'm going to do the same.

Being trans has allowed me to truly discover myself, to know for sure who I am and that sureness has made me stronger, wiser, more compassionate, more honest and happier (which was still true even through the darkest depths of my mental health issues).

Being trans has allowed me to become close friends with people - both cis and trans - who are themselves beautiful, strong and full of compassion, people that I would never otherwise have known.

Being trans has opened up the world for me in a way that I would never have seen if I had not taken this step. It has shown me some of the most base, vile and grotesque sides of humanity but it has also - and more often - shown me the beauty, dignity and joy that the best of humanity can exhibit.

It's not just about hormones and make up and clothes - in fact, none of it is about that. It is rather about truth and trust and honesty.

Tea, Comics and Gender

Being trans is really fucking difficult - some days it feels impossible - but it's also the best thing ever. I am so proud of who I am and what I am doing. I don't think I would change it even if I could.

I have so many people to thank and I'm sure I'll forget half of them. If I do, please accept my apologies.

Firstly, there are my parents, Carol and Shaun (and their new partners, John and Molly), my big brother Sean, my ex-wife C and my wonderful kid, M. Without them, I would never have made it this far or have this much confidence in myself.

Then there is my chosen family: Amy, Rachel, Dylan, Karen, Katrina, Pete, Lesley and Nicky. I love you all and treasure my friendship with you.

My trans army: Katie, Gemma, Steph, Jay, Kirizal, Stargirl, Eleanor (my authorsis!), Cal, Piper and Peter.

My work colleagues who have been by my side and supported me through all the shit of the last couple of years: Karen, Sharon, Ryan, Deb, Elaine and Laura (and everyone else at the Trust who aren't part of the e-rostering team but who have proven themselves to be the best colleagues a trans girl could wish for).

There's the Readers of the Lost Art - Louise, Aaron, Chris, Jean, Steven, Nicole, Alistair, Gemma, Rachel, Simon, Tim and Sophia. I can't wait for this apocalypse to be over so I can get back to seeing you in the flesh.

There are my Patreon Patrons. One of the 'perks' that people get when signing up for my Patreon (at $5 a piece or more!) is that I name them in the acknowledgements.

Therefore, I am legally obliged to say thank you to Mike Wilkinson, T.C. O'Neil and Karen Nayler. Without you (and the other Patrons who that I haven't mentioned but to whom I am still very grateful), there is every chance that this book would not have happened. And I promise I'll write something new I can share with you soon.

Finally, I want to thank you for reading this piece of pretentious wankery. I have found it enjoyable (apart from the bits that made me cry while writing them) and cathartic (which is mainly those bits that made me cry) and I hope you come away from it happy as well.

Ellen.

www.ingramcontent.com/pod-product-compliance
Lightning Source LLC
Chambersburg PA
CBHW070459120526
44590CB00013B/689